T0351257

Law and the Economy
in Colonial India

Markets and Governments in Economic History
A series edited by Price Fishback

Law and the Economy in Colonial India

TIRTHANKAR ROY and
ANAND V. SWAMY

The University of Chicago Press
Chicago and London

Tirthankar Roy is professor of economic history at the London School of
Economics and Political Science.

Anand V. Swamy is professor of economics at Williams College.

The University of Chicago Press, Chicago 60637
The University of Chicago Press, Ltd., London
© 2016 by The University of Chicago
All rights reserved. Published 2016.
Printed in the United States of America

25 24 23 22 21 20 19 18 17 16   1 2 3 4 5

ISBN-13: 978-0-226-38764-2 (cloth)
ISBN-13: 978-0-226-38778-9 (e-book)
DOI: 10.7208/chicago/9780226387789.001.0001

Library of Congress Cataloging-in-Publication Data

Names: Roy, Tirthankar, author. | Swamy, Anand V., author.
Title: Law and the economy in colonial India / Tirthankar Roy and Anand V.
  Swamy.
Other titles: Markets and governments in economic history.
Description: Chicago ; London : University of Chicago Press, 2016. |
  ©2016 | Series: Markets and governments in economic history | Includes
  bibliographical references and index.
Identifiers: LCCN 2015047755| ISBN 9780226387642 (cloth : alkaline paper)
  | ISBN 9780226387789 (e-book)
Subjects: LCSH: India—Economic policy. | India—Economic conditions. |
  India—History—British occupation, 1765-1947.
Classification: LCC HC435 .R68 2016 | DDC 349.5409/034—dc23 LC record
  available at http://lccn.loc.gov/2015047755

⊚ This paper meets the requirements of ANSI/NISO Z39.48-1992
(Permanence of Paper).

To Jyotika and Sudakshina

CONTENTS

ILLUSTRATIONS

Maps

Tables

Figures

ACKNOWLEDGMENTS

The two authors of this book met at a conference on law and economic development at the University of Utrecht in 2007. This and subsequent interactions at the World Economic History Congresses in Utrecht (2009) and
Stellenbosch (2012), and at a conference on Indian economic history at the
University of Warwick in 2011 helped shape this book. We are grateful to
the organizers of these panels and conferences. We would also like to thank
Bishnupriya Gupta and Latika Chaudhary, who, in addition to friendship
and support, have generously allowed us to draw on ongoing work in chapters 4 and 6. Price Fishback, the editor of the series of which this book is a
part, and two anonymous referees provided invaluable comments.

We have also separately incurred many debts. Roy presented earlier versions of chapters 2 and 7 in seminars at the University of Oxford, Cambridge
University Centre of South Asian Studies, University of Warwick Global
History Centre, and Pranab Sen Memorial Lecture of 2011 in Kolkata. The
discussions generated in these meetings led to major revisions and improvements in the text. He wishes to thank the organizers and conveners of these
events, especially David Washbrook, Joya Chatterji, Maxine Berg, Giorgio
Riello, and Rama Sen. Chapter 7 draws materials from a paper published in
the *Economic History Review*. Conversations with colleagues and friends and
reading their work have contributed to the chapters, often in unseen ways.
A special mention must be made of Raj Brown, Debin Ma, Marina Martin,
and Frank Tough.

Swamy benefited from the opportunity to be Erasmus Mundus Global
Studies Scholar based at the London School of Economics for two weeks in
the summer of 2013, which allowed face-to-face interaction with Roy. The
India Growth Center at the LSE supported work on chapter 4 of this book,
allowing him to use the British Library, whose staff was very helpful. Swamy

would particularly like to acknowledge the extraordinary resourceful and responsive Interlibrary Loan office at Williams College, whose support has been critical. Chapter 4 draws on a paper published in the *Journal of Development Economics*, written jointly with Rachel Kranton. Jerry Caprio, Bill Gentry, Peter Montiel, and Steve Nafziger have read portions of the book and provided useful comments. Gaurav Dutt, Doug Gollin, Mukul Sharma, and Aseem Shrivastava have helped hugely, often by disagreeing. Swamy also thanks Roger Betancourt, Gopi and Rekha Boray, Charu Gupta, Brian Greenberg, Meg Greene, Santhi Hejeebu, Vrinda Kadiyali, Rachel Kranton, Nadia Loan, Mandar Oak, Arvind Rajagopal, Anupama Rao, Sanjiv Sahai, Arijit Sen, Shalini Sinha, and Arafaat Valiani. Finally, he acknowledges, but cannot sufficiently thank, his family in Bengaluru, Delhi, and Munsiari, and Jyotika, whose presence sustains his life and work.

ONE

Introduction

The Problem

Since economic liberalization policy was adopted in the 1990s, the Indian economy has grown rapidly and attracted global capital on a significant scale. While such rapid growth and foreign investment typically require a well-developed legal infrastructure for doing business, including property and commercial law, there is a widely shared view that India's legal infrastructure is in urgent need of reform.[1] Contract enforcement takes a long time, land laws differ from state to state, labor laws are more restrictive than in other emerging economies, and personal law that is religious in origin exists side by side with secular laws in matters of inheritance and succession of property. Some of these problems emerged or grew in the years between India's independence from British colonial rule (1947) and the onset of the economic reforms (the early 1990s). In this period, the state expanded in size and made numerous regulatory interventions. But many of the weaknesses of the legal infrastructure, as much as the infrastructure itself, were creations of British colonial rule in South Asia.

The British East India Company came into possession of large and populous regions of India around 1765, acquired new territories thereafter, and ruled over these until 1857. Much of the Indian subcontinent was ruled by the Crown between 1858 and 1947. The British Empire in India, or the Raj for short, reconfigured Indian laws in two ways that were often connected—by representing a state that was more bureaucratic, more in favor of formalization than previous regimes, and by being a foreign cultural import that interfered with indigenous social norms, legal ideas, and institutions. The historical process by which Indian laws were reshaped by the colonial power is of great importance to understanding how law works today, because some of the failings of the legal infrastructure derive from the manner in which the British redesigned Indian law. This book is a study of the evolution of British Indian law in the colonial period with a view to discovering why the process might have made market exchange more difficult, perhaps increasingly so. Our analysis will also contribute to a literature that explores how European colonial rule aided or obstructed institutional modernization in the non-European world.

Contribution of the Book to Institutional Economic History

Over the last two decades, many economists and economic historians have emphasized the importance of secure property rights and cheap and reliable contract enforcement as conditions for long-run economic growth. In its simplest version, the argument is compelling, even commonsensical: a farmer will not dig a well if he/she might lose the land tomorrow; a multinational corporation will not build a factory if it fears nationalization; a lender will not provide credit if the borrower can easily default; long-distance trade will not occur without a mechanism for ensuring that the buyer will eventually pay. This perspective is closely identified with the New Institutional Economics, especially the work of Douglass North, and, in this general form, it is widely accepted.[2] However, controversy emerges quickly when we ask, How do societies develop (or not) law and institutions that protect property rights and reliably enforce contracts?[3]

There are of course a range of answers to this broad question, some which do not directly concern this book. But two influential hypotheses, developed in the last two decades, which apply especially to the former colonies of the European empires, are relevant. One of these suggests that in regions where the European colonizers did not settle, they looked for quick returns and set up "extractive" institutions that did not protect property rights.[4] However, where they did settle in large numbers, they imported institutions from Western Europe, which ensured security of property. In both cases, the early institutions showed considerable persistence, influencing economic growth to the present day. We will refer to this as the "extractive states" hypothesis. The second view, in contrast, does not directly focus on colonization, but on the origins of the legal systems of developing countries around the world. These writings assume that importation from Europe has played a large role in the evolution of the legal systems of many developing countries. This hypothesis further assumes that importation from some places, especially England, has led to better legal and economic outcomes than importation from France specifically, and from civil-law-based traditions more generally.[5] We will call this the "legal origins" hypothesis. Researchers have now begun to test these arguments with country-specific analyses.[6]

Another area of scholarship that deserves a mention in this discussion is the historiography of colonial empires. Bearing a resemblance to the extractive states hypothesis, the historiography of colonial empires tends to see colonial law mainly as a means to regulate the social and political order, ultimately with a view to sustaining the empire itself.[7] This literature, however, does not focus on institutional quality in relation to economic growth, nor does it explore the historical roots of the quality of present-day institutions. Therefore, it is of less relevance to this project.

The two perspectives derived from institutional economic history differ in their predictions for India. On the one hand we may think, following the extractives states hypothesis, that because the British did not settle in India, their inclination should have been to put in place extractive institutions, rather than the institutions present in Britain. On the other hand the legal origins hypothesis highlights the significance of importation of English law into India, even suggesting that because it had roots in English common law or, more broadly, British precedent, Indian law represented a more efficient system than that of many other colonies.

Our narrative history suggests that a straightforward application of these ideas to colonial India is difficult. For example, consistent with the extractive states hypothesis, the company government did display a conservative attitude toward importing British laws into India. But did this conservatism represent a choice in favor of extraction, or was it a defensive reaction? In the eighteenth century, indeed throughout the career of the Raj, colonial power was limited by the vast imbalance of numbers between the Europeans and the indigenous residents. British political confidence, and hence the willingness to effect institutional change, varied over time. But limited confidence was surely a factor, especially in the early years of company rule.

Furthermore, the unstated assumption of the extractive states and legal origins perspectives is that non-European and Western legal systems were fundamentally different. This assumption may not have been shared by the eighteenth-century administrators in India. There were, in fact, similarities between precolonial India and preindustrial Europe in the structure of economic laws. For example, as the British discovered by perusing Sanskrit, Persian, and Arabic texts in the eighteenth century, the notions of legality and rule of law were as developed in India as in Europe. In some of these texts that they translated for use in the courtroom, the meaning of private property and the theory of the sanctity of contract closely resembled their

European counterparts. Like in Europe the legal tradition in India "grew—in part—out of the structure of social and economic interrelationships within and among groups on the ground."[8] These groups included merchants, artisans, tribal communities, and landholders. Since indigenous norms were so deep rooted, and carried moral force, it would have been natural as well as expedient for a foreign power to preserve them.

In short, on the one hand, the theoretical assumption that a colonial state that was conservative with regard to importing European institutions was so because it was extractive in aim seems inappropriate for a history of colonial law in India. On the other hand, the decision to incorporate indigenous tradition suggests that it is difficult to read British Indian law as an importation of a British common law model into India.

And yet, this literature does supply helpful pointers for our project. The extractive states hypothesis, as well as the historiography of empires, suggest that it is necessary to study the evolution of colonial law as an expression of a project to gain political control, especially control over economic management. The legal origins hypothesis directs our attention to the role of law as a means for dispute resolution.[9] By doing so, it suggests that it is necessary to evaluate colonial law in this role. We follow both these leads in our narrative of Indian law and economy and find them relevant in different spheres of legislation. In addition, we see a problem which, while surely not unique to India, was particularly severe: the need to devise law with broad applicability across very diverse settings. Thus, multiple and potentially conflicting aims were being served by law derived from different sources.

Colonial Law in India: Multiple Aims and Means

In many cases of economic legislation, law embodied a policy or political goal. Some of the earliest important legislation pertaining to the definition of "proprietary rights" in agricultural land and the allocation of these rights was driven by the state's need to raise tax revenues. We show in chapter 3 that even if the allocation of rights could be described in vague or confusing ways in legislation, it was usually clear who owed the land taxes. In the second half of the nineteenth century after the Indian Mutiny (1857) and other rural protests such as the Santhal Rebellion (1855) and the Deccan Riots (1875), the Raj legislated extensively to preserve the stability of the rural social order. In some regions this took the form of protection of tenants from eviction and rent increases. The Raj also explicitly rejected laissez-faire notions as inapplicable to India when it enacted legislation restricting the transfer of land (chapter 4). Each of these enactments was preceded by extensive discussion where combatants in the debate might draw not only on Indian precedent (the understanding of which evolved, a major subject in its own right), but also the history of Irish tenancy, American homestead laws, and the sanctity of the Raj's prior commitments. But the political objectives were paramount. Political considerations also influenced the *absence* of legislation in some areas, such as the protection of sharecroppers (chapter 3). And through all of this the Raj struggled with the bewildering variety of preexisting land tenure arrangements, which could vary greatly even across adjacent districts. For instance, as the reader will see, even within a region the commonplace word *zamindar* (landholder) could refer to people of hugely different social and economic status, complicating the task of devising law to regulate landlord-tenant relations.

In the 1930s, in response to political protest and a growing Indian role in provincial governance, there was a slew of legislation pertaining to the moneylender-borrower relationship: usury laws, laws requiring record keeping and documentation by lenders, and eventually laws aimed at providing debt relief, that is, allowing borrowers to repay less than what they owed contractually. Again, this was law driven by political considerations, with the state aiming to alter relationships of power between specific sets of economic actors.

As modern industry grew, legislation was again driven by diverse political pressures. British capital pushed for legislation to protect workers in India, which would make Indian labor more expensive and Indian products less competitive. Legislation was also motivated by the need to accommodate or undermine the organizational capacity and militancy of Indian industrial workers. Finally, pressures from humanitarians and from organizations like the International Labour Organization led to measures intended to protect the vulnerable. These included limits on work by children, and a ban on underground work (in mines) by women.

It would, however, be simplistic to focus only on political motivations to explain legislation even in the most explicitly political contexts. By contrast with agricultural land or industrial labor, where the focus, implicitly or explicitly, was on politics, the sphere of commercial law foregrounded the disputant as a market actor. The compulsion to legislate was often supplied by the context of the economic activity, and perceptions about how laws best protected trade (and indirectly, tax revenues). But, then, this drive was counteracted by a political imperative dictating that conventions be left alone. It was only when conventions failed to resolve disputes, and judges had made numerous departures from convention, that statutory intervention took shape. This dynamic was most clearly evident in the sphere of contracts and corporation law. As chapter 7 will show, the Indian Contract Act (1872) was indirectly motivated by the experience of disputes between peasants and planters around indigo cultivation (1859–60) that threatened to turn into a political problem. We see in chapter 8 how indigenous institutional forms such as the managing agency remained underlegislated for a long time because law followed British precedent too faithfully, while slowly adapting to the need to devise stronger protection of minority shareholders.

Chapter 5, on inheritance and succession of property, explores another large field of conflict between aims, to preserve indigenous tradition as a matter of political expediency and to serve efficiency and equity. The conflict arose because preserving tradition, being defined in religious terms, boiled down to acknowledging the rights of the joint family, males, and agnate (male-based) lines of descent over individual members of the family, women, and cognate (female-based) lines of descent. Judges often thought that these rules, traditional or not, were iniquitous. The disputes that came to court caused new principles and priorities to be added and eventually to new legislation, such as those strengthening the testamentary powers of individuals (i.e., their right to will their property)

We can draw two lessons from this brief description of the historical process of the making of economic laws. First, there was a persistent tension between what politics dictated would be a safe choice for the colonial state and what the immediate context of the dispute suggested would be a fair or efficient choice. Second, the physical space where the conflict was often negotiated was not the legislating office of the governor general, but the courtroom as well as the offices of provincial administration. These offices engaged with the day-to-day problems of economics. They were closer to the litigants, studied norms, prepared the digests, argued in courts, and were friendly with the judges and pleaders. Therefore, in choosing sources, we decided to focus on these local and courtroom discourses.

Why Colonial Law Became Dysfunctional

The system that British colonialism built became less and less user friendly within the time span studied in this book. As far as we can measure, the relative intensity of disputes continued to rise from 1880 (chapter 9). Appellate cases piled up, and suits took a longer time to conclude. There were two particular sources of the distortion. In land law particularly, parallel evolution of federal, provincial, and case law created enormous complexity, a problem which persists to the present day. And in matters of succession or in commercial law, even as the state added new statutes, the old principles were never declared obsolete. Simultaneous codification in related fields meant that one subject was dealt with by several laws, prompting disputants to try their luck under different provisions. For example, contract law was covered not only in the Indian Contract Act (1872), but also by civil procedures, negotiable instruments, specific relief, laws on wager and game, and several other minor acts. The result was overlegislation across the board.

There was a further source of distortion: the slowing pace of expansion of the legal infrastructure. From the interwar period, legislation slowed down and the scale of the colonial judicial system failed to grow in step with either population or the size of the economy. Around 1930, the British Indian state sharply reduced expenditure. The pace of enactment of new laws decelerated. The start of provincial legislatures (with Indian participation) in 1919 and again in 1935 reduced the federal legislative motivation. At the same time, crises in the global economy, the collapse of commodity trade, and population pressure on land added strains to market transactions all around. Independent India inherited a legal system that not only had serious design defects but also had grown much too slowly for too long. The legendary tardiness of the Indian courts system in the present times has its origin in this prehistory of deceleration and accumulation of huge backlogs that began in the late colonial times.

The overarching thesis of the book, then, is that the inherited defects and problems of the colonial Indian legal system derived from the fact that civil law was set up to meet distinct aims (politics, efficiency, and applicability in diverse terrains) with an eclectic choice of means (indigenous ideas and borrowed), leading to complexity and overlegislation in all fields. Some dysfunctional features of the judicial system in independent India, such as overburdened courts and delays, had emerged by the end of the colonial period. Multiple aims and origins complicated the Indian judicial system long before independence in 1947.

Sources

In attempting to understand this complex process we have the good fortune to be able to draw not only on a large secondary literature but also on abundant primary sources. The sources we use come from several bodies of material, of which the three most important are policy discussions such as the deliberations of the law commissions or proceedings of the Deccan Agriculturists' Relief Act, judicial proceedings, and commentaries by legal professionals. The heavy use of the second resource in this book is an innovation at two levels. First, it reflects our belief that institutional change was

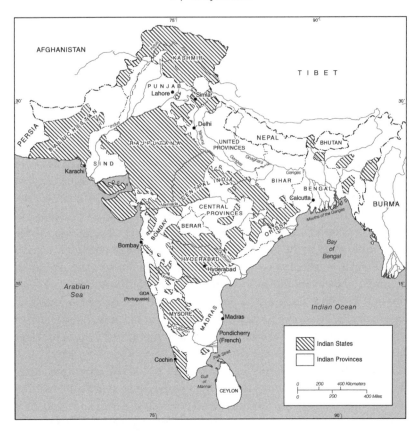

Map 1.1. India, 1939.

made and unmade by the judges as much as the state officers. And second, it has remained little utilized as a resource in the discussion on institutional change in colonial India.

In the present day, the archives on proceedings of court cases are located in the regional high courts, though the condition and cataloging of the resource are variable. Few historians have used this resource despite a growth of scholarship on law. The judgments of cases tried in the high courts (civil and criminal) were compiled for printing from the late nineteenth century.[10] The first comprehensive compilation of civil suits alone was published in 1910.[11] Throughout the book, case law will be used intensively to gauge reasons behind perceptions of judges about the need for legislation or the effects thereof.

The official compendium of statistics, the *Statistical Abstracts*, started publishing some data on the judicial system from the 1870s. The presentation style and level of detail changed in the next sixty years, so that not all of the information can be used to construct continuous time series. But we can identify some basic trends. Other statistical sources used include the *Annual Reports on Civil Justice* and many one-off surveys.

Plan of the Book

The contents of individual chapters have already been introduced, and we will avoid repetition. But the sequencing needs a brief explanation. Loosely speaking, the first half of the book focuses on private property, and the second half on commercial law. Two chapters on the legal system provide bookends. We begin with a chapter (2) describing the early development of the British-Indian legal system under colonial rule. The next three chapters (3, 4, and 5) deal with the colonial state's central preoccupation: property, especially landed property. The choices made in this domain had implications for a range of outcomes, from family disputes to taxation to the development of credit markets and, importantly, the incentives and capacity to invest, especially in agriculture. We do not discuss common land and forests. Forays into these important topics would greatly expand the scope of this already wide-ranging project.

We then move to a discussion of labor markets (chapter 6), where the colonial state's interventions were perhaps less consequential, except in the modern factory sector, which became significant only from the late nineteenth century onward. In this chapter we also discuss the Raj's controversial retention of penal contracting (especially in plantations) until 1926, long after its abolition in Britain. We then turn to legislation necessitated by newer forms of economic activity and the expansion of market activity more generally, in chapters on contracts and corporations (7 and 8). A chapter on procedural law (9) documents the rise and decline in judicial activism in the period of Crown rule in India and the emerging dysfunction in the legal system. The concluding chapter of the book revisits our main themes and explores continuity and rupture between the colonial and the postcolonial periods.

TWO

The Process of Legislation, 1772–1857

The Indian Law is generally a codified one. . . . There is no analogy between the status of this codified law and the common law of England; and Courts in India are not justified in relaxing the Statute Law in the same way, as Courts of Equity in England deal with rules of common law.

—Judgment, *Gujar Mal Ram Lal v. Sita Ram Urjan*, ca. 1900

The British East India Company came into possession of a large and populous territory in eastern India about 1765. By 1818, it ruled over more than half of the Indian subcontinent, and by 1858, this territory had been taken over by the Crown. The early history of colonial legislation usually starts from 1772, when the British parliament began taking part in the governance of the company's territories in India. The first systematic policy on British Indian law was framed around this time. By the middle of the nineteenth century, the judicial system was well established, but key elements of the older framework were being given up. This chapter will describe the evolution of the British Indian judicial system and suggest why it needed change.

The most important idea was that the joint family was the rightful owner of property in India, and that this had been sanctioned in Indian religious codes. This was the basis for the codified law of property in late eighteenth-century Bengal. By 1850, the belief in a religious source of the idea was weaker than before, because the judges made frequent departures from the code. The claims of the joint family continued to be respected, and the codes remained, but the authority and the commitment behind them disappeared.

The initial impetus to legislation was partly political. Nevertheless, deep changes were introduced in the process of legislation as well as the process of litigation in the first century of British rule in India, partly because British ideas about Indian society frequently were at odds with the reality of the dispute in the courtroom.

The Establishment of British Power, 1660–1772

The company was doing business from ports located on the vast seaboard of South India from the early-1600s. The question of law did not become a pressing matter for the company before 1660, because it did not own territory yet. This changed in the decade of the 1660s. Change came from three sides. For twenty years already, the company had been in possession of a small stretch of land in and near Madras town. Here as elsewhere, it employed a number of people. The royalist-leveller contest in England made governance an awkward issue in Madras and made it necessary to clarify the nature of the company's jurisdiction. Should the company legislate and appropriate sovereign powers, or should it rule in the name of the sovereign by means of English law? The acquisition of Bombay in the 1660s from the Portuguese Crown consolidated the company's status as landlord in India and, in view of existing Portuguese land tenures in the area, necessitated a policy on tenancy. As if anticipating such issues, the charter granted in 1661 by Charles II authorized the company to appoint governors with "power to judge all persons belonging to the said Governor . . . in all causes, whether civil or criminal, according to the laws of this kingdom, and to execute judgement accordingly."[1] It was further agreed that the company could legally wage war in defense of its territory and subcontract the power to wage war. In matters of security and good governance, the company was allowed a certain degree of freedom to legislate.

Important though these steps were, courts existed only in name and only in Madras until the end of the 1670s. But progress was rapid thereafter. In 1677 a charter was granted empowering the company to issue currency in its name; in 1683 admiralty courts were established with royal approval; and in 1687, James II extended a royal prerogative to issue charters to municipalities to the town of Madras. In fact, jurisdictional matters had already come up in the court of James II because the company was in the habit of making proclamations in Madras in the king's name. These measures saw the first municipal courts (known as mayors' courts) being established in Madras. Bombay soon followed.

Progress in this front had to be shelved when the Glorious Revolution (1688) made the company's own standing shaky in London politics, subjected its monopoly to trade in India to parliamentary regulation, and eventually paved the way for a rival company. When the dust settled, and the two companies merged to form a single entity (1709), attention turned again to India. A charter of 1726 allowed reconstitution of the mayors' courts in Madras, Bombay, and Calcutta (Calcutta had come into existence in 1690). Although Madras was briefly occupied by the French during the War of the Austrian Succession (1740–8), the judicial system did not see a significant disruption.

What law did the mayors' courts follow? On this question there is a dispute among legal historians.[2] One opinion is that English statutes became automatically valid in the company's territories in India. Another opinion holds that the charter of 1726 effectively made the legislation process autonomous for the company's courts. It is possible that the mayors' court judges themselves were not quite clear on this question. But it would not be too wrong to assume that English law was the default law of the land where no other guidance was available or when the disputants wanted settlement under English law.

We do know that the scope of such debate was limited to commercial law. As the three towns grew in population and became homes to many Indian merchants, merchant litigants dominated the proceedings of the mayors' courts. Histories of family firms in Bombay show how readily the merchants of these towns resorted to company courts for dispute resolution.[3] Simultaneously, there was decay, or at any rate turmoil, within intracommunity courts, whatever form these had taken earlier. The clearest instance of such turmoil can be seen in the case of the Parsis who migrated to Bombay from Surat. Their community court, the Parsi Panchayet, was racked by dissensions and conflicts, partly because an alternative platform to settle disputes was available.[4]

The Battle of Plassey (1757) extended the landholding of the company to several large districts of Bengal, and the Battle of Buxar (1764) made the company effectively the ruler of Bengal, Bihar, and Orissa. Officially, the company assumed charge of the finance ministry of Bengal, Bihar, and Orissa, with very few institutional or informational resources available to perform this task, little political capital, a tiny army, and pervasive fear of being attacked and deposed. Among some of its employees, the new authority came as an opportunity to extort money from local rulers. To the company as a whole, access to the revenue of the state by itself did not make it feel like a government. It only obviated its need to import silver to carry out a profitable trade in Bengal textiles. Ruling the country was not yet the plan.

The acquisition of territory, however, had drawn Parliament's attention. A weak attempt at regulation (Lord North's Regulating Act of 1772) allowed the establishment of a Supreme Court in Calcutta. The intervention had also succeeded in the appointment of Warren Hastings (1732–1818, head of the company state in India, 1773–84), a former employee who had established a reputation as a publicist and spoke eloquently on the company state in Bengal, as the governor and later the governor general of the company's territory in India. All of these moves made fiscal and legal reforms an imperative matter for the new regime.

In principle, acquisition of vast agricultural lands and assumption of governing power meant that the company was about to confront a problem of law of a far more serious order than any it had dealt with so far. Commercial law had been the main element in its jurisdiction, but now land tenure and land revenue law were added to it. Land was an exceedingly complex issue, even more so for a foreigner to understand and intervene in. There were two particular sources of complexity. First, depending mainly on dates of settlement of the cultivable land frontier, terms of use of landed property could differ greatly between locales and sometimes within a village. Second, property right almost everywhere was a conjoint right, the right to raise taxes for the state and the right to cultivate, and these two rights usually belonged to different sets of people.

Good governance, then, required of the state intimate knowledge of local custom, and either a co-option of the military aristocracy who held fiscal rights to land or their removal from the scene. Between 1764 and 1772, these questions were set aside as far as the company could manage. But then the company was being monitored by Parliament, and a famine in 1770 and continued warfare within India made fiscal reforms an urgent matter. Induced by these pressures, the company started looking into land tenure. In turn, this task involved looking into the indigenous law of property, and the indigenous system of justice.

What did it find?

The Precolonial System of Law and Justice

There was little documentary evidence on jurisprudence in action. In part, this was due to the fact that many eighteenth-century states that succeeded the Mughal Empire (1526–ca. 1720) were struggling to establish firm institutions of governance in their realms. But the absence of documentation also suggests a more fundamental feature of precolonial law: that there was no known substantive law of the land at all. Courts established by the states did exist, but these courts usually settled cases according to canon law if the disputants (and the king) were Muslims, or sometimes heard cases that arose among aristocratic and elite urban residents irrespective of the religions of the disputants. For the rest of the population, civil law was defined as codes of conduct of local collective bodies, and administered by institutions that these local collectives set up. The state extended a token approval of the juridical autonomy of communities. This is undoubtedly a stylized picture, but so far no historiography of precolonial institutions has revealed anything that suggests a substantially different picture.

The Muslim law ruling in India, a version of Hanafi codes, represented a segment of the Islamic *fiqh*, or the body of law in theory applicable to all Muslims.[5] The emergence of an Indic Islamic law, or Hindiya, as it was sometimes known as in the Middle East, was enabled by the presence of two books that were widely accepted as authoritative in precolonial India. One of these was the Hedaya, or al-Hidaya, a commentary originally compiled in Arabic by the twelfth-century jurist Burhan al-Din al-Marghinani, and first translated into English (from Persian) by the scholar and company officer Charles Hamilton (1752?–92). The second resource was the Fatawa-e-Alamgiri, a compilation based on the sharia, prepared under instruction of the Mughal emperor Aurangzeb (1618–1707, reigned 1658–1707). The British Indian courts continued to follow these codes but also made a big departure. They began to compile and make use of precedents, whereas formally, sharia law would not privilege custom in the same way.[6] In any case, too little material was available on proceedings in the Islamic courts.

What was the law of the land, and how were agreements sanctioned by law, outside this sphere? Not much more than snapshots are available on the administration of justice by locally autonomous bodies. Even less is known on the contents of law and the process of framing these. One work on the peshwa domain in the eighteenth century suggests that the panchayat, or local assembly consisting of village notables, and sometimes prominent families, administered justice.[7] "The state was not allowed to interfere with its customary right to deliver justice."[8] An interesting speculation advanced in this work is that the framing of succession rights by the local assembly had the effect of making it harder for outsiders to settle in the village, implying that this might have been the intention. Another work dealing with local justice after the British takeover of the Peshwa's territory (1818) suggested that the panchayats were in decline for some time because of the "glaring defects and dangerous abuses" of the system.[9] The statement was not sufficiently explained. It is possible that the British policy on land settlement interfered with the local notables' attempts to exclude migrants. Further, panchayats took a long time to settle complicated land disputes and often found themselves powerless to enforce their orders.

The evidence on the continuance of panchayats is contradictory. A statistical work on the administration of justice twenty years after the British annexation of western India reported: "A feature in the administration of civil justice in Bombay is the frequent reference of matters in dispute by the parties to a panchaet, or jury of five persons, who give their voluntary aid to decide between the litigants."[10] The author of the report published a later document suggesting that the panchayats were rarely used (see chapter 4, note 12). Neither report refers to any counterpart of these bodies in northern or eastern India. An almost contemporary work on castes also observed that among bankers (sahukars) of Poona (later Pune), formal councils existed and routinely engaged in property and contractual dealings.[11] However, the description did not make any reference to the involvement of the councils in disputes, whereas frequently the government is mentioned as a point of reference in matters of dispute, which together suggest that these bodies performed mediating roles in matters of contract, partnership, and succession but did not function as courts of justice if mediation failed.

As for the other regions, a useful early nineteenth-century snapshot comes from the journal, kept by Francis Buchanan (later Buchanan Hamilton) and published in 1807, of a trip through Mysore, where indirect rule by the East India Company came to be established from 1800.[12] Buchanan reports the presence of caste councils, hereditary chiefs, headmen, religious gurus, and local assemblies of other sorts in settling disputes. Whereas in Buchanan's description all of these bodies were deeply interested in the question of purity of women, their involvement, if any, in property and contract appears to have been minimal. On the other hand, individuals who were somewhat prominent in the village on account of privileged tenure, such as the local accountant, possessed some authority in land disputes as well.

In eighteenth-century Bengal, the company at first made use of the still quite solid structure of state law and state courts in existence in the 1760s. The state followed Islamic law and procedures. It had two parts. Property and other civil matters were supervised by the dewan, the finance minister, through the dewanny court, or the "adawlut dewanny." Criminal jurisdiction was vested in the local ruler, the nawab nazim, and his officers and courts, the chief court being known as the "adawlut al alea" and later the "nizamat adawlut."[13] The local courts headed by the *qadis* (judges in Islamic courts) heard cases of both kinds, joined in negotiations between disputants, and presided over religious ceremonies. The reach of these Islamic courts was limited both socially and geographically. On the other hand, descriptions of local justice resembled the situation in Peshwa's domain or Mysore. In the 1830s, a survey of Bihar villages found that village elders and chiefs took part in settling disputes among their tenant farmers.[14] An almost contemporary survey of Bengal discovered the presence of caste gatherings and assemblies.[15] These assemblies were probably in general decline, for they received no mention when rural Bengal experienced a series of disputes over indigo sale in the 1850s.

At the turn of the nineteenth century, then, there were sufficient, if vague, references to the panchayat, or administration of civil justice by village headmen—enough for a section of the administration to recommend (in 1814) that this option should be included in the official "regulations" (on regulations, see below). The argument was sound enough. "No arrangement . . . can proceed . . . which has not a reference to the ancient and long established customs and institutions of the country."[16] Further, the local headmen were in possession of more information than were the judges in district towns. In the context of an explosion of suits involving the zamindari estates, numerous disputes over boundaries of property, and a flood of suits that the lower courts found unable to deal with, this was an attractive alternative. Nothing, however, came of it. The panchayat did not become part of the code of legal procedures. They were quietly ignored by the disputants as well as by the state.

In this vacuum, the first attempt at creating a system of law took shape.

The Hastings Project, 1772–81

The 1770s saw determined steps toward the definition of the executive and judicial branches of the government in Bengal. The company tried to retain control of both, but Parliament successfully obstructed these efforts. A council of four was to advise the governor general. And, as mentioned before, a Supreme Court was established in Calcutta, as the ultimate appellate court, for trying cases involving the state, and for those involving European subjects. Whereas until 1772, law and justice in the interior were responsibilities of the nawab, the structure of criminal and civil justice was streamlined and brought under one authority by Hastings's reforms.

Quarrels between the council and the court vitiated these efforts toward centralization. The chaos claimed one high-profile casualty, Nandakumar. Nandakumar was a senior tax officer of the nawab's court and brought in a charge of bribery against Hastings. Nandakumar was probably acting on behalf of the anti-Hastings lobby, and the charge may well have been fabricated. In any case, to clip Hastings's power, his vocal critics in the council gave the charge a sympathetic hearing. Hastings was himself a member of the council but stormed out of the meeting. Before the council could act on the charge, Nandakumar found himself in the Supreme Court on a charge of forgery of documents. The chief justice of the court, a friend of Hastings, tried Nandakumar for forgery and quickly sentenced him to death. The death sentence, carried out on August 5, 1775, was generally perceived as a judicial murder and symbolized the dangerously discordant nature of government in Bengal. It also represented a legal watershed in two distinct senses. Possibly for the first time in recent Indian history, the judiciary ruled against the executive. Not for the first time, the judiciary also played a political part. The second problem the incident exposed was the great uncertainty then prevailing over procedural law.

Notwithstanding these and other scandals, Warren Hastings's ten-year rule over Bengal laid the foundation for an institutional reform that was both unprecedented and revolutionary. There were two senses in which it was both of these. First, the new rule of law was founded on the principle that state civil law encompassed all inhabitants irrespective of their faith. The canon law practiced in the nawab's court did not have universality. Second, in order to implement one framework over all, it was necessary to have a properly organized system of courts. The only substantial thing known about the indigenous legal system was that courts of law had existed earlier, but their reach was exceedingly limited and they did not follow either a universal law or uniform procedures. This was where reform was needed. A universal system was needed, even though the users were to be given the choice to continue with their old ways.

What was to be the *lex loci*? Hastings represented a lobby that believed that substantive law in India should grow from indigenous roots rather than be imposed from the outside by the colonists. Local practices and principles of governance should be the basis for legislation. In choosing which practices to use as reference, a bias was expressed in favor of religious law. The foundation of rights and torts was seen to be religious. As we have seen, the law prevailing in the regions formerly under Islamic rule was Islamic law, and it was decided that this should be followed for the Muslims. Hindu, rather Brahminic, code books on law and conduct were full of injunctions about the superiority of caste, community, family, notions of purity, and the importance of being virtuous by maintaining the rules of the caste and the collective order. The code books offered little, by contrast, on courts and procedures. Nevertheless, influenced by this discourse, the British rulers decided that the foundation for law among Hindus was religious, just as it was among the Muslims.

The Hastings project led to an attempt to understand, reconstruct, and preserve indigenous religious codes; gave employment to scores of legal scholars—that is, pandits (Hindu scholars) and ulemas (Muslim religious scholars); and saw the start of schools of Hindu and Islamic traditions in Benares and Calcutta. The drive to define, codify, and preserve indigenous common law was led by scholars-linguists-jurists, including William Jones (1746–94), Henry Thomas Colebrooke (1765–1835), Thomas Strange (1756–1841), and the father and son Francis (1763–1843) and W. H. Macnaghten (1793–1841). All of them worked as judges in the company's courts. Jones was a contemporary of Hastings. The last named was a judge in the Sudder Dewanny Adawlut, the chief civil court of Calcutta in the nineteenth century. The digests on law that this energetic and innovative scholarly enterprise produced were expected to be used by judges as guidebooks.

The concrete effect of this project was that property right among the Hindus, Muslims, and Buddhists tended to be delivered to a joint family, something in between a unitary family and a kinship group. The precise definition of the joint family was left open. The understanding was that under Indian religious tradition, property was usually held in common among descendants of an original ancestor. This was the principle of impartible inheritance, and it worked in conjunction with a flexible concept of the joint family (see also chapter 5 on property).

The legal regime that Hastings had set in motion tried to be neither a completely new order nor a completely traditional order. It tried to be traditional in molding law after religious codes; it tried to be modern in creating a single procedure valid for all. Colonial law followed the English common law precedence in two very qualified senses: (a) allowing access to English law in the towns, to expatriates, and in the towns to those indigenous disputants who chose to be subjected to it, and (b) creating a "due process." A single referee and uniform procedures would arbitrate many players. Neither of these principles had existed in India before.

Regarding the system of courts, the 1770s innovation was to establish two appellate courts, a Sudder Dewanny Adawlut, or chief civil court, and a Fowzdarry Adawlut, or chief criminal court. The latter was an adaptation of its indigenous counterpart, whereas the former was in effect a new institution. With these moves, the mayors' courts were no longer needed. Supreme courts were established in Madras in 1801 and in Bombay in 1823. These courts had jurisdiction over the three port cities, or "presidency towns," and over all British subjects. The judges were Crown appointees. In the provinces, officers managed district courts. Seventeen of these were established. These were headed by revenue officers mostly, thereby giving rise to a persistent overlap between the executive and the judiciary in the interior, which was the subject of much discussion at the turn of the nineteenth century.

In all cases, the law in question in the case of property disputes was religious for Indian disputants. Commercial law in the port cities could refer to English precedence. Commercial law in the interior remained a black hole, despite a steady flow of European merchants and planters into the countryside in this period. In part, the gap was bridged with penal law in the case of certain breach-of-contract suits, but this practice raised more problems than it solved. Expatriates were thought to be protected from the chaos by the rule that they could be tried only by European judges. But then the judicial service in the interior saw steady recruitment of Indians. When on Thomas Macaulay's recommendation (see below) the privilege of Europeans to be tried only by Europeans was withdrawn (1836), the move provoked a fierce reaction. The European merchants called it the "Black Act" and unsuccessfully tried to block its passage.

Council Era, 1781–1861

In 1773, a crude system of legislation for the company territories was initiated. The council could pass a law but had to have it ratified by the Supreme Court. All laws needed the king's formal approval, but this was not a condition for their execution. A further proclamation in 1781 conditionally empowered the council to pass laws valid for the provincial courts without reference to the Supreme Court. The Supreme Court was not necessarily bound to these laws. This system of legislation by a committee prevailed with changes in detail for the next sixty years and was strengthened further by a proclamation in 1833 that reduced the Supreme Court's say further. The laws thus passed were called "regulations." The first compilation of these regulations appeared in 1793. Parliament informally ceded to the council the power to legislate for the provincial courts. Initially subjected to the authority of Calcutta, Madras received legislative autonomy in 1800, and Bombay in 1807. In 1807, a second and more comprehensive compilation of the regulations was published in Calcutta.[17]

Far from simplifying the legislative process, the regime complicated it hugely. Contradictions piled up as more regulations were added in response to new needs, such as taxation or new types of business like European plantations. There were many sources of contradiction. English parliamentary acts and the English common law were by default valid in India; indeed, the Supreme Courts functioned with reference to these. The provinces, the main field of legislative drive, saw a completely different set of laws constructed out of custom and religious codes. These codes covered property and debt much better than they did contracts and procedures. Practices in Bombay,

Madras, and Calcutta concurred in some respects but more often diverged. On matters of procedure, such as limitation (see chapter 9), the divergence caused a great deal of confusion.

Along with these administrative difficulties, the regime gave rise to huge anomalies in the application of religious codes to the context of property ownership and inheritance. These contradictions, which influenced subsequent legislation and case laws, are dealt with more fully in the chapters on property (3, 4, and especially 5). A general problem was that many more private family disputes than before were now flooding into the state courts. Earlier, communities settled civil disputes by means of their own courts following their own rules. The state did not need to care about the constitution of these bodies or the procedures that they followed. But now the judges in British Indian courts settled community disputes by means of common procedures that applied to all. With this shift, the problems began. The judges needed to spend time on interpretation of religious codes that provided conflicting guidelines. For example, impartible inheritance worked on the condition that women who married into the joint family had restricted claims on property. Otherwise, remarried widows threatened a division of the estate. But these legally valid claims of distant male relatives to be allowed a share in the joint estate conflicted with the moral claim of the immediate family of the head of a household to succeed.

Finally, there were too many fields overlooked by Hindu and Muslim law. As one authority remarked apropos the situation in the 1830s, "Setting aside Hindu and Mahomedan law, there was no law of contract, no law of succession, no territorial law, no law of evidence, [and] no law of administration of deceased estates."[18] Customary laws were not specified in enough detail to meet the needs of modern forms of business. Informal contract enforcement systems did not succeed in the sphere of transactions between parties who did not know each other well enough. It was not as if systematic procedures of business did not exist in precolonial India.[19] The problem was that impersonal and secular laws of business could not be found written down fully. At the same time, the scope of business transactions between parties that did not share either the same custom or an intimate knowledge of each other expanded enormously from the eighteenth century. The growth of trade in the nineteenth century increased the interactions between communities, leading to both more cooperation and more disputes. Sanskrit, Arabic, and Persian codes that the British Indian courts made use of were almost never successful in settling trade disputes or tort cases that came to these courts.

In practice, businesses exporting agricultural or craft goods from India tended to rely on middlemen. The middlemen had social power; that is, they were sufficiently stronger than the peasants or the artisans to be able to coerce or persuade the latter to fulfill the contracts. The middlemen also carried knowledge power; that is, they were better informed than the contracting merchants, often Europeans, about the peasants and the artisans. They therefore took advantage of the weakness of the one and the ignorance of the other to cause serious trouble to both. Agents and middlemen, in short, were part of the problem rather than the solution. As a result of the reliance on such agents, contractual disputes exploded in Indo-European trade and often took on violent character. Transactions in cotton, wheat, textiles, silk, opium, and indigo involved serious disagreements, which turned political in the indigo case (see chapter 7).

The mid-1830s saw two significant developments in response to these problems. The earlier event was the royal proclamation of 1833 that curtailed or removed the legislative authority of the Supreme Court and provincial councils, making the governor general in council the supreme legislative authority. The provinces got back their power to legislate in 1861, but under informal direction of the governor general. The 1833 proclamation also led to the establishment of a Law Commission that would enquire into the desirability of new substantive laws and suggest areas where reform and streamlining would be necessary.

The second event was the appointment of T. B. Macaulay (1800–1859) as the first law member of the new Governor General's Council, a position he held between 1834 and 1838. Macaulay, a historian, classicist, Whig politician, and defender of equality in the eyes of law (he had earlier advocated equality for the Jews in England, and later between the English and the Indians in India), was also a staunch critic of the ideological foundation underlying the Hastings project. He did not think much good would come of governing India by its own cultural precepts. In an infamous "minute" on Indian education, he rooted for Westernization of the school curriculum. The minute was influential, but not because Macaulay was persuasive. Rather, the minute came at a time when the Hastings project was collapsing under its own contradictions. Even among influential Indians, there were few admirers in the 1830s of Sanskrit and Persian authority in matters of law and, in turn, education. These languages were still widely taught, but demand for them was dwindling. English was in ascendance both as a lingua franca of business in the port cities and as the language of legislation and legal proceedings. Macaulay's minute struck a sympathetic chord among literate ambitious Indian elites for these reasons.

Independent of these events, the Hastings project had been losing support among the judges. In 1815, the governor general could still write of the old regime expressing the hope that "time" would heal the inequity that adopting Hindu religious guidance entailed. In this case, he was referring to the religious sanction to caste discrimination. "A judicial administration," he wrote, "which makes no distinction between the Brahmin and the soodur [Shudra, outcaste], cannot be popular in India."[20] The time to correct these biases had come in 1840.

The reference to religious codes was never the preferred guideline in areas outside Bengal. India, however, was a plural society, with not one but many religions. Codes differed also between sects within a broad religious fold. Not only were the Hindus a diverse group, but also Muslim law in practice had little uniformity, and in Burma, indigenous Buddhists and Buddhist migrants from China followed different personal law. Although such complexities did not bother the early codifiers much, they would become a headache for the judges a generation later. In practice, all of these codes apparently existed more as ethos rather than as positive law. The very principle of decentralized jurisdiction would have made any top-down written code irrelevant. In this scenario, the government could only accord all reasonable claims and many unreasonable ones equal status. And in order to maintain strict equality, it instituted universal procedures and a universal system of courts.

Even in Bengal, the Regulation of 1832, while reaffirming the Hastings project, expressly qualified it by the statement that religious codes "shall be held to apply to such persons only as shall be *bona fide* professors of those religions at the time of the application of the law to the case, and were designed for the protection of the rights of such persons, not for the deprivation of the rights of others."[21] The so-called Lex Loci Act of 1850 further affirmed that excommunication from caste could not lawfully lead to deprivation of property. Bombay regulations, which came thirty years after the Bengal ones, were from the start skeptical of religious guidance and gave precedence to local usage or customary law instead. Punjab, which became part of British India in 1849, expressed a stronger preference for customary law over scriptures, an idea often identified with the Punjab Civil Code and the Punjab school of administration.

The fifteen years that elapsed between the first Law Commission, of 1842, and the Indian Mutiny of 1857 were years of exceedingly slow progress in matters of legislation and policy. A proclamation of 1853 that allowed for provincial representation in the Governor General's Council notwithstanding, there was very little real change, and hardly any new laws were passed.

Several of the Law Commission's recommendations were left to gather dust. But after the Mutiny, progress was extremely rapid and many sided. The first major move to reform was the 1861 one that allowed the reestablishment of provincial legislatures, a semipolitical step taken to allow some heads of princely states to share in the legislative process.

The High Courts Act of 1861 allowed the establishment of high courts. By 1866, high courts were established in the major cities, and the cluster of civil courts below these courts were organized in a tiered structure. The new regime superseded the older one, which had consisted of three Supreme Courts in the three presidencies, mainly following English common law and statutes, and the "sudder adawluts" and district courts in the interior, following a diluted version of indigenous custom. The new system was formed of a concentric hierarchical structure of courts which continued after 1947.

If such was the origin of the legal system, what were its results?

An Inefficient System

In the winter of 1814–15, a series of reports conducted in all the provinces revealed a growing backlog of suits at all levels of the judiciary.[22] Concerns over the efficiency of the courts were raised from the very beginning of the formation of the company's system. Governor General Cornwallis (1738–1805, in office 1786–93) worried that the growing backlog of suits (1793) struck "at the very root of the prosperity of the country."[23] Since the majority of these suits concerned disputes between landholders and tenants or between one farmer and another over land, justice delayed led to violent "affrays." In 1793, the large estates possessed armed retainers, which added to the worry. The cost in time and money of accessing the courts was enormous, and delay added to these costs.[24] The common remedy to which all administrators agreed was increasing the number of lower and small-causes courts headed by Indian judges, though few believed this was the ideal solution. And in any case, it failed to redress the problem effectively. It is interesting to observe how the problem was diagnosed by contemporary authorities.

Almost all interpretations seem to agree that the main problem was the unusually long time that even simple proceedings were taking around 1800. Why was that the case? The Madras statesman Thomas Munro (1761–1827) hinted at a disconnection between communal loyalty and public honesty. On the one hand, an Indian made business deals all the time, "with comparatively few disputes," and yet without any formal contractual document or receipt, manifesting "a high degree of mutual confidence . . . [and] conviction of the probity of each other." On the other hand, the same individual would "perjure himself in a litigation respective water, boundaries of villages, and privileges of caste. He will also perjure himself, with little hesitation, in favour of a relation, a friend, or an inhabitant of the same village."[25] Whether this description was fair or generalizable or not, it was not just communal ethic that delayed the proceedings.

The governor general's diagnosis of the problem was that much time was wasted in matters "extraneous" to the case, leading to the high proportion of appeals made.[26] In making an explicit comparison with England, a report written by the secretary to the government of Bengal (1814) suggested that the contents of the legal codes were the main obstacle. Not only did the codes complicate proceedings, but also they erected obstacles to easy access to legal information, without which a common law court can become paralyzed. "The diversity of the law, composed as it is of the Hindoo and Mahomedan codes, with numerous additions . . . the want of fixed and established principles in the conduct of the business of the courts of judicature, and . . . the consequent want of uniformity in the decisions of these courts" combine to "deprive" the "community" of litigants as well as judicial officers of "legal information."

The state of affairs caused "moral hazard," attracting lawyers who were "extremely illiterate" and yet good at "promoting litigation" by withholding information, among other means.[27] In the newly conquered areas, where peasant property rights were established (called raiyatwari), the village officers and headmen were constantly summoned to courts located fifty or a hundred miles away as witnesses, causing great trouble to their own affairs. In these regions, therefore, the local officers had developed a general aversion to the Bengal system of setting up state courts and gave opinions in favor of village panchayats and local courts of justice to settle small causes as far as possible. As we have mentioned before, this discussion did not lead anywhere, and the village courts were not integrated into the institutions of justice. Their proponents did not seem to have much knowledge of these courts as real-life institutions.

A second survey, conducted in the 1830s, suggested a slight improvement in the situation. The number of total and appellate cases had more than doubled between 1800 and 1840, but the pace of disposal of cases had improved too, and the worry over backlog was absent in the 1840s survey (table 2.1). The latter report does not suggest why the situation improved. The number of judicial officers had increased rapidly (see also chapter 9).

Table 2.1 Suits pending in the Sudder Dewanny Adawlaut

	Number of Cases Pending	Net Addition during the Year
1802	105	−15
1814	2,667	52
1838	736 (Bengal only)	−71

Sources: British Parliamentary Papers, *Papers Relating to Police, Civil and Criminal Justice under Governments of Bengal, Fort-St.-George and Bombay, 1810–19* (London: HMSO, 1819): 101, 105; Sykes (1843).

But alongside that, the judges departed from their earlier adherence to Hindu and Muslim code books far more frequently than before. The situation improved (that is, the net addition to the backlog fell) because a judicial principle of blindly following traditional codes was collapsing all round.

Conclusion

The legal framework that the East India Company instituted in India was modeled on a set of codes derived from religious scriptures. The only way this system could possibly work was jurisdictional fragmentation that would make available one code for one religious group and another for another group, allowing some scope for crossovers between codes. These crossovers and the availability of English law for expatriates involved an incorporation of English statutes and the spirit of the English court of equity. But the scope of such convergence was initially narrow.

By 1850, the desire for reform had gained a following. The acquisition of large territories in western and southern India and more recently in Punjab and Awadh had made it imperative to fit property rights with a different land revenue system from that prevailing in Bengal. The new framework privileged local custom over religious codes. A deeper process of reform began shortly thereafter, induced by judgments in appeals cases and by the Law Commission. The general sentiment was that *lex loci* could not be constructed on the foundation of Hindu or Islamic law. A representative statement is the one made by Erskine Perry (1806–82), chief justice of the Supreme Court of Bombay. In Perry's opinion, "a jurist qua jurist has only to deal with human laws, he recognises the existence of divine laws, . . . but . . . does not recognise them as enforceable in Courts of justice any further than the secular power has ordained." The 1772 pronouncement which had established religion as the basis for Indian codification he dismissed as a political act. "I think it is quite clear that the clause in question was framed solely on political views, and without any reference to . . . the purity of any particular religious belief."[28]

In the second half of the nineteenth century, a legislative drive led to the creation of a number of specific laws, commercial laws, and provincial laws. In all cases, there were departures from Indian tradition in general, and from religious codes in particular. Curiously, all courts were entitled to try suits by both old and new sets of laws. Like an archaeological excavation site, different legislative principles devised in different times formed layers, and all of these layers were available to the judiciary of the late nineteenth century. In this way, while the legislature solved some problems, it also sowed new seeds of discord and delay, by encouraging litigants to try their luck with reference to different laws (see also chapter 9 on procedures), and to be more willing to go to appeals. The process was unusually information intensive, because appeals would need to go over the same ground.

The earliest of the layers consisted of laws relating to agricultural land and land mortgage (1793–1885). At the end of the eighteenth century, land revenue sustained the state, and raising it and securing it was a life-and-death issue against the backdrop of wars breaking out on many fronts. Thereafter, the framework of law relating to agricultural land and agricultural classes entailed its own trajectory and momentum of change. This large subject is addressed in the next two chapters.

THREE

Landed Property:
Security and Incentives

What the British established in India might be described, in fact, as an imperfect or *kaccha* kind of private ownership of land.

—Daniel Thorner[1]

The attitude of the colonial state towards a hypothetical capitalist transformation of agriculture was notoriously ambiguous.

—David Washbrook[2]

Introduction

The history of land law in colonial India is, to put it mildly, dense and complex. Land tenure varied greatly across space and time, with a corresponding proliferation of administrative terminology. So there is a compelling need, despite the risks, for some simplification—to identify some broad categories through which to approach the subject. Typically, the literature has relied on the distinction between two types of proprietorship, zamindari and raiyatwari, representing ownership by "landlords" and "cultivators," speaking loosely. This is a useful distinction, which has stood the test of time. However, as economic historians focused on investment and growth, we feel the need for a richer typology. We have created this by considering two other axes: the security provided (or not) to tenants, and the transferability (or not) of land, which is potentially the most valuable collateral against which to obtain credit. Thus, in our framework we have eight types of land tenure regimes, depending on the type of proprietorship, the presence or absence of tenant protection, and the transferability or lack thereof of land rights. We use this structure to organize the discussion of this chapter and a portion of the next chapter, though some of the eight potential categories are thinly populated.

We begin in this chapter with the first two dimensions of the typology, rights of owners and rights of tenants, and add the third dimension, transferability, in the next chapter. The discussion of land transfer leads naturally to credit markets and legislation to regulate them. This exposition allows us to describe legal and institutional nuances, while retaining a focus on the investment incentives and capacities they generate.[3]

The Three Dimensions of Regulation: Proprietorship, Tenancy, Transferability

Imagine for a moment that when it conquered each new region, the company or the Raj had found a clean slate: it could write land law as it wanted. What would it have done? We can be fairly sure that in the early stages of the rule, when the company needed funds for trade as well as for military adventures, it would have looked for substantial tax revenues. But subject to this need, it would have sought to maximize growth. From the outset the company and the Crown understood that the British would gain more revenue from India if it prospered.[4] Based on the economic thinking of the late eighteenth century it would have sought to promote investment, by providing secure property ownership. To whom would it have given ownership? The English "improving landlord" was one obvious model: given a secure right, the owner of a large property would develop his estate, prospering alongside his tenants, whom he would treat well with his own long-term interests at heart. As we will see below, these were indeed the terms in which land tenure was discussed by company officials in India. But, in theory, there were other alternatives: secure ownership rights could have been given to cultivators who would prosper by working hard and investing. Transferability of land would be important, because it would allow land to be used as collateral for loans, and also to be transferred to the more productive user (see below). These conjectures regarding the company's intuitions must sound very familiar to many readers. They have survived in mainstream economics to the present-day.[5]

The company did not, of course, find a blank slate. How did the evolution of land law actually play out? To retain coherence, much of our focus in this chapter will be on the Bengal and Madras Presidencies, the earliest regions to be colonized, with only brief excursions into other regions, some of which we will discuss more fully in chapter 4.[6] As we mentioned earlier, the two grand categories used by the company in its formulation of land law were zamindari and raiyatwari. In the former, the owner was not expected to be the cultivator: he or she would be a landlord, it was hoped of the progressive, investment-oriented variety. In the latter, the owner would also cultivate—the dynamic peasant would drive the agrarian economy. The distinction between these categories, as theorized, was clear. But it was blurred in practice: a diverse set of arrangements could exist under each of these umbrella names.

We have organized our discussion of the evolution of land law into three sections, using more familiar categories: state and owner, landlord and protected tenant, and unprotected tenant. We will argue that the relationship between state and owner was typically not problematic in a legal sense. The law could be harsh, but it was clear and usually enforced rigorously. Relations between landlord and tenant, in contrast, were often complex. Early legislation left the legal status of the tenant ambiguous, subsequent clarification in court and legislation was a long time coming, political combat between landlord and tenant spilled over into courts, and by the end of the colonial period the legal system was overburdened and sometimes overwhelmed. The incentives for investment probably deteriorated over time in some important regions. In short, the ideal structure of property rights we described above was far from realized in some important regions. But our discussion is incomplete until we turn to the next chapter, where we examine the transferability of land and its connection to credit markets. Eventually, we tell a story of variability across space and time. In some times and locations land law and legal institutions may well have limited economic growth. In others, the picture was not nearly so bleak.

State and Owner

The East India Company's conquest of Bengal via the Battles of Plassey (1757) and Buxar (1764) is often identified as the key to its eventual domination of the Indian subcontinent. Bengal was a rich region, and its resources would prove valuable to the company. Resources from Bengal could be used to buy the textiles the company was exporting in huge quantities to Europe, they could pay for the company's frequent wars, and in the early years they were a source of "corruption" for company officials. But first they had to be accessed. Indeed, collection of taxes was the company's primary role as the Dewan (roughly, finance minister), the title it had acquired from the Mughal emperor. Who would collect the tax, and from whom? This question was, from the outset, linked to the allocation of property rights.

The answer to this question was by no means straightforward. The company was now administering a large area with a variety of land tenure arrangements. The bundle of rights associated with a single piece of land might lie with different people: one might have the right to collect taxes for the nawab of Bengal, others might have the right to undisturbed *use* so long as they paid customary rent, they in turn might have the right to sublet the land, and so on. There were also areas that were de facto small kingdoms, with the landholder controlling enormous tracts of land, managing law and order, administering justice, and maintaining public goods. There were barely 250 officers in the company's civil service in Bengal in 1773, and the population they were governing was well in excess of twenty million.[7] Given the scope and complexity of the company's task, it had to rely on local intermediaries.

The beginning was not auspicious. The company tried to rely on the existing tax administration but was unable to supervise it adequately. Amid allegations of corruption and poor governance, a devastating famine struck Bengal in 1770, when as much as a third of the population may have died in some regions. Under severe criticism from various parties in London, including Parliament and the press, the company was forced to take a more active role. Still, its next choice—tax farming—continued to reflect its limited administrative capacity. Moreover, since farms were auctioned to the highest bidder, it was somewhat predictable that auction theory's "winner's curse" would apply, and that revenue farmers would default.[8] Eventually the company settled on an administratively simple solution. A diverse group of people, many previously connected with tax collection, were declared "proprietors," and the tax they owed was fixed in nominal terms in perpetuity— hence the term "Permanent Settlement." If owners did not pay the tax, their land would be seized and auctioned. The proclamation of the Permanent Settlement in 1793 reserved the option to protect the rights of tenants situated lower in the agrarian hierarchy. The option was, at the time, only lip service, but subsequently it turned out to be important.

The Permanent Settlement was preceded by decades of discussion in which investment incentives were front and center. Indeed, the proclamation of the Permanent Settlement (Regulation I, Article VI, 1793) explicitly argued that benefits would flow from the owner's secure right to the *entire* return on any investment:

> The Governor General in Council trusts that the proprietors of the land, sensible of the benefits conferred upon them by the public assessment being fixed for ever, will exert themselves in the cultivation of their lands, under the certainty that they will enjoy exclusively the fruits of their own good manage-

ment and industry, and that no demand will ever be made upon them, or their heirs, or successors, by the present, or any future government, for an augmentation of the public assessment in consequence of the improvement of their respective estates.[9]

What if the zamindar could not pay the tax, and the land had to be sold? Philip Francis, an early proponent of the Permanent Settlement, was not troubled by this possibility: "A transfer of landed property to monied people, who are able to make improvements, will be in some degree advantageous to Government and to the country."[10]

The theoretical discussion notwithstanding, the case can be made that the Permanent Settlement was really driven by the company's need to "outsource" its tax collection. Had the company sought to immediately protect tenants' rights, it would have had to investigate the structure of land rights. Had it linked the tax to output, or retained the right to raise it, it would have had to keep track of changes in cropped area and value of output. The Permanent Settlement required none of this. The development of a bureaucracy that would engage with the nitty-gritty of agrarian structure and production could wait until the second half of the nineteenth century, when British rule had both expanded in area and consolidated in authority. We are, therefore, inclined to agree with Peter Robb that the Permanent Settlement was "to an extent just another quasi-feudal response by a weak state."[11] The Permanent Settlement in Bengal also became the model for portions of the Madras Presidency that were settled under regulations enacted in 1802.

Now that the company had laid down the law, how would it be enforced? Two sets of relationships needed to be regulated: between the state and the zamindar, and between the zamindar and the tenant. The company decided that if the property right of the zamindar was to be secure, it had to be protected even from the state. So disputes between the zamindar and the state would no longer be adjudicated by revenue officials—they would now go to the civil courts described in chapter 2. This clean separation did not last very long, and by the early nineteenth century, probably on grounds of convenience and speed, such matters were adjudicated in "revenue courts."[12] But civil courts remained available for appeals, and the idea that the courts were a check on the power of the state had been enunciated clearly, a development that was to have important long-term implications. An example of how this could play out in court is provided by *Collector of Moorshedabad v. Bishennath Rai and Sheonath Rai* (ca. 1802), wherein a zamindar successfully disputed the state's right to tax a portion of his property, on the grounds of prior exemption.[13] Such disputes did not proliferate, because the company, and later the Crown, kept its word on a central point: the land tax was never raised.[14]

The Permanent Settlement was perceived very negatively in some official circles. Many zamindars could not pay the high land tax, and their lands were sold. In some instances, the high land tax led to rack renting by zamindars, and the peasants deserted.[15] In some regions there was a proliferation of intermediaries between the zamindars to whom tax collection was delegated and the actual cultivator, a phenomenon known as "subinfeudation." Amit Bhaduri has argued that zamindars did this for insurance against risk, in the face of high land taxes.[16]

After early experience in those South Indian regions where the state relied less on powerful intermediaries, Thomas Munro, a former military officer who became an influential administrator, pushed for an alternative to the Permanent Settlement which aimed to provide ownership (and tax obligation) to the cultivator, thereby creating a direct relationship of the state with the cultivator. Facing the prestige and influence of the Bengal school, Munro took a long time to win the argument, but, after a period of experimentation the raiyatwari system was introduced in the bulk of the Madras Presidency in the 1820s, and then shortly after in the Bombay Presidency.[17]

The case for raiyatwari was made via a critique of zamindari, and its alleged unsuitability to Indian conditions.[18] But raiyatwari was also a more administratively demanding arrangement, because the state was now entering into agreements with a much larger number of people. Raiyatwari required that the company officials and its Indian intermediaries engage with the countryside at a micro level, because taxes had to be based on productivity. Officials had to make judgments about prevailing rents and sometimes even the quality of soil. Lack of information could lead to poor choices, such as unfair allocation of the tax burden. Officials often discussed the appropriate level of taxation in theoretical terms, the Ricardian theory of rent being at the center of the discussion.[19] But administrative considerations and revenue needs eventually drove the decisions.[20] And, as in the case of zamindari, the government was prompt in selling the property of defaulters. The state was rigorous, even harsh, in enforcing its rights, but there was little legal ambiguity.

Relations between state and owner, as pertaining to the state's right to tax, did become a source of controversy, in both zamindari and raiyatwari areas, when it came to inam land. *Inam* can be translated as "reward." In precolonial India, such land was given at a low rent to religious institutions or persons, for military service, for holding hereditary office, for maintenance of irrigation facilities, and even for minor governmental functions. The extent of inam land was substantial. In 1885, of the 90.4 million acres shown by the Survey Department in the Madras Presidency as a whole, roughly 8 million acres were under inam, with the proportion being much higher in some areas.[21] Inams varied greatly in size. The Inam Commission (1869) complained that, before conquest by the company, individuals might hold whole villages "under conditions of service which was neither rendered nor called for under the British administration."[22] Still, by and large, the company and then the Raj honored existing inams.

Why would the company's administration give up so much potential revenue? The Inam Commission clarified.[23] Referencing an insurrection by a certain Narasimha Reddi in Cuddapah (Kadapa), the Court of Directors in a judicial dispatch (October 14, 1847) warned against disturbing long-held rights: "The arbitrary resumption of tenures and the ill-advised transfer of landed property in India, whether effected by Courts of Law or by the Officers of the Government, are almost invariably followed by disaffection and disorder." After some more back-and-forth correspondence, the Court of Directors came to a decision: "They accordingly directed that all Inams enjoyed uninterruptedly since the introduction of British rule, whether held under Sanads [governmental decrees] or not, should be confirmed to the holders."[24] In practice, the required period of uninterrupted holding was reduced to fifty years, and a light tax was assigned. The extent of inam is a very clear indication of the political constraints on land taxation policy. Without these constraints, it is hard to see the cash-strapped company/Raj forgoing substantial amounts of tax revenues.

The *inamdar*, like the zamindar, was also protected by the state as judiciary from the state as executive. In a case heard in the Bombay High Court in 1873, Vasudev Patil, who had been given the inam of a village by the government in 1818, sued the collector (official in charge of land revenue administration) for interfering with his property rights by opening a quarry and taking stones and sand. Ruling for Patil, the high court argued that once the Inam Commissioner had ruled, the executive had to respect its decision. The case summary is worth quoting because it is quite specific about the principle in question: "The Inam Commissioner's decisions, under Act XI of 1852, on matters falling within his jurisdiction, are final, except when, and as modified by an appeal to the Government in its judicial capacity under the Act; and binding not only upon the *Inamdar*, but upon the Government itself in its executive capacity: and where a Government officer infringes the rights of an *Inamdar* thus determined, an action lies against him in Civil Court."[25] We have argued thus far that relations between state and owner, primarily pertaining to taxation, were generally defined clearly, and enforced rigorously, in both zamindari and raiyatwari areas. What was the *level* of this taxation? If taxes were set at a high and "extractive" level, the clarity of legal status would not confer substantive security of property rights. Our understanding of this issue varies by region, perhaps even more by period. In the late eighteenth and early nineteenth centuries the cash-strapped company did set land taxes at a high level. According to one authority, the taxes associated with the Permanent Settlement were "unbearably high."[26] Another work suggests that in 1793 the tax burden was approximately 18%–20% higher than it had been in 1757.[27] It is also likely that the company was more effective in extracting its stated tax demand and more rigid (in the sense of not providing remissions when crops failed) than precolonial regimes. There was significant turnover of land, and sale of zamindaries. Even in raiyatwari regions land taxes were high and defaults could lead to land sales, especially in the Madras Presidency. According to one estimate "coercive processes" (land sales) were applied to collect 4%–5% of taxes in each of the years 1870–71, 1871–72, and 1872–73.[28] So the case for an "extractive" state as described by Acemoglu and Robinson (2013) can be made for some regions for parts of the nineteenth century.[29]

However, with the passage of time, the tax burden declined. In the zamindari regions under the Permanent Settlement this was inevitable—after all, the tax had been fixed in nominal terms in perpetuity, whereas cultivated area and population grew. But even in the temporarily settled zamindari areas and raiyatwari areas (see map 3.1), in which the state could periodically increase taxes, political compulsions led the state to seek other sources of revenue. By 1900–1901, land taxes were only 5% of gross agricultural output, and this figure had declined to 2% by 1946–47.[30] Indeed, one can make the case that, far from being "extractive," in the twentieth century the Raj taxed too little, and provided too few public goods.[31]

We now turn to the relations between landlords and tenants whose pre-existing rights the colonial state did not intend, in principle, to abrogate. To simplify this exposition we have divided it into three sections, the first two dealing with the experience of the Bengal and Madras Presidencies and the third summing up.

Landlord and Protected Tenant: Bengal Presidency

If the zamindar of the Permanent Settlement was to pay taxes, he or she had to collect rents from tenants. How much rent could the zamindar charge? And what if the tenant did not pay? When the Permanent Settlement was

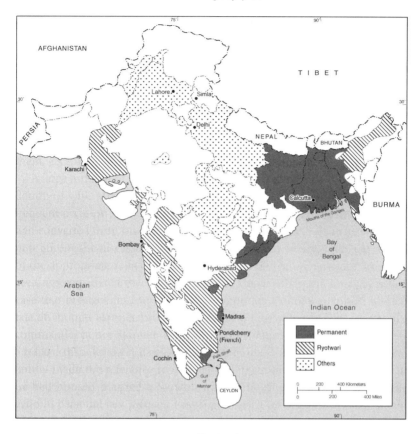

Map 3.1. Types of land settlements, 1858.

proclaimed, Lord Cornwallis (governor general at the time) was clear that (a) tenants had customary rights regarding rents and protection from eviction; and (b) the company's government did not have enough information to define these rights in law. In a minute dated February 11, 1793, Lord Cornwallis wrote that the "vague term of usage was the only rule for deciding upon any question respecting the Revenue and the rights of those concerned in the payment of it," and "precedent might be pleaded in justification of every species of exaction and oppression."[32] So the proclamation of the Permanent Settlement took two steps: it warned the zamindar not to act arbitrarily against the tenant and reserved the government's right to intervene to protect these rights in the future. Regulation VIII of 1793 warned the zamindar not to impose "any new abwab or mathot [fines or fees] upon the ryots under any pretence whatsoever."[33] And, in words that were to have impact far into the future, the regulations reserved the following right for the government:

> The Governor-General in Council will, whenever he may deem it proper, en-act such Regulations as he may think necessary for the protection and welfare of dependent talookdars, ryots, and other cultivators of the soil; and no ze-mindar, independent talookdar, or other actual proprietor of land, shall be entitled, on this account, to make any objection to the discharge of the fixed assessment which they have respectively agreed to pay.[34]

These regulations are worth quoting because they point to the ambiguity at the heart of the Permanent Settlement. The only thing permanent was the tax the zamindar would pay. Much else—especially the tenant's right to occupancy as well as the rent he or she would pay—was left to be clarified. As the reader will see, this would lead to disputes over a century and a half.

The company's information deficit persisted into the nineteenth century. In the discussion preceding new regulations passed in 1812 an official argued that "there was actually no sufficient evidence of the rates and usages of pergunnahs, which could be appealed to" to decide how landlord-tenant relations should be regulated.[35] Following this, Regulation V of 1812 (known as Panjam, meaning fifth) ostensibly passed to give some protection to the tenant (see below), used language that some interpreted as giving the zamindar the right to set rents as he or she chose. Indeed, the Court of Directors' interpretation in 1819 was that, as the law now stood, zamindars "are authorized, by the existing law, to oust even the hereditary Ryots from possession of their lands, when the latter refuse to accede to any terms of rent which may be demanded of them, however exorbitant."[36]

The company gave the zamindar considerable powers to recover rent. The Haptam (seventh) Regulation of 1799 was notorious in this respect. It allowed the zamindar to seize and sell the defaulting tenant's property while waiting for a judicial decision.[37] If a zamindar filed a legal complaint against the tenant, he could be arrested even before any investigation.[38] But, perhaps most important, "no part of the existing Regulations was meant to deprive the Zemindars and other landholders of the power of summoning, and if necessary of compelling the attendance of their tenants, for the adjustment of their rents, or for any other just purpose."[39] This gave the zamindar license to personally coerce the tenant. The 1812 regulation subsequently placed some restrictions on the zamindar's rights to sell the tenant's property, but the provision permitting coercion remained in place until 1859.

The ambiguous laws and the substantial privatization of rent recovery inevitably implied conflict between landlord and tenant. How did this power struggle play out? At one level, we have the example of Jaykrishna Mukherjee, zamindar of a large estate called Uttarpara near Calcutta. Even his sympathetic biographer acknowledges that "his methods of dealings with his tenants were of a rather summary nature" (!) and mentions his use of enforcers who used clubs (*lathiyal*).[40] This was apparently common practice among zamindars. Jaykrishna Mukherjee also filed (and usually won) a large number of suits against his tenants—for instance, for resumption of lands which they had claimed were rent free. But we can also find descriptions of zamindars who were more constrained: it has been persuasively argued by Ratnalekha Ray that many zamindars had to come to terms with tenants who were in fact powerful landholders at the village level (jotedars).[41] Jotedars were in physical control of the land. They might cultivate some, lease out the rest to sharecroppers, and also operate as moneylenders.[42] Ray's view of the status of the jotedar is reflected in an unusual description: "peasant landlord."[43] The zamindars could not increase the jotedars' rents at will and had to share the surplus they exacted from the sharecroppers with them.

Ray's identification of the jotedars depends to a large extent on surveys by Francis Buchanan, one of which was in Dinajpur District.[44] Buchanan states that of the 7.2 million bighas (a third of an acre), 1.09 million were under "principal farmers" who had about 165 bighas each, and 0.66 million were under "great farmers," who had about 75 bighas each.[45] He classified 7% of the farmers as "principal" or "great." Most of their land was cultivated via sharecroppers, and they loaned money "both to those who cultivate for share, and to their other necessitous neighbours."[46] Buchanan's comments about the incentives for investment are striking. He claims that "in almost every part of the district the leases are granted in perpetuity and the tenant will not accept of any other." Moreover, "in some places, they even pretend to a right of perpetual possession *at the usual rent* [our italics], if they have occupied a farm for ten years." Therefore, he writes, "the landlord [zamindar] has no incentive to lay out any money in improvement."[47] Here Buchanan turned the rationale for the Permanent Settlement on its head: Governor General Cornwallis had argued that security of tenure and tax would motivate the zamindar to invest. But if the zamindar could not raise rents on his tenant, it was the tenant who would gain from output growth, and he would have the incentive to invest. This illustrates the potential gap between the structure of incentives the Permanent Settlement intended to create and what actually came into being.[48]

In this context it is worth noting that the claim of a perpetual lease at fixed rent was not limited to Dinajpur, and such claims could be taken to court. There was a tenure called "Istimrari," acknowledged in regulations passed in 1793, in which the tenant had such rights. In 1803 Durpnarain Rai and others took Chintamunee Mustofee to district court in Nuddea (Nadia), claiming the defendant had attempted to oust them from their fixed-rented land. The plaintiffs showed a decree from the zamindar of Nadia in 1737 confirming their fixed rents. The district judge ruled in favor of the plaintiff, and his decision was upheld by the provincial court as well as the Sadar Diwani Adalat.[49]

From early on, some company officials argued that legislation was required to clarify tenants' rights. A regulation to protect tenants was proposed in 1826. But the company was unwilling to change the law because of administrative worries and a reluctance to alter rights in property that it believed it had granted. If disputes had remained at the level of individual landlord and tenant, in court or outside, discussion of tenant protection might not have become urgent. But political unrest emerged, which eventually led to legislation. Some of the early protests were in the regions inhabited by the so-called tribes, whose religious and cultural practices differed from the Hindu mainstream, and which sometimes practiced shifting cultivation as opposed to settled peasant agriculture.[50] The power given to the zamindar by the Permanent Settlement had disrupted their traditional sources of authority, such as the village headmen. Moreover, rent increases, indebtedness to immigrant moneylenders, and abuses by government functionaries had fueled resentment. The Kol insurrection in Chota Nagpur in 1831–32 had to be suppressed by troops brought from other areas, who on one occasion faced a rebel force of three thousand men.[51] Zamindars and moneylenders were targeted in the large-scale Santhal insurrection of 1855. And it is likely that the Indian Mutiny (1857), which led to a profound questioning of the company's policies in India, reinforced the position of those arguing for intervention to protect tenants and stabilize agrarian society. Sir Rivers Thomson, who was lieutenant governor of Bengal, said in the Imperial Legislative Council in 1883: "It was only when . . . the oppressions of the landlords threatened an agrarian revolution that the Government stepped in by a legislative enactment to arrest the natural increase of rent in Bengal, and the result was the land law of 1859."[52]

Eventually, a weak law, the Bengal Rent Act of 1859, was passed, with a view to protecting tenants from arbitrary evictions and enhancements of rent. A tenant who had occupied a piece of land continuously for twelve years was declared an "occupancy tenant." He or she could hold the land in perpetuity, subject to paying a rent that was "fair and equitable." But the words "fair and equitable" had to be translated into a more precise criterion. The manner in which this was done is an interesting lesson in the role of English precedent. In 1862 a darpatnidar named James Hills sought to increase the rents of his tenant, Ishwar Ghose, because output had increased "otherwise than by the agency or at the expense of the ryot."[53] The additional judge of Nuddea (Nadia) had argued that the proportionate increase in rent could not exceed the proportionate increase in output. Since the increase Hills had demanded was smaller than this amount, the court had ruled in his favor. Ghose appealed to the high court, which delivered a decision that fundamentally undermined the intention of the act of 1859 to protect the tenant. Justice Peacock agreed with the lower court in ruling against Ghose but disagreed with its rationale. Peacock argued that the 1859 act said nothing about the rule of proportions. Quoting Mill and Malthus, Peacock defined rent in Ricardian terms as the return to the landowner after all costs, including the cost of capital, had been accounted for. In effect Peacock had said an occupancy tenant could be charged a competitive rent.

The issue had not been settled. In 1865, two high court judges received an appeal from a plaintiff (tenant) whose rent increases had been upheld by lower courts. Since a ruling in a later case had conflicted with Justice Peacock's decision in *Ghose v. Hills*, the judges asked for a full bench ruling regarding whether a competitive rent should be charged or whether rent should be determined by custom. And if the latter, how should enhancement be determined if the customary rate had not changed? This came to be known as the Great Rent Case.[54] Justice Trevor, with whom the majority concurred, also quoted Mill, but in opposition to Peacock's position. Competition, which prevailed in England, was "comparatively modern," and in times past "custom" had prevailed "as protector of the weak against the strong."[55] India was still at the stage where custom applied.[56] After a lengthy discussion of the history of land tenure and taxation in India, Justice Trevor concluded that custom required that the zamindar get a fixed fraction of the gross produce, so that the rent should rise in proportion to the increase in output, with the benchmark output being the average for three to five years before the increase. An interesting aspect of this case is that only one justice out of twelve (Justice Peacock) dissented. Perhaps, consistent with a more cautious post-Mutiny official sensibility, there was broad agreement in the judiciary that, as Justice Trevor put it, "any reasoning drawn from facts peculiar to England must be fallacious."[57]

Not surprisingly, the 1859 act was not very effective. It had decreed that a tenant could obtain protection by obtaining "occupancy rights," if he had occupied a piece of land for twelve years. Zamindars were able to evade this law by switching tenants from plot to plot.[58] In the 1870s tenants' discontent received organized political expression via the formation of the Agrarian League in Pabna, in central Bengal, which withheld rents and challenged zamindars in court.[59] The tenants, some of whom were of substantial means, received support from urban-educated English-speaking middle-class activists. Zamindars, of course, had their own association and complained about the difficulties in realizing rents. It was evident that the 1859 act was not satisfying either tenants or zamindars. Legislation aimed at addressing the zamindars' concerns was passed in 1878, but strengthening tenant protection was to be more of a challenge. Eventually, the Bengal government decided that a complete overhaul of the Rent Act was required. It took a while longer. There was a Rent Commission, a draft bill (1880), public commentary on the bill, and a revised bill responding to the commentary. During this period important officials on different sides of the issue came and went. Eventually the Bengal Tenancy Act was passed in 1885.

During the debate the Raja of Darbhanga, who was zamindar of an enormous estate (2,400 square miles) in Bihar, warned the government against "broken faith" and reminded it that "the foundation of British rule in India is justice."[60] He also made an argument based on affinity: the tenants belonged "to the same castes as the zamindars," and the zamindars often had "many of their own kith and kin among their ryots." Therefore, relations between them were good. The collector of Dacca (Dhaka) was among those who argued that "the action of the proposed law will only be to make the occupancy tenant the rack-renter instead of the present landlord."[61] Part of the difficulty was that there was considerable variation in the relative status of zamindar and tenant across regions. The collector of Moorshedabad (Murshidabad) argued that while "in some parts of the country it may be that the ryot is unable to look after himself . . . in many others the zemindars have by no means the best of it."[62]

An 1883 official report examining reactions to the proposed bill, and providing some revisions, made the case for tenant protection. It was quite clear, it argued, that "the rights of proprietorship conferred upon the zemindars were not 'absolute' rights such as are involved in the notion of proprietary rights in England."[63] The government had reserved the right to intervene to protect tenants in the original proclamation of the Permanent Settlement, and both justice and the need to promote prosperity dictated that tenants should have security and protection from arbitrary rent increases.[64] Eventually, the bill that passed had as its key provision the creation of a category called the "settled raiyat." A settled raiyat was someone who had held land anywhere in the village for twelve years. This person would get occupancy rights, meaning security of tenure conditional on payment of rent and pro-tection from arbitrary rent increases, on any land currently held.[65] Settled raiyat status could not be sold. It was the status of a person. But a piece of land could be sold with the occupancy right, if permitted by custom. So, eventually, settled raiyats had occupancy rights on all the land they held, but every occupancy tenant was not a settled raiyat.

How was the rent of an occupancy tenant to be determined? It was, as in the 1859 act, to be "fair and equitable," but now there was more clarity. The current rent was assumed to be the right one unless the zamindar could make the case to the contrary. A zamindar could raise the rent under certain conditions such as an increase in prices, but there was a 12.5% ceiling on the increase. And once increased, it had to be left untouched for fifteen years. How would these rules be applied? The revenue department and the judi-ciary would need detailed field-level information. So Chapter X of the act permitted a survey and record of rights. Many such surveys were conducted, some of which we will use below.

To what extent was the Bengal Tenancy Act implemented? There are three issues. First, did tenants acquire the legal status of settled raiyats or occu-pancy tenants? Second, were they actually protected from rent increases? Third, did the Bengal Tenancy Act reduce the number of court disputes? We will also comment briefly on the impact of the Bengal Tenancy Act on economic growth.

Detailed surveys of rents and rights called "settlement reports" carried out under the aegis of Chapter X of the act showed that most of the land was recorded as being in the possession of occupancy tenants. Table 3.1 provides figures for several districts in Bihar. The percentage of area under settled and occupancy tenants varied between 69 and 87. Table 3.2 shows similar fig-ures for Chittagong, in eastern Bengal. In a purely formal sense, the act did work. Did it protect tenants from arbitrary rent increases? The answer varies by location, not only across districts, but even within them, depending on the relative strength of tenant and zamindar. A later settlement report from Jessore from 1925 puts the matter of rents as well as illegal fines or taxes very plainly. Regarding rents it reported, "The rents of the raiyats and tenure-holders of this district holding under zamindars and big talukdars have re-mained practically unaltered for the last 50 years. The Narail, Gobardanga, and Hatbaria zamindars are the only ones who have enhanced the rents of tenants recently. They are, however, too powerful for tenants to dispute their rents."[66] Regarding illegal charges (*abwabs*), the report noted that they were "fast dying out," except for payments that went to the landlord's staff. The legal system was not particularly relevant. The tenant was paying illegal

Table 3.1 Percentage of land under occupancy and settled raiyats and others, Bihar, ca. 1912

District	Proprietors and Tenure Holders	Raiyats at Fixed Rates and Rent-Free Raiyats	Settled and Occupancy Raiyats	Nonoccupancy Raiyats
South Monghyr	11.7	2.17	83.67	2.46
North Monghyr	13	1.25	81.25	4.5
Bhagalpur	8.45	1.71	87.22	2.62
Purnea	29.8	6.51	69.40	3.20
Darbhanga	14	2	83	1
Muzaffarpur	19	5	74	2
Saran	10	5	84	1
Champaran	9	4	84	3

Source: P. W. Murphy, *Final Report of the Survey and Settlement Operations (under Chapter X of the Bengal Tenancy Act) in the District of Monghyr (South), 1905–12* (Ranchi: Bihar and Orissa Secretariat Printing Office, 1914): 80.

Table 3.2 Percentage of land under occupancy and settled raiyats and others, Chittagong, ca. 1908

Types of Cultivator	Aggregate Cultivated Acres	Percentage of Cultivated Area
Ryots at fixed rents	54,064	17
Settled ryots	201,816	62
Occupancy ryots	17,383	5
Nonoccupancy ryots	16, 481	5
Rent-free holders	5,786	2
Under-ryots	30,977	9

Source: L. S. S. O'Malley, *Eastern Bengal Gazetteers: Chittagong* (Calcutta: Bengal Secretariat Book Depot, 1908): 105.

charges because he was afraid of the zamindar and did not have the courage to take him to court.[67]

The extraction of abwabs by the employees of the zamindar seems to have continued to the end of the colonial period. It seems this was one way for the zamindar to reduce costs, given rent ceilings: pay employees very low wages, and let them engage in extortion. A 1930s report stated that "in view of the low rates of pay which these collecting staff are allowed by their masters, the practice [of taking abwabs] cannot be stopped, and the tenants themselves recognize this, and again there has not been a single instance of their applying under Section 75 of the Bengal Tenancy Act for relief."[68]

Did the Bengal Tenancy Act reduce court disputes? It did not. There is, first, the simple fact that the number of rent law suits steadily increased. There was a huge expansion of rent law suits in Bengal over time. In 1878, Bengal (including Bihar) had 126,902 rent law suits. In 1946 Bengal alone

Table 3.3 Rent law suits in Bengal, subordinate courts

Province	Year	Percentage Rent Law Suits	Rent Law Suits	Suits for Money and Movable Property	Title and Other Suits
Bengal + Bihar	1878	0.40	126,902	158,406	34,629
Bengal + Bihar	1900	0.46	284,288	257,675	71,666
Bengal	1912	0.45	283,049	276,130	66,962
Bengal	1923	0.56	323,407	194,792	63,710
Bengal	1937	0.70	468,375	146,089	59,207
Bengal	1940	0.75	397,590	82,670	49,802
Bengal	1946	0.76	375,642	62,514	54,705

Sources: Figures for 1878 and 1900 are from Bengal, *Report on the Administration of Civil Justice in the Lower Provinces of Bengal* (Calcutta: Government Press, 1879 and 1901); for 1912 and 1923 they are from Bengal, High Court, *Report on the Administration of Civil Justice in the Presidency of Bengal* (Calcutta: Bengal Secretariat Book Depot, 1913 and 1924); from 1937 onward they are from Bengal, High Court, *Report on the Administration of Civil Justice in the Province of Bengal* (Calcutta: Government Press, 1938, 1941, 1947).

(Bihar excluded) had 375,642. The trends can be seen in table 3.3. Several serial publications on the administration of civil justice divided cases into three categories: rent law, money and movable property, and title and other. Not only did the number of rent law suits grow; they steadily increased as a fraction of total suits. The vast majority of rent law suits were for arrears of rent. Of course, the fact that rent suits increased *after* the Bengal Tenancy Act does not prove that they increased *because* of the act. However, various officials suggested that the precise definition of the correct rent which the act permitted encouraged litigation. Now that a clear benchmark had been laid down, the injured party had a greater chance of getting a favorable decision in court. The author of the district gazetteer of Bakarganj commented on "the greater number of rent-suits filed as a result of the settlement operations, which enabled landlords to bring such suits without excessive expense."[69] Another district gazetteer made a similar argument in somewhat more detail.[70]

By the mid-1920s, when the Civil Justice Committee produced its report, the Bengal civil justice system was overloaded, substantially due to rent suits.[71] The committee reported that rent law suits congested the munsifs' courts.[72] By the end of the colonial period, a commission of enquiry reported that it was "common knowledge" that a rent law suit in Bengal could "not infrequently" take three or four years. The legal process was "expensive and harassing to both landlord and tenant."[73] Not all of this was due to legislation. Tenant movements, which we know emerged before the Bengal Tenancy Act, were stronger in the 1920s and 1930s, and included "no-rent" campaigns. The Great Depression lowered prices and made payment of rents more difficult, so there was more reason for landlords to go to court. Still, at the minimum it is clear that the Bengal Tenancy Act of 1885 did not reduce the number of disputes that went to court.

How did this long and complex history of landlord-tenant relations affect economic growth in Bengal? A comprehensive answer to this question is beyond the scope of this book, but we can comment briefly on the available evidence. It is useful to distinguish performance in three dimensions: the extensive margin, the intensive margin, and public infrastructure, specifically, large-scale irrigation works. The Permanent Settlement may have been useful in a world in which the land frontier had not been reached. A zamindar who owed the state no taxes for additional land he or she brought under cultivation had strong incentives to do so, especially if tenant protection was limited. Writing in 1918, J. C. Jack, whom we have quoted before, claimed that cultivated area had expanded greatly in the nineteenth century. Rents had also increased substantially, and the increases after the Bengal Tenancy Act were illegal. However, he argued that the rents had initially been fixed at very low levels "owing to the need of attracting colonists." In his view, there was "considerable justification for the increase in rent."[74] Jack also suggested that the much-criticized phenomenon of sub-infeudation, with several intermediaries between zamindar and cultivator, had emerged as part of this process of reclamation in a densely forested area. The delegation of rights continued until, at the lowest rung, the plot was of manageable size. Jack described a type of tenure called *hawala*, which he called "most characteristic" of the district. It was a "small lease for the reclamation of forest granted to a man who was prepared to make his home in the grant and personally to supervise the reclamation."[75]

We have referred earlier to Jaykrishna Mukherjee, zamindar of Uttarpara. His biographer, Nilmani Mukherjee, who referred to his harsh methods of collecting rents, also depicted him as an "improving landlord."[76] On acquiring new estates he would often find substantial uncultivated areas. He used various devices to bring the land under cultivation, including employing labor, and offering prospective tenants loans and low rents. He also encouraged them to introduce new crops appropriate to the soil.[77] After the land was in cultivation for a few years, he would raise rents. Nilmani Mukherjee claimed that "one half of Bengal was waste" in 1793, and by 1858 zamindars had increased their rent rolls by four times, by a combination of expanding the area under cultivation and increasing rents.[78] To the extent the Bengal Tenancy Act made rent enhancement more difficult, it would have discouraged such efforts.

Perhaps the clearest evidence of a negative impact of the Bengal Tenancy Act on productivity comes from regions such as South Bihar, which were dependent on large-scale irrigation works. The terrain was sloping, and embankments and facilities for storage and distribution of water were critical. This could be organized (potentially) in three ways: coordinated action (1) by large numbers of peasants, (2) by the state, or (3) by the zamindar. The first option became difficult as numbers increased.[79] The state's incentive to take on this task had been diluted by its tax collection being fixed in perpetuity. But the Permanent Settlement, especially in its early years, when rents could be raised, created incentives for the zamindar to maintain and improve irrigation works. Sharecropping, in which the zamindar would get a share of increases in output, was prevalent in places like Gaya (Bihar). As late as the 1890s, there were good relations here between landlords and tenants.[80] Landlord-tenant relations deteriorated in the twentieth century. Tenants in Gaya and elsewhere applied, under a provision of the Bengal Tenancy Act, for "commutation," that is, conversion of shared-produce rents into fixed cash rents. This led zamindars to neglect irrigation works on their properties.[81]

Overall, it is possible that in Bengal and Bihar law and politics were more favorable to agricultural growth in the nineteenth century than the early twentieth. The protection of tenants, while a just cause, may have slowed economic growth.

The Protected Tenant: Madras Presidency

As we have mentioned earlier, the Permanent Settlement in the Madras Presidency was introduced in 1802, and roughly one-third of the area of the Madras Presidency was eventually under the zamindari, or Permanent Settlement.[82] The history of the system in legislation, in politics, and in court disputes has several parallels with its Bengal counterpart. The stated intention to protect tenants was a shared feature. So were the consequent disputes in court, a court interpretation that (like *Ghose v. Hills* in Bengal) undermined tenant protection, subsequent court decisions which (like the Great Rent Case in Bengal) undid the damage, and, finally, legislation attempting to define the rights of tenants more clearly.

According to the Pattah Regulation XXX of 1802, clause IX, the Madras zamindar did not have a free hand with rent: "Where disputes may arise respecting rates of assessment in money or of division in kind, the rates shall be determined according to the rates prevailing in the cultivated lands in the year preceding the assessment of the permanent jummah [tax] on such lands; or, where those rates may not be ascertainable, according to the rates established for lands of the same description and quality as those respecting which the disputes may arise."[83] In 1822 a regulation was passed to clarify that though a zamindar was allowed to "distrain" property if the tenant did not pay the rent, the intention was not "to define, limit, infringe, or destroy, the actual rights of any description of landholders or tenants; but merely to point out in what manner tenants might be proceeded against, in the event of them not paying the rents justly due from them."[84] A Rent Recovery Act was passed in 1865 to further clarify processes for rent recovery.

However, in 1870 *Chockalinga Pillai v. Vythealinga Pundara Sunnady* undercut tenant protections.[85] In this case the tenant's father had signed an agreement with the government in 1837, specifying the rent he would pay. Now the land was in the hands of a temple which had found someone who was willing to pay more. It wanted to evict the tenant. After lower courts had ruled for the temple, the case came to the high court. The heart of the matter was whether or not the tenant had, by default, an occupancy right at a fixed rent. The court (Justice C. J. Scotland) ruled that "neither the Rent Recovery Act nor the Regulations operated to extend a tenancy beyond the period of its duration secured by the express or implied terms of the contract creating it."[86] It ruled the tenant could be evicted. The case created a sensation because, though it had arisen in the context of land originally leased from the government, it was broadly interpreted to mean that the default status of even a zamindari tenant was that of a tenant-at-will.

As in Bengal, a subsequent case overturned this decision. The Madras High Court took a quite different view in *Appa Rau v. Subbanna and Others*, which was decided in 1889.[87] It shifted the onus of proof onto the zamindar. The case was complex: a tenant had borrowed against his land and then defaulted on the loan. His creditor had bought the land at auction. The zamindar sued on the grounds that the land was not the tenant's to transfer to begin with. The high court ruled against the zamindar. Having reviewed various cases, Judge Muttusami Ayyar argued: "It seems to me that the foregoing cases show that unless the landlord has a *prima facie* right to evict the tenant, he must start his case and show how such right accrued. . . . It would be monstrous to hold that every tenant in a zamindari is presumably a tenant at will."[88] The creditor was allowed to keep the land he had seized. The argument for the tenant's occupancy right was made even more clearly in *Venkatanarasimha Naidu v. Dandamudi Kotayya*, decided in 1897: "A raiyat cultivating land in a permanently-settled estate is *prima facie* not a mere tenant from year to year, but the owner of the kudivaram [occupancy] right in the land he cultivates."[89]

The Madras equivalent of the Bengal Tenancy Act, the Madras Estates Land Act of 1908, tried to clarify and strengthen the tenant's claim to an occupancy right.[90] However, it still left ambiguous the rights of the tenants of an inamdar (who owned land on which he owed low or no taxes). In a case before the Privy Council in 1918 the issue was whether an inamdar had the right to evict a tenant. The claim was that the land had been given to the inamdar by a Reddi king in 1373. The inam had been confirmed by the government. The question was, had the king given the inamdar only the right to collect rent or also the right to permanent occupancy? If the former were true, the Madras Estates Land Act of 1908 would apply, and the tenant was entitled to the occupancy right. However, the Privy Council ruled that "there is no presumption in law that the grant of an inam by a Native Ruler prior to British rule conveyed only the *melvaram* (revenue due to the state)."[91] Therefore, the land was not an estate and the Madras Estates Land Act did not apply. It took another eighteen years for the issue to be resolved by passing legislation bringing inam land under the purview of the Madras Estates Land Act. The tenant had to pay the inamdar a year's rent to obtain the occupancy right.

In Madras, as we have earlier seen in Bengal, the strengthening of legal rights of tenants and their growing political conflict with zamindars led the latter to neglect the management of irrigation facilities. After legislative reforms, when the Congress Party came to power in Madras in 1937, it set up the Prakasam Committee (T. Prakasam was a Congress leader and the revenue minister) to investigate the Madras Estates Land Act.[92] The Prakasam Committee did not have any immediate impact because the Congress government soon submitted its resignation, but it did researchers a favor by compiling and printing an enormous number of documents, including the responses of peasants' associations to its questionnaire. These responses are filled with complaints regarding the neglect of irrigation facilities by zamindars. A memorandum submitted by the North Vizagapatam District Ryots Association commented on the Parlakimedi estate, the "largest and most important in North Vizagapatam," consisting of 526 villages. It noted that the estate had "many fine tanks of large size" but they were in "bad state of repair."[93] Also, feeder channels were neglected, and when the farmers reported this to the estate, they were asked to go to the men they had voted for in the election.[94] Various other tenants' representatives made similar complaints.[95] As we might expect, zamindars' own reports painted a more favorable picture.[96]

There was one respect in which the Madras zamindari was different from Bengal zamindari: legal disputes were resolved more quickly. In Madras

Table 3.4 Methods of rent recovery: Madras Presidency

Year	Suits for Landholder to Recover Arrears of Rent (A)	Notices of Intention to Sell (B)	A/B
1913–14	22,631	28,099	0.81
1914–15	23,562	30,695	0.77
1915–16	21,640	53,244	0.41
1916–17	20,492	41,229	0.50
1917–18	19,480	31,773	0.61
1918–19	19,621	45,449	0.43
1919–20	17,163	40,084	0.43

Source: Madras, Revenue Department, *Report on the Working of the Madras Estates Land Act, 1908, during Fasli 1329* (Madras, 1921): 2.

cases went to the revenue courts, where revenue officials were the judges. These were quicker than civil courts, because procedures were less formal. Further, the Madras Estates Land Act allowed a "certificate procedure." This involved the zamindar directly applying to the collector (not filing a suit) and getting permission to sell the occupancy tenant's holding for arrears of rent.[97] Zamindars fairly quickly adopted this more direct procedure. As table 3.4 shows, suits for rent recovery via court were replaced by notices of intention to sell via the collector. Though legislation passed in 1934 made the sale procedure more cumbersome, rent recovery via legal process in Madras remained quick compared to Bengal. The Floud Commission's report of 1940 estimated that it took nine months in Madras zamindari areas, compared to the three to four years it could often take in Bengal.[98]

The Protected Tenant: Summing Up

Not all zamindari settlements were permanent. It was possible to have a broadly similar system in which land taxes could be periodically increased. Of course, there was regional variation. The 1898 Central Provinces Tenancy Act "was certainly the most comprehensive one in India."[99] In his report on Jabalpur (in the Central Provinces), the settlement officer, Crosthwaite, reported in 1912 that even though ordinary tenants could buy occupancy rights by paying two and a half years' rent, they did not bother to do so because "ordinary tenants are to all intents and purposes 'protected' tenants, and this they know and understand."[100] In contrast, in Awadh the administration sought the loyalty of the talukdars (the zamindar equivalents) who had been active against the British in the Mutiny, and hence tenant protection came slowly and grudgingly.[101]

Overall, legislation in all the zamindari areas was in the direction of creating parity between the status of the tenant of the zamindar and the status of the raiyatwari owner. An 1883 report from Bengal we have cited earlier was explicit that rental rates for occupancy tenants should be similar to the taxes paid to the government by owners in the raiyatwari regions: "The rates should be fixed with reference to existing rents, change of prices, and all other matters such as are taken into consideration in carrying out a ryot-wari settlement."[102] Jabalpur's Settlement Officer Crosthwaite sought parity between the rent of the occupancy tenant of the malguzar (zamindar equivalent) and the land tax of the maliq maqbuza (the raiyatwari-type "government tenant"). In Madras too, the trend was toward seeing the zamindar as simply a collector of governmental revenue. Under this interpretation the zamindar's occupancy tenant was similar to a raiyatwari landholder, except he was paying rent to an intermediary (who kept a portion of it) rather than a tax to the state.

But even if the zamindari regions created a class of protected occupancy tenants, does this mean the actual cultivator had security? Our next section addresses this question.

The Unprotected Tenant

In principle, raiyatwari had sought to eliminate intermediaries between the state and the cultivator. The Madras Presidency, in which the system originated, is the ideal location to assess the extent to which practice corresponded to theory. They could part ways for two reasons. The first was that, from the outset, the company had to make concessions to existing inequalities. The second was the emergence, especially in the twentieth century, of a new category of tenants. We will discuss these two issues sequentially.

It is true that in some raiyatwari regions the company did not encounter the supravillage rural magnate of the zamindari regions. But there was inequality within the village itself. Regarding the Madras Presidency, one historian writes that in "several districts the settlement [assignment of ownership rights and taxes] had to be made with landholders who were clearly not cultivators." The state then did not provide protection to tenants in raiyatwari regions because of "the fiction that the raiyat as registered in the Government records was the actual cultivator."[103] The key to understanding this issue is to recall that in the early nineteenth century, in many areas, labor, rather than land, was the scarce factor. The original settlers of a village, the *mirasdars*, might collectively owe taxes. It was in their interest to attract settlers who would help pay these taxes. Over time, the settlers had acquired rights that were hereditary. This was especially true in some areas in which the mirasdars were Brahmins, who abided by religious injunctions to not participate in agricultural work, in particular by not touching the plough.

The company sometimes gave raiyatwari ownership rights to these settlers (which the mirasdars resisted), and sometimes it did not. But, in a style with which we are now familiar, while not providing explicit sanction to customary rights, the company did not deny these rights either. So a tenant on land "owned" by a mirasdar, faced with the threat of eviction, could contest it in court. The courts took the position that the onus was on the tenant to prove right to occupancy by "custom," "contract," or "title." But judges still had considerable discretion and in some instances ruled in favor of the tenant even when these conditions were not satisfied. An interesting case that ended up in the Privy Council involved mirasdars suing to have their tenants ejected. There was no dispute regarding the fact that mirasdars held title to the land, that there was no contract establishing permanent occupancy rights, and the tenants' rights could not be established on the grounds of prevailing custom. And, this being a raiyatwari area, the onus of proof was on the tenant. Still the Privy Council ruled in favor of the tenants, primarily on the grounds that they had "immemorially been in possession of the lands" at a uniform rent, had brought it under cultivation, and had made improvements to it.[104] The dispute had begun in 1897, and the Privy Council finally resolved it only in 1918.

Legal ambiguity notwithstanding, it is likely that in the early nineteenth century, because labor was scarce, the lack of legal protection may not have affected the de facto security of some tenants. However, by the twentieth century, after population had grown, the status of the tenant was weaker. There were also new entrants into the ranks of tenants. These included families whose owned land was not adequate for increased family size, former owners who had defaulted on land revenue payments whose land had been auctioned by the state, and others who had defaulted on loans and lost land to professional moneylenders who did not wish to cultivate and had kept them on as tenants. It also appears that even rich peasant households, when they acquired more land than they could cultivate, typically did not set up "capitalist" farms using hired labor. The surplus land, beyond what could be cultivated by the family, was leased out, often to sharecroppers. The reluctance to cultivate on a large scale was common across regions: the occupancy tenant in Bengal, the raiyati owner in Madras and Bombay, and even Punjab's famed "peasant proprietors" (whom we will discuss in the next chapter) were all reluctant to cultivate their own land beyond what could be cultivated with family labor and usually rented the land out to sharecroppers. Absent economies of scale in cultivation, sharecropping was a sensible choice, addressing the difficulty of monitoring workers as well as the need to protect them from risk.[105]

Statistical evidence of the extent of this tenancy-at-will is fragmentary, but the estimates are consistently in the range of 20%–30% of cultivated area. A survey of seventy-seven randomly selected villages in Bengal in 1944–45 identified land held under "some temporary arrangement such as barga [sharecropping], temporary lease, or usufructuary mortgage" as 2,999 acres of a total of 13,493, which is 22%.[106] Of these 2,999 acres, 91.8% were under share-cropping. Regarding tenancy in the raiyatwari areas, the best data we have been able to find are from the Bombay Presidency. From 1932 onward, the Land Revenue Department in its quinquennial survey of holdings began to define a category of persons who "receive rent only without themselves taking part in cultivation."[107] In 1931–32 and 1936–37, the raiyatwari areas under pure rent receivers were 30% and 31%, respectively.[108] These are underestimates of the area under tenancy, because they exclude land rented out by cultivating households. In Madras raiyatwari areas a survey conducted in 1912 showed variation in the percentage of occupied area leased out: Tirunelveli (40%), Coimbatore (37%), North Arcot (16%), and Cuddapah (33%).[109]

Proposals to protect tenants of raiyatwari owners as well as tenants of zamindari occupancy tenants received political attention in the late colonial period. These issues gained prominence with Indian participation in provincial governance in the 1920s and 1930s. In Bengal the sharecroppers did not have adequate political representation for meaningful legislation in their favor.[110] In Bombay the Maharashtra Provincial Congress Committee made the case for it, and the Bombay Tenancy Act was passed in 1939. On the whole, though, further legislation to protect these tenants-at-will had to wait for Indian independence. It was not easy to implement even then (see chapter 10).

Conclusion

The story told in this chapter has a paradox at its center: on the one hand, as early as the late eighteenth century, the British administration in India believed that economic growth required clear and secure property rights; on the other, well into the twentieth century, disputes about what rights they had conferred on a proprietor were finding their way right up to the Privy Council. These disputes were not about arcane subtleties or points of detail. They pertained to a central question: Who had the right to occupy the land?

How did this paradox emerge? At the outset the company knew it did not have a blank slate, that there was a preexisting structure of land rights. But these rights were complex, variable across space, undocumented, and difficult to understand. The company did not consider it prudent, or perhaps even possible, to wipe the slate clean. It therefore chose to define new rights, while proclaiming its intention to not undermine rights already in existence.[111] But there was a contradiction here: if existing rights were not known and identified, how could one know whether or not they were consistent with the new rights being defined? This ambiguity fueled more than a century of political struggle, legislation, and court disputes.

Another characteristic of early British-Indian land law was the creation of a pseudouniformity, in which terminological similarity masked enormous substantive differences. This feature of early legislation then affected subsequent attempts at reform as well. As we have noted, a Bengal zamindar under the Permanent Settlement could fit the image of a king ("raja") with many thousands of acres of land, or fit a more conventional image of a "landlord" with fifty acres of land. Both had "tenants." Both sets of tenants received protection under the Bengal Tenancy Act. But the raja's tenant was often a large landholder in his own right with many tenants of his own, and the landlord's tenant could be a small peasant with a few acres. So the impact, not only of the Permanent Settlement itself, but even of attempts at reform such as the Bengal Tenancy Act or the Madras Estates Land Act, varied greatly.

We have, therefore, been cautious in speculating on the aggregate impacts of various laws.[112] It appears that in the first half of the nineteenth century, the zamindar's property right in Bengal could be relatively clear, and with his or her taxes fixed in perpetuity, this created incentives for expansion of cultivated area and maintenance of irrigation facilities. By the late nineteenth century the frontier had been reached in many places, and there was growing conflict over land rights. Especially after 1885, disputes between zamindar and tenant increased, as a consequence of stronger legal rights of tenants as well as political mobilization. There is evidence that this hurt the maintenance of irrigation facilities, and it is likely that this also hurt other investments. A broadly similar story can be told for zamindari areas in Madras as well. In the raiyatwari regions of the Madras Presidency there was considerable ambiguity regarding the legal status of the tenant, but conflict in courts and outside the courts did not approach zamindari levels. We speculate that raiyatwari regions in Madras represented a more growth-supportive environment.

A third theme of this chapter, which emerged most clearly in the case of

Bengal, is of court disputes as a dimension of political combat. This probably had a self-reinforcing character. If tenants did not pay rent, landlords could take them to court. But if enough tenants did this, courts would slow down. This would make the option of not paying rents even more tempting. But the overburdening of the legal system had other sources as well, and also occurred in regions where disputes were not primarily about rents and eviction. We will see examples of this in the next chapter.

Many of the conclusions of this chapter have been driven by the study of two zamindari regions, in Bengal and Madras. As we move to the next chapter, focusing on the issue of transferability of land, much of our discussion will be on other regions, including the Punjab, with quite different tenurial histories and economic outcomes. We will then revisit some of our conclusions.

FOUR

Landed Property and Credit

We cannot draw an indictment against half the people of India; and we may be
quite sure whether we can see it or not, that we and our institutions are in the
wrong, and not they.

—Denzil Ibbetson[1]

Introduction

We began the previous chapter by identifying three dimensions of land
rights—the type of ownership, tenants' rights, and the right to transfer—to
categorize the diversity of land tenures in colonial India. Chapter 3 focused
on the first two dimensions, the type of ownership (raiyatwari and zamindari) and the rights of tenants. This chapter introduces the third dimension,
transferability. This leads us to discuss credit, for two related reasons. In a
largely agricultural economy once population has grown sufficiently and
land becomes the scarce factor, it is potentially the most important form of
collateral. And to the extent land is actually used as collateral or seized in
lieu of repayment, credit transactions can become a cause of land transfer.

The discussion of credit raises the issue of contract enforcement. Credit
involves two transactions, borrowing and repayment, which are separated
in time, leaving room for opportunistic behavior by both parties. The lender
is, of course, worried about repayment. The borrower, especially if illiterate
or financially unsophisticated, may be concerned about fraud. These issues
need to be addressed if credit markets are to function smoothly. So we study
the regulation of credit contracts, not only via legislation, but also in the
functioning of the courts and the implementation of their decisions. Finally,
putting together our discussion of land and credit markets, we will venture
some hypotheses regarding how the structure of property rights and contract

enforcement might have affected the incentive to invest and the availability of funds for investment.

Rural credit was not a central concern of the company at the beginning of its rule. Its stance changed by the second half of the nineteenth century, with the growth of population, the expansion of cultivated area, and increasing cultivation of crops for sale. The demand for credit grew, and, in parallel, there was an increase in the value of the most important form of collateral, land. It was inevitable that some peasants would borrow against their land and lose it after defaulting, or would sell it to pay off loans. One might have expected that the state, especially given the influence of laissez-faire views in Britain, would view this phenomenon with some equanimity as part of the normal functioning of a market economy, in which there are winners and losers. However, this was not to be. When land loss by peasants led to protests and even "riots," the Raj reacted with great anxiety, second-guessing the legal and institutional changes it had introduced and legislating extensively (in some regions) to prevent or discourage land transfers in relation to repayment or default on debt. Why did the Raj react so strongly?

The Mutiny of 1857 was one reason. This made the Raj fearful of rapid social change, which they believed to be its cause. But there was also a prior and subsequent history of agrarian rebellion and protest. Taken together, they led the Raj to be cautious, to not introduce policies that might undermine the agrarian social structure. This required an understanding of the key elements of this structure. The notion of the "village community" provided an organizing idea. From the early nineteenth century at least, British officials in various regions had embraced to different degrees a view of the Indian village as a largely self-contained entity. It had internal systems of governance. It was somewhat disconnected from the larger polity—regimes could come and go without affecting it significantly. The ownership of land and responsibility for paying taxes was shared within the community. The village itself contained providers of various services, from priests to carpenters.[2] The "village community" formulation received particularly strong support from officials in the North-Western Provinces, with Charles Metcalfe's observations regarding villages near Delhi being especially influential.[3] And following the final annexation of Punjab (1849), observation of social organization in its "tribal" northwestern region (discussed below) provided further impetus to the notions of "jointness" of ownership of property and village political cohesion. In 1889 Henry Maine wrote: "It was not till the English conquest was extending far to the north-west, and till warlike populations were subjugated whose tastes and peculiarities it was urgently necessary to study, that *the true proprietary unit of India* [our italics] was discovered."[4]

Given this understanding, the Raj concluded that political stability required the maintenance of the economic and political cohesion of the village, which would be undermined if "immigrant" and or "nonagriculturist" lenders took possession of land. Legislation was passed in several regions in the late nineteenth and early twentieth centuries to discourage such transfer, seeking to undermine the use of land as collateral in credit transactions, or disallow its seizure after default. The spirit of these laws was to protect the reckless and naive borrower both from the lender and from himself.

After late nineteenth- and early twentieth-century discussion and legislation pertaining to land transfer, the next (potentially) important legislation was the Usurious Loans Act of 1918. And after the Depression, legislation to protect borrowers from predatory lenders and reduce their debt burdens was driven by a new set of factors—the growth of nationalist and peasant movements, and the participation of Indians in provincial governance. By this point, the shortcomings of the judicial system, which made it hard to enforce credit contracts, had also been exposed in some regions.

The remainder of this chapter describes and analyzes this history, linking it to our discussion of landownership and tenant rights. We first discuss law pertaining to the transferability of land in the raiyatwari regions, where there was little or no legislation to protect tenants. We then consider zamindari regions, where, as we have seen in chapter 3, tenants were protected to varying extents. Punjab, a late and major conquest, is often considered sui generis, so we devote a separate section to it. A discussion of issues of enforcement of credit contracts, especially as pertaining to land transfer following court decrees, follows. The last two sections of this chapter discuss developments in the late colonial period, when aggressive policies to reduce debt burdens and regulate lenders were introduced, and the strain on the judicial system became more visible in some regions. In the conclusion we will argue that because law and institutions were so variable across regions and time, it is difficult to generalize regarding their implications for economic growth. We can identify locations in which at specific times law probably constrained growth. But there are also instances where, if growth did not occur, the causes will have to be found elsewhere, not in property rights or contract enforcement.

Raiyatwari Regions: Bombay and Madras

The region known as the Bombay Presidency was conquered piece by piece, but a key date was 1818, the defeat of the Maratha peshwa based in Poona (Pune), in the Bombay Deccan. Subsequent company rule introduced several

changes that affected credit markets. The evolution of debtor-lender relations over the next several decades led to the passing of the Deccan Agriculturists' Relief Act (DARA hereafter), an important and influential legislation.

There were two critical innovations introduced by British rule. Under the
raiyatwari system there were now clear titles to land which could be sold,
pledged as collateral, or seized in lieu of debt repayment.[5] Second, the adjudication of disputes moved out of the village, where methods were informal,
to the district courts established by the company where procedures were
more formal and documentary evidence more important. The net effect of
these changes, and increases in the value of land, was to encourage inflow of
lenders, including immigrants who did not have strong local connections.
This had one clear potential benefit: there was more credit available. But,
as official reports and some historians tell the story, it changed borrower-
lender relations in ways that hurt the peasants.

It appears that, in the precolonial setting, a rural lender-borrower dispute
was usually adjudicated by a panchayat, or village council (see also chapter 2).[6] Since the Bombay Deccan was a poor and dry region, immigrant
lenders were an important source of credit.[7] They were at a disadvantage
when disputes were adjudicated, because they were appealing to members
of village councils to rule against their peers. The panchayats also seem to
have practiced what we would today call limited liability, in the sense that
they would not take the shirt off the borrower's back.[8] There was, furthermore, a ceiling on the amount the panchayat would award the creditor—
twice the outstanding principal, irrespective of how much interest had accumulated. This rule, known as *damdupat*, has a long history.[9] There are many
references to it in treatises on Hindu law dating back almost two thousand
years.[10] There was also a rule favoring the creditor, called the Pious Obligation, which made the sons and even grandsons liable for their ancestor's
debts, even beyond the extent of their inheritance. Like damdupat, the Pious
Obligation could be found in ancient texts, but perhaps more to the point,
it was honored in practice.[11] The panchayat did not necessarily enforce its
decrees. The lender and his employees were allowed to use coercive methods
up to a point. This probably limited the geographic scope of any lender's
activity.

Mountstuart Elphinstone, the governor of Bombay and a "conservative"
in the sense of favoring gradual institutional change, wanted the panchayat
to remain an important judicial institution. Accordingly, the regulations of
1827, which underpinned the legal structure that was to develop, allowed a
role for it. However, the institutions of the new political order were the ones
that commanded more respect. Panchayats, therefore, were hardly used.[12]

Dispute resolution moved to the hierarchical system of courts, modeled on the Bengal/Mughal judicial administration set up by the company.

The new judicial system differed from the panchayat-based adjudication in several ways. The courts placed more weight on documentary evidence. Dispute resolution did not occur in the village. In fact, the district court was often several days of travel away for the borrower. The state itself would enforce contracts. And though the Regulation of 1827 placed limits on what assets could be seized in lieu of debt repayment, imposed an interest-rate ceiling (12%), and retained damdupat, imprisonment was one possible punishment, which diluted the impact of borrower protections.

The impact of these changes depended on who the borrowers and lenders were. But much of the discussion and legislation in the Bombay Deccan was driven by the relationship between the professional trader-lenders, especially immigrants, and the peasants. As the nineteenth century unfolded, several British officials made a plausible case that institutional innovations had favored the lender. The latter was more at home with new legal procedures, more adept at bookkeeping, literate, and could better bear the costs and time associated with litigation. The adjudication was now not being done by a group of the borrower's peers. There was now a judge, driven by the letter of the law, relying heavily on the written word. Finally, the lender could rely on the state to help enforce its judgment, including seizure of land. After an early period of heavy taxation, taxes were lowered significantly by 1850. Population, cultivated area, and commercial agriculture expanded. As the demand for credit increased, more immigrant lenders moved in, relying on the new British-Indian legal apparatus for loan recovery.

From quite early on, British officials were concerned about two related outcomes of this process: they worried, first, that unsophisticated peasants were being defrauded by lenders and, second, that land was passing from the hands of traditional cultivators to the immigrants who had no connection with land. The following comments in 1852 by Captain George Wingate, an important land revenue official, are illustrative: "The facilities which the law affords for the realization of debt have expanded credit to a most hurtful extent. In addition to ordinary village bankers, a set of low usurers is fast springing up. . . . All grades of people are thus falling under the curse of debt, and should the present course of affairs continue, it must arrive that the greater part of the realized property of the community will be transferred to a small monied class."[13] As we noted in the introduction, the Mutiny exacerbated concerns regarding the political implications of land transfer.[14] In parallel with the political fears there was, at the ideological level, what Thomas Metcalf has called "the creation of difference"—the notion that

Indian (at least agrarian) society was not prepared for British institutions.[15] In our context, Raymond West, a judge in the Bombay High Court, provided a clear statement of this perspective. West wrote a highly influential monograph in 1873 entitled *The Land and the Law in India*, arguing that it was a mistake to allow land to be transferable. It gave the peasant too much access to credit (the full value of land), but he or she was not capable of handling it appropriately. This sentiment was echoed by officials in other regions, and the right to borrow against land was often described as a "fatal boon."[16]

The 1860s saw a boom in cotton cultivation in the Bombay Deccan, suitable due to its black soil, because the American Civil War disrupted the supply of cotton. Debt expanded considerably in this period. Prices fell after the Civil War ended, and in the late 1860s and early 1870s there were other "shocks" to the system, such as increases in land taxes and adverse weather conditions. Peasants defaulted on loans and lost their lands to moneylenders. As resentments grew, moneylenders were sporadically attacked, but the crisis finally came in 1875, when peasants in four districts (Poona, Ahmednagar, Sholapur, and Satara) "rioted." The riots occasionally took the form of violence against moneylenders, but more often the rioters simply wanted to destroy the "bonds" that were proof of their debts. Some historians have questioned the magnitude of the Deccan Riots, and Neil Charlesworth once provocatively described them as a "minor grain riot."[17] But for many of the Raj's officials this was confirmation of their fear that British innovations in land rights and law were destabilizing Indian society in a politically threatening way.

What was to be done? The Deccan Riots Commission was set up to address this question. After it produced a voluminous report, the DARA was passed in 1879, applying to the four districts where the riots had occurred. The act did not accept Raymond West's radical suggestion—a ban on land transfer—and focused instead on the legal process. The act had numerous provisions. Village-level "conciliators" were appointed to facilitate arbitration, and nearby courts with munsifs (judges, usually Indian, in lower courts) were set up to adjudicate disputes involving small sums. Mortgages had to be registered, and ex parte judgments (absent the defendant) were discouraged. The interest rate ceiling, which had been abolished in 1855 after the abolition of usury laws in Britain, was reinstated. But the most important change was that judges were empowered to "go behind the bond," that is, investigate the entire history of transactions, and use their discretion to reduce payments, or order payment in installments.

Meanwhile, what of the two measures in Hindu law, the Pious Obligation and damdupat? The Pious Obligation had lost its bite after the passing of the Bombay Hindu Heirs' Relief Act of 1866, which declared that a son was liable for his father's debts only to the extent he inherited his property. Damdupat was part of the 1827 regulation, as mentioned above. It was included in the DARA. It remains on the books in Maharashtra and a few other places in India.

The impact of the DARA, which was extended to Sindh in 1901 and the rest of the Bombay Presidency in 1905, was controversial. While the officials associated with its formulation and implementation praised it, critics also alleged that it was driving out the lenders and credit was drying up.[18] Borrowers and lenders colluded to side-step the DARA by disguising loans as sales. The borrower would "sell" the land at a certain price, and buy it back later at a higher price, with the interest embedded in the price differential. The DARA had to be modified so that even land sales could be scrutinized.

Recent research shows that the DARA achieved some of its procedural goals: for instance, the incidence of ex parte decrees declined dramatically.[19] Judges used their discretion to reduce repayments to creditors. However, while credit did contract, this does not seem to have hurt "real" outcomes such as cropped area and yield. This finding is consistent with work on present-day India which suggests that greater access to credit does not necessarily promote agricultural growth.[20] It appears that the DARA was, overall, a moderately successful intervention, giving the borrower some protection without materially undermining the supply of credit. It can be interpreted as an exercise in moderation, moving away from an extreme in which the lender had too much power vis-à-vis the usually illiterate borrower, to one where they were more evenly matched.

Meanwhile, what of the other major raiyatwari region, Madras? The Madras administration's attitude to land transfer was in complete contrast to that of Bombay. It argued that in Madras most lenders were local "agriculturists," not immigrant trader-lenders (see table 4.1). So, even if land did change hands, it would not cause political unrest. Moreover, the inspector general of registration of Madras argued that the new owners "in addition to capital have sufficient education and intelligence to adopt improved methods of cultivation when they are found to be profitable."[21] His understanding of the credit market was directly at odds with the spirit of the DARA. The DARA had worried that loan recovery was too easy for the lender. The Madras inspector general thought interest rates were high because loan recovery via the courts was too costly.

The Madras inspector general's view of the credit market (among many other subjects) is fleshed out in a famous report he published in 1893.[22] He provides estimates of the legal costs incurred by a creditor making a claim

Table 4.1 Registered loans in Madras Presidency, 1889–1891

Profession of Lender	Percentage Mortgages Greater Than 100 Rupees	Percentage Mortgages Less Than 100 Rupees	Percentage Simple Bonds
Agriculturists	61	65	64
Nonagriculturists	34	31	32
Farmers combining other professions with agriculture	5	4	4

Source: India, *Note on Land Transfer and Agricultural Indebtedness in India* (Simla: Government Press, 1895): 65.
Note: The data are from sale/transfer registration figures and pertain to ten districts.

of 50 rupees or less. This is based on the experience of a judicial officer who had experience in Tanjore, Tinnevelly, and Trichinopoly Districts (currently spelled Thanjavur, Tirunelveli, and Tiruchirappalli, respectively). The inspector general concluded that to recover 50 rupees, a successful litigant would have to spend 34 rupees. Even if he won and were awarded court costs, he would fail to recover 11.5 rupees.[23] Thus, the lender would lose 23% of the principal in legal costs. The recovery cost estimate was conservative in that it assumed the lender lived close to the court. The percentage lost by the lender would fall as the size of the loan increased—12%, 5% and 3% respectively, for loans of rupees 100, 500 and 1,000. The inspector general argued that if the loan were 10 or 20 rupees, the cost of recovery might exceed the value of the loan. This was why it was "impossible for the poor peasantry to obtain small loans at anything like reasonable rates of interest" even when they offered good security.[24]

Given this discussion and that of the previous chapter on security of ownership and tenancy legislation, what can we conjecture regarding the incentives for investment in raiyatwari Bombay and Madras in, say, 1900? Stressing the word "conjecture," our sense is that the legal and institutional structure per se was not a major obstacle to investment. Raiyatwari ownership was generally secure. Even when land was leased out, owners' incentives to invest were not undermined because tenancy was at will, and landlords could raise rents (though, as we have seen, there could be disputes when tenants claimed occupancy rights). Land could be used as collateral to raise funds for investment (with some scrutiny in Bombay). Legal costs of enforcing contracts could be high, as a proportion of loan size. But this is not unusual for a developing economy, when loan sizes are small and there are fixed administrative costs.[25] Overall, we do not see the structure of property rights or formal contract enforcement as being major obstacles to economic growth. And, we have noted, in the case of the DARA statistical analysis has not yielded evidence of any adverse effect on economic growth.

The Zamindari Regions: Bengal and Madras Presidencies

We have argued in the previous chapter that, before the tenancy acts, zamindars in Bengal and Madras (under the Permanent Settlement) had good incentives to invest, since they would reap the benefits, with no additional taxes to pay.[26] And, of course, there were no restrictions on their right to transfer some or all of the zamindari, so they did not, in principle, lack access to funds.[27] However, after tenancy legislation was passed, incentives for landlords weakened because it was more difficult to raise rents, or evict tenants. But the strengthening of tenants' rights meant that they could now have greater confidence in profiting from their investments. Where would the funds come from? The obvious option was to mortgage the occupancy right. Was this permitted? Depending on the zamindari region and the period in question, the answer was "Yes," "Maybe, or "No." We discuss these cases sequentially.

The "yes" case, in the Madras Presidency, is easy to explain. We have seen above that in the late nineteenth century the Madras administration had rejected out of hand the idea of restrictions on the transfer of raiyatwari rights. When the Madras Estates Land Act was passed in 1908, the intention was to give the zamindari occupancy tenant a status similar to that of raiyatwari owner. So there were no restrictions on transfer of the occupancy right, or on borrowing against it. In principle, the Madras zamindari occupancy tenant had both the incentive to invest (because of protection from arbitrary rent increases and eviction) and the capacity to invest, because of the ability to collateralize the occupancy right.

The "maybe" case is more complex. The framers of the Bengal Tenancy Act of 1885 had left the issue of whether the occupancy right was transferable to "custom" or "usage." In 1894 the government of India, driven by the political concerns we have discussed, communicated with various local governments including Bengal on the subject of restrictions on land transfer. The government of India suggested to the Bengal government that "the effect of the Bengal Tenancy Act has been in many instances to place the raiyats at the mercy of the moneylenders." The government of Bengal responded that since the passage of the Bengal Tenancy Act there had indeed been a substantial increase in the number of transfers of occupancy right registered, though some of this may have been simply better reporting. But most of this was not to moneylenders. Moreover, moneylenders in Bengal were not "the grasping and foreign moneylenders of other parts, but persons who are agriculturists themselves, and who have a little capital which they lend out at usury."[28] Supporting this view, the government of Bengal enclosed a long letter from M. Finucane, who was a strong supporter of tenant rights. Using data on more than forty-seven thousand transactions, Finucane argued that land was mainly going to other peasants, and only one in seven transfers was to Mahajans (moneylenders). And, he argued, "of these so-called Mahajans, however, but a small portion were probably other than substantial raiyats themselves, for these are the chief money-lenders in rural Bengal."[29] Far from being concerned about land transfer, the government of Bengal worried that though "custom" usually allowed free land transfer by occupancy tenants, courts might not endorse this view. The 1894 letter quoted above (note 28) worried that "it is possible that the technical and narrow views which the Civil Courts may take of the evidence required to prove 'custom' . . . may cause an ever-widening breach between the law as administered by the Courts and the general practice, so that it may eventually be necessary to interpose by legislation to set the Courts right."[30]

This concern was well founded, as illustrated by *Palakdhari Rai v. Manners and Others*.[31] In 1895, Palakdhari Rai, a zamindar, brought fourteen suits against Manners and Others regarding their purchase of occupancy rights in his estate. The central issue was whether or not transfer without the consent of the landlord was consistent with "custom." The munsif's court had ruled for the plaintiff (the zamindar), but this decision had been reversed by the subordinate judge. The zamindar appealed to the high court, which, citing a prior judgment of the Privy Council, held that for the transfer to be valid "it would be necessary in these cases either to prove the existence of the usage on the landlord's estate, or that it is so prevalent in the neighborhood that it can be reasonably presumed to exist on that estate."[32] Criticizing the subordinate judge, the court noted that the documents he had cited showing transfers "all relate to other villages," and it was not clear what bearing this had "upon the question of the existence of usage in the two villages in which the holdings have been purchased by Manners and which are the subject matters of this suit."[33] The high court required the case to be retried. This ambiguity in law was resolved only when the Bengal Tenancy Act was amended in 1928, explicitly allowing the occupancy tenant to transfer his or her right upon payment of 20% of the sale price to the zamindar. This requirement of 20% payment was removed in 1937.

The transferability of the occupancy right thus remained in legal limbo for a considerable length of time, left to the best judgment of the court regarding "custom." It is likely that this undermined the tenant's ability to borrow against this right. Land law in Bengal in (say) 1900 thus seems to have undermined the zamindar's incentive to invest (because the Tenancy Act made it harder to raise rents or evict tenants), and the tenant's capacity to invest (since the occupancy right could not necessarily be used as collateral). It is likely that some investment did occur, in part because, as we have seen in the last chapter, the provisions of the Tenancy Act were evaded, with zamindars illegally raising rents. And tenants could borrow from their zamindars, with their occupancy right as de facto collateral: the surrender of occupancy right could then be described as being due to default in rent. Still, even if the Bengal Tenancy Act was beneficial on grounds of equity, the uncertainties created by it may have undermined economic growth. Later legislation (see below) aggravated the problem.

The "no" case pertains to strong "protective" legislation in colonial India, which was passed in the *adivasi* areas. *Adivasi* translates roughly as "original inhabitant." Adivasis' cultural and economic practices could differ significantly from those of the more numerous Hindu peasant communities. In the colonial period they were called "tribes," and in today's official parlance "Scheduled Tribes." We will use the term *adivasi*, because it is more respectful. It will also help avoid confusion with a different use of the word "tribe" in the section on Punjab, below. As we noted in the last chapter, conflict between adivasis and the colonial state, zamindar, and moneylender had begun as early as 1832 in the portions of eastern India under the Permanent Settlement. Our focus here is on the Santals, adivasis who were proficient at forest clearing. By the mid-1850s they had a substantial presence in an area within the present-day Indian state of Jharkhand, where, depending on location, they were raiyatwari-type owners or zamindari tenants. After protracted tensions with zamindars (over evictions and rent increases) and moneylenders (over land transfers) the Santals rebelled in 1855. This was a large-scale insurrection, which the colonial state eventually dealt with harshly, militarily, with perhaps as many as ten thousand Santals killed.

After the rebellion was crushed, the administration attempted to address its causes. A new district called the Santal Parganas was created, which was designated a "non-regulation" area in that the rules and laws passed for the rest of British India would not automatically apply. According to Act XXXVI of 1855, "No law which shall hereafter be passed by the Governor-General of India in Council shall be deemed to extend to any part of the said districts, unless the same shall be specially named therein." There would be a more paternalistic form of administration, with a strong role for the executive, especially revenue officials. However, in 1863, the advocate general declared the formulation quoted above ultra vires, so the "non-regulation" status became invalid. Following this, under the provisions of the weak Bengal Rent Act of 1859 (discussed in the previous chapter), zamindars increased rents. A rule imposing an interest rate ceiling of 25% was now declared void, and "the district was fast relapsing into the position from which it had been rescued by Act XXXVII of 1855." Renewed political unrest in 1871 led to fresh legislation in 1872. The advocate general's decision was declared erroneous, and Santal Parganas were declared "non-regulation" again.[34] Santals in the zamindari areas were given occupancy rights and protection from eviction and rent increases.[35] Officials would conduct village-level investigations to "settle" rents and rights.

A valuable occupancy right had been created, and, predictably, some of this was lost to moneylenders. Again, to forestall political trouble, regulations were passed in 1887 forbidding the transfer of the occupancy right, unless the "custom" of transfer was found to prevail when officials entered the villages to "settle" rents. This custom was sometimes found in villages inhabited by Bengalis, but never in the Santal villages. So, de facto, land transfer was banned. Officials even rescinded illegal transfers that had already occurred.

What were the implications for investment? Zamindars would not invest because they could not raise rents. The occupancy tenants would not be able to raise the funds for investment, because the land could not be used as collateral. Our confidence in this assessment is strengthened by the commentary of H. McPherson, whose famous settlement report we have quoted extensively above. McPherson was proud of the protective legislation passed. He estimated that in the previous thirty years the population had grown by only 44%, whereas cultivation had increased by 66% and the standard of living had increased by 30%. He writes: "A 30% improvement in the standard of comfort spread over 30 years must be admitted to be a striking testimony to the value of Sonthal Parganas legislation. To that legislation is due the unhampered extension of cultivation, the controlled enhancement of rent, and the general protection of weak and ignorant cultivators who would otherwise have become the prey of their wilier and stronger neighbours."[36] However, if we read McPherson's analysis closely, it suggests that legislation could have reduced growth. Regarding the zamindars he notes that the "system militates against enterprise on the part of the proprietor" because "he can get no appreciable return to expenditure till settlement revision, and then his return is dependent on the will of Government and is liable to be limited by rules of settlement regarding classification and rates."[37] On the tenants his observation was that they had "every inducement" to " extend and improve cultivation," but also that they took very few loans (from the government) under the Land Improvement Act because "raiyats cannot offer their holdings as security, their rights not being transferable."[38] Thus, the combination of tenant protection and restrictions on land transfer may have promoted equity at the expense of growth.[39]

Thus far in this chapter we have mainly discussed regions that were conquered in the early phase of British rule in India. We now turn to a major and late acquisition, Punjab.

Punjab

The vast area of Punjab warrants some introduction before we turn to issues of land and credit. The year 1849 is usually identified as the date of Punjab's annexation, though some portions were seized earlier, and some areas were later added or removed from the province.

Punjab can be thought of as three regions: western Punjab (now in Pakistan), central Punjab (roughly present-day Indian Punjab), and the southeast (roughly Haryana in India).[40] Western Punjab was largely Muslim, the southeast was largely Hindu, and central Punjab had substantial Hindu and Sikh populations.

Western and southeastern Punjab were dry, and rainfall was more abundant in central Punjab. But there were five major rivers which provided opportunities for irrigation. After 1885 the Raj constructed a network of canals that eventually made more than ten million acres of formerly barren land in western Punjab cultivable.[41] The land was settled with migrants, many from densely populated central Punjab, who were given land grants by the state. The Canal Colonies' history is quite different from that of the rest of Punjab in the extent to which policies of land settlement were connected with the Raj's military goals, so we do not discuss it further in this section.[42]

As we noted in the introduction to this chapter, the notion of a largely self-contained "village community" had been developed in the North-Western Provinces, and early administrators in (the contiguous) eastern Punjab believed that they had found this community in perfected form in Punjab. Punjab was, therefore, largely given the land tenure system developed in the North-Western Provinces. The presumption was that the village belonged jointly to a set of proprietors. A lump sum tax was imposed on the village, which was then divided among owners. It is not entirely clear how meaningful this "jointness" was in practice. Because the property rights and tax obligations of individuals were clearly identified within the village, this was de facto not necessarily very different from raiyatwari. George Campbell, who had worked in the Punjab, noted: "Practically, the settlement made with a community is very nearly ryotwar, with the difference that Government deals with the united body, and not directly with each individual separately."[43] It was also inevitable that in such a huge region there would be places where there was no tradition of joint ownership or joint liability for taxes. How was the Raj able to impose these unfamiliar practices? B. H. Baden-Powell provided the example of Kangra, a hill state, and argued that though joint responsibility for taxes was novel, it was "rarely enforced" and was a "very shadowy" thing."[44] This reinforces the point that land tenure in Punjab was in practice close to raiyatwari.

The view of the village as a cohesive and self-contained entity received further impetus from western Punjab, especially the northwest frontier, where tribes were identified in Peshawar, Hazara, Dera Ghazi Khan, Dera Ismail Khan, and Bannu.[45] The dominant tribe in these areas is usually referred to as Pathan or Pashtun. The theory was that following conquest of a contiguous area by a tribe, the land was divided into smaller regions sometimes known as *ilaqas* and then into villages. The joint nature of land ownership and the sense of political unity came from this shared tribal heritage. The Raj extended the notion of tribe to other parts of Punjab as well. For instance, in central Punjab, Jats constituted the most numerous cultivating tribes.[46] For our purposes British theories regarding how Indian tribes originated are not of great consequence. What is noteworthy is that a new and influential category, not of religious origin, was in play.[47] The state's goal was now to understand and uphold what it understood to be the "customary law," which would preserve village cohesion.[48] The way to ensure this was to put decisions, revenue-related and judicial, in the hands of the executive, rather than rule-bound courts. Therefore, like the Santal Parganas, Punjab was declared "non-regulation."

Consistent with their views regarding village social organization, British officials found that when land was sold, by "custom" other owners in the village had the right of first refusal, or the right of preemption. The *Punjab Land Administration Manual* explains how this custom was translated into law.[49] An 1852 circular required that a landowner who wished to sell his share of land had to offer it first to the village community or to another owner in the village at a price upon which they agreed, failing which a revenue official and three assessors would arrive at a price. This rule was then brought into the Punjab Civil Code in 1854 and was extended to sales in execution of a court decree and to foreclosures on mortgages. In 1856 the chief commissioner extended the right of preemption to usufructuary mortgages (in which the lender got possession of the land). Efforts were also made to limit land transfer via the exercise of executive discretion. According to an

1866 regulation no land sold could be sold to satisfy debt without official sanction.[50]

However, the broader processes at work in the rest of British India were not to be denied. The long process of codification of law, begun in the 1830s, was coming to fruition. The Code of Civil Procedure of 1859 was extended to Punjab in 1866 (with some restrictions). A chief court was set up in Lahore in the same year, and a formal court system slowly emerged. In 1874–75 regular civil courts were established, which now adjudicated suits for debt, replacing district officers and other officials, who could now focus on their primary tasks. The judges were mostly of urban origin, with little awareness of rural customary law.

The right to preemption ran into trouble in court. Suppose a *bania* (trader-lender and not a member of the village "brotherhood" of owners) acquired a foothold in the village. The chief civil court found that he would have the right of preemption. With this interpretation, an officer complained, "a proprietor by purchase, though a stranger to, and at bitter strife with, the original village brotherhood, had as good a title to claim pre-emption as any member of it."[51] We will see below that the government addressed this issue in 1905. Preemption remained a significant contributor to litigation until the end of the colonial period.[52] In 1938, of 135,912 suits before all courts, 5,203 were for preemption.[53]

By the 1870s, a Bombay-Deccan-like process emerged in the Punjab. Land values rose during British rule because land taxes were lower, communication and trade improved, and cultivation expanded. Land titles were now clearer and could be transferred. The volume of debt, the number of suits in court for loan recovery, and transfers to land titles all increased.[54] As we have seen, by the mid-1890s the government of India itself was concerned about land transfer and sought the views of various local governments on the need for a law to restrict land transfers. It is interesting to see its *Note on Land Transfer* struggle to make the case (see table 4.2) that there had been large-scale transfer of land to nonagriculturists.

These figures do not make a compelling case for a social transformation in which the traditional peasantry was being expropriated. Arguing that "statistics regarding so large an area are of less importance than information of a more localized character,"[55] the *Note* had to cherry-pick areas where its case could be made: in particular, Ambala in eastern Punjab (in present-day India) and Gujranwala in western Punjab (now in Pakistan). The statistics for Gujranwala, pertaining to *tahsils* (subdistricts) are provided in table 4.3.

Still, the Punjab government responded enthusiastically to the proposal to restrict land transfer. The lieutenant governor warned that in the districts

Table 4.2 Transfers to nonagriculturists or new agriculturists (NNA), Punjab

Year	Percentage of Total Area Sold to NNA during the Period	Percentage Transferred to NNA of Total Area Sold during the Period	Percentage of Total Area Mortgaged to NNA during the Period	Percentage Transferred to NNA of Total Area Mortgaged during the Period
1875–78	0.3	38.2	0.9	60.4
1879–83	0.5	31.5	1.2	42.9
1884–88	0.6	30.6	1.7	39.0
1889–93	0.6	20.5	1.6	32.3

Source: India, *Note on Land Transfer*, 48.

Table 4.3 Transfers to nonagriculturists, 1868–91, in Gujranwala District, Punjab

Tahsil	Percentage Cultivated Area Sold	Percentage of Sold Area Going to Nonagriculturists	Percentage of Cultivated Area Mortgaged	Percentage of Mortgaged Cultivated Area Going to Nonagriculturists
Gujranwala	14	60	13	75
Wazirabad	12	53	15	75
Hafizabad	10.5	50	6.5	60

Source: India, *Note on Land Transfer*, 50.

where the "alienations are most extensive there may be a great probability that, unless some check is at once applied, we may in the near future reach a point at which the amount of land alienated and the number of proprietors reduced to the condition of tenants or even of labourers would constitute a political danger of formidable dimensions."[56] These fears should be understood in the context of Punjab bordering Afghanistan, and the large Sikh presence in the British-Indian army. If something had to be done, the lieutenant governor continued, it had to be much more than legislation along the lines of the Deccan Agriculturists' Relief Act, which he characterized as "*placebos.*"[57] Eventually, in 1900, the Punjab Land Alienation Act was passed with the goal of limiting transfer of land from "agricultural tribes" to others.

A key provision of the Land Alienation Act was that a member of an agricultural tribe could not "permanently alienate" (e.g., sell, will, or gift) land to someone who was not a member of an agricultural tribe without the permission of the deputy commissioner. Such permission would be granted only under special circumstances.[58]

The Punjab Land Alienation Act and the laws regarding preemption were in contradiction: the alienation act sought to prevent transfer to nonagri-

culturists, but according to prevailing law, as discussed above, a nonagriculturist owner of land in the village had the right to preempt. The Punjab Pre-Emption Act was revised in 1905 so that a person who was not of
an agricultural tribe could not preempt unless he was of the same tribe as
the seller, and he or a male ancestor had held land in the same village for
twenty years.[59]

The Punjab Land Alienation Act had to contend with two problems. The
first was defining who belonged to an agricultural tribe. The definition was
district specific. Thus, for instance, the agricultural tribes in Hissar District
were defined as Jats, Rajputs, Pathans, Syads, Gujars, Ahirs, Mughals, Dogars,
Malis, and Arains.[60] The second was that its goals had to be achieved without
undermining access to credit so much that it hurt productive activity. Therefore, mortgage of land had to be permitted without allowing it to become a
permanent transfer.

Usufructuary mortgages were permitted from a member of an agricultural tribe to a nonmember in two forms.[61] Under the first, there was
automatic redemption. For a maximum period of twenty years the mortgagee could use the land; at the end of the period the land went back to
the original owner and the loan was automatically extinguished. Under the
second the mortgagor retained the rights of an occupancy tenant, and the
rent (which would serve as interest) had to be limited to twice the land tax
plus other cesses. Conventional mortgages in which the land of a member
of an agricultural tribe was used as collateral for a loan from a nonmember
were permitted, but if the borrower defaulted the lender could only apply
to the deputy commissioner. The deputy commissioner would convert the
transaction into a usufructuary mortgage for a term not exceeding twenty
years, using his discretion to decide on principal and interest. The act also
banned (for all parties, agricultural tribes or not) the so-called conditional
sale, in which the land would automatically go to a lender (without court
intervention) if the debtor did not repay by a certain date.

The Punjab Land Alienation Act had three perverse effects: lobbying to
be included in the list of agricultural tribes; misrepresenting one's tribe to
engage in a land transaction; and doing a *benami* transaction—that is, getting someone else to buy the land on one's behalf.[62] Still, various types of
evasion notwithstanding, it appears the act favored the rich-peasant lender
over the professional trader-lender, strengthening the former in the credit
market. The weakened position of the professional moneylender can be
seen in the number of cases brought by them against agriculturists, which
fell from 105,598 in 1901 to 86, 646 in 1904 to 62,769 in 1905 to 59, 895 in
1906.[63] A district judge in Ambala (southeastern Punjab) noted, "Every year

brings it home more forcibly to the money-lender that he must seek new investment for his capital, and in this district there appears to be some advance toward industrial enterprise on the part of the capitalists."[64] A later small-scale study conducted by the Board of Economic Inquiry, Punjab, pertaining to twenty-six villages in Ferozepur District, confirmed that in fact lending and mortgage were primarily done by agriculturist lenders.[65] The Punjab Banking Enquiry Committee (1930) reported that the nonagriculturist rural moneylender considered the Land Alienation Act the "most serious obstacle to his business."[66] Still, obstacles notwithstanding, nonagriculturist trader-lenders continued to come into the Punjab because of growing business opportunities. H. C. Calvert reported that the number of moneylenders paying taxes on incomes above one thousand rupees increased from 8,400 in 1902–3 to 15,035 in 1917–18.[67]

As in previous sections, we end with some speculations regarding how law relating to land and credit might have affected economic growth in Punjab. Tenancy legislation was not particularly relevant. Though there was a category of occupancy tenants, they occupied only a small fraction of the area and had very secure rights, and were de facto owners. Most tenancy was at will. As a first approximation, we can think of Punjab (especially central Punjab) as a raiyatwari-type region, with additional frictions in the credit market due to the Land Alienation Act and to lesser extent due to the laws on preemption. How important were these frictions?

It is possible that in the poor and dry regions with many large landlords (e.g., southwestern Punjab), the weakening of the nonagriculturist lender did some damage. It may have strengthened the position of the large landlord, who was now powerful in both land and credit markets, with some market power to use to his advantage. However, in regions with more even distribution of irrigated land, there would have been many agriculturist lenders with surplus capital to lend, and the weakening of the nonagriculturist lender may have been of less consequence. The extensive presence of Punjabi agriculturists in the army also meant that their savings and remittances were available.

It is difficult to estimate the actual volume of agricultural debt, but a valiant effort was made by a colonial-era official, Malcolm Darling, using figures reported by various provincial banking enquiry committees whose reports were published around 1930 (see below).[68] As a multiple of the value of annual agricultural output, agricultural debt in the Punjab, at 1.48, was relatively high.[69] Even the mortgage debt as a percentage of total agricultural debt was not particularly low in the Punjab compared to other provinces.[70] There is no doubt these figures have to be used cautiously. Still, at the least, there is nothing to suggest that the Land Alienation Act greatly undermined the availability of credit in Punjab.

In sum, then, Punjab had approximately raiyatwari land tenure, and limited tenancy legislation, and credit markets were active. So we cautiously come to the same conclusion that we did for raiyatwari regions of the Madras and Bombay Presidencies: land law and institutions in themselves were probably not a major obstacle to growth. This conclusion is reinforced when we show below that the judicial system in Punjab worked faster than in some other major regions. Of course it is possible that in Punjab and Bombay policies that weakened the position of lenders had a long-run detrimental impact on the development of the financial system, and hence an adverse impact on growth. This is a subject for future research.

Earlier in this chapter we told the story of the Bombay Deccan in the period when the British-Indian judicial system was being introduced in the nineteenth century. By (say) 1925 it had been in place more than a century in some regions. How effectively did this system adjudicate disputes between lenders and borrowers? Apart from court costs, there was also the problem of execution of court decrees, especially when they involved the seizure of land. We discuss these issues in our next section. We obtain evidence from scattered sources, but this is sufficient to show considerable variability across space, and deterioration over time in some major regions.

Enforcement of Law

In 1923 the Civil Justice Committee was appointed to study the performance of the judicial system. The committee found the problem of delay in courts "serious" in several major provinces, and not so in others.[71] The figures in table 4.4 pertain to suits in the courts of the subordinate judges and the munsifs. Munsifs were usually the lowest tier in the legal system, where the bulk of the work was done. Between 20% and 28% of contested cases were pending for more than a year in Assam, Bengal, Madras, and Bombay. The corresponding figures for Agra and for Bihar and Orissa were much lower (2.67% and 3.91%).[72] The Madras Provincial Banking Enquiry Committee reported that the average contested suit in the munsifs' courts took ten months. In District Judges' courts the average duration had risen to 560 days.[73] Even in the Punjab, which the Civil Justice Committee identified as *not* having a "serious" problem, our examination of civil justice reports reveals a trend toward increasing duration, which seems to taper off after the mid-1920s (see figure 4.1).

Even after the court had reached a decision, it had to be executed. A judge

Table 4.4 Delays in adjudication of suits in lower courts, 1922 (subordinate judges and munsifs)

Province	Number of Decisions (1)	Number of Contested Decisions (2)	Number of Suits Pending More Than a Year (3)	Ratio of (3) to (2) (%)
Bengal	464,184	56,373	16,052	28.45
Assam	22, 099	3,587	903	25.17
Madras	122,007	64,745	14,069	21.88
Bombay	59,574	28,833	5,682	19.70
Bihar and Orissa	136,066	25,207	986	3.91
Agra	86,466	26,232	703	2.67

Source: India, Civil Justice Committee, *Report* (Calcutta: Government of India Central Publication Branch, 1925), 17–18.

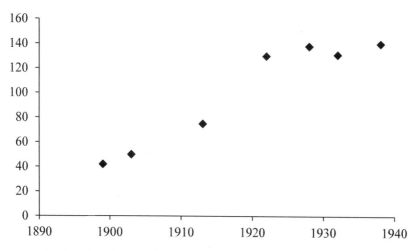

Figure 4.1. Duration of contested civil suits in subordinate courts in Punjab, in days. Source: The figures from before 1922 are from *Report on the Administration of Civil Justice in the Punjab and Its Dependencies* (Lahore: Civil and Military Gazette Press) for the respective years. From 1922 onward they are from *Note on the Administration of Civil Justice in the Punjab* (Lahore: Superintendent of Government Printing).

of the Privy Council complained in 1872 that "the difficulties of a litigant in India begin when he has obtained a decree." In several regions a large percentage of decrees were "totally infructuous." For instance, the figure was as high as 63%–71% in mofussil courts in several Bengal districts.[74]

We need to be cautious in interpreting these figures. First, it is possible that the two parties simply settled the transaction informally, avoiding the transaction costs of dealing with courts. Second, the winner might not want to execute the decree, and could simply use it as a device to "sweat" the borrower—for instance, a moneylender may not have any use for land, and might prefer to let the original owner nominally own the land, while paying a heavy "rent."[75] The Civil Justice Committee also points out that some lenders might just have taken their chances. They would charge a high rate of interest up front, allowing for the fact they might not recover their money. But these caveats notwithstanding, the various provincial banking enquiry committees which produced reports around 1930 acknowledged that execution of court decrees, especially seizure of land, was difficult. Even the Bengal Banking Enquiry Committee, which was quite unsympathetic to the lender (see below) acknowledged that "the delay in execution proceedings is often very great, particularly in mortgage suits."[76] The Bombay Banking Enquiry Committee also commented that delays in disposal of suits and execution of decrees were "bound to have an adverse effect on credit facilities, especially the rate of interest charged."[77]

Why was it difficult to execute decrees? In part this was because of numerous procedures the creditor had to follow, as well as appeals available to the debtor.[78] It is also true that foreclosure is costly the world over, especially in rural areas, where an urban or nonagriculturist banker will not be popular with the neighbors of the original landowner. And in India, as elsewhere, efforts to protect the debtor were misused. For instance, the Madras Banking Enquiry Committee complained that debtors were exploiting the provisions of the Insolvency Act of 1920 to evade repayment.[79] The Central Provinces Banking Enquiry Committee noted, in a similar vein, that the cultivators had realized that "two can play at the law court game."[80]

Creditors also faced the risks posed by benami. This was the practice of one person holding the title to property on behalf of another who was the real owner. Benami was legal. It could be done with good intentions, for instance, when an adult would hold the title for a minor. But it was also used as a method of protecting property from creditors. Anticipating a court decision favoring a creditor, A might transfer property to B. Of course this exposed A to risk, since B might then appropriate the property. But courts could be quite indulgent in protecting A. In *Jadunath Poddar v. Rup Lal Poddar* (1906), the plaintiff openly admitted that he had relinquished property to the defendants in anticipation of losing a court case. But he won the case, and did not need to perpetrate the fraud he had planned. He now wanted his property back. Ruling for the plaintiff, Justice Rampini concluded that "when the intention to commit fraud has not been carried into effect, a beneficial owner is entitled to sue for a declaration that a deed of transfer executed by him is *benami*."[81]

Benami reinforced the weaknesses of the system of registering property ownership. There were two ways one might determine who owned a piece of land. One was via the records of the revenue (tax) department. But that merely reported who owed the tax on the land. As the Madras Provincial Banking Enquiry Committee put it, "A patta [revenue department record] is not a title to land; it is merely a statement of account and is in the name of the person believed to be responsible for the payment of the sum but there is no guarantee persons whose names are in the patta, or any other such record, are the rightful owners of the land, nor does it prove that they have any title to the land."[82] The Registration Department had its own records of transactions such as sales and mortgages, but the committee tells us: "Although the statement is authoritative with regard to every transaction so registered, it does not follow who is the rightful owner of the land, except in cases where an outright sale has been registered, assuming no *benami* transactions can be recognized. It must be admitted that if *benami* transactions are to be recognized a record of rights loses very much its value."

Thus, by the late colonial period a creditor would probably have a difficult time in court, both in obtaining a decree and in executing it. These issues needed to be addressed if private lending was to work smoothly. Especially after the Depression, India went in a quite different direction.

Protecting the Borrower, Again

Even after legislation had been passed to restrict land transfer (in some regions) the need to protect the borrower had remained on the policy agenda. The judge's right to go "behind the bond" was introduced in an important India-wide law, the Usurious Loans Act of 1918. Judges could reduce interest payments they considered excessive. The Usurious Loans Act was viewed as necessary because judges were taking a narrow view of provision in the Indian Contract Act pertaining to unconscionable bargains and undue influence. The Usurious Loans Act was preceded by the usual consultation with local governments and was modeled on the provisions in section 1 of the Moneylenders' Act passed in England in 1900.[83]

The Usurious Loans Act was fairly well received by the Madras Provincial Banking Enquiry Committee, though it noted that the law had loopholes: the principal on the loan could be overstated, and the law would not help if the defendant did not show up in court. The Madras Banking Enquiry Committee noted, approvingly, that the Usurious Loans Act had not specified a particular rate of interest because the cost of capital could vary. And despite the loopholes the act was not a "dead letter."[84] Of 24,807 cases it had examined, courts had reduced the interest rate in 1,958.[85]

The Bengal Banking Enquiry Committee reported, however, that "the consensus of informed opinion is that it [the Usurious Loans Act] is inoperative and has failed to give the relief that it was intended to afford."[86] The judges complained about several rulings of the high court and the Privy Council which made them reluctant to act to protect debtors. One had concluded that a 12% interest rate could not necessarily be considered excessive, even with good security.[87] According to another, compound interest at 12% could not necessarily be considered excessive. The Bengal committee recommended fixing a maximum rate of interest and banning compound interest. It was not sympathetic to the lenders, arguing that while they "have a tendency to condemn many provisions of civil law as obstacles against realization of their claims," relaxing these provisions would provide them "a handle for oppression."[88]

After the Great Depression tensions between lenders and borrowers increased. With the growth of peasant and nationalist movements and Indian participation in governance of provinces, a slew of acts was passed in the 1930s to regulate moneylenders and to provide relief to debtors.[89] In Bengal this took the form of the Bengal Moneylenders' Acts of 1933 and 1940, and the Bengal Agricultural Debtors' Act of 1935. The moneylenders' act had familiar elements, concerned with documentation, keeping accounts, providing receipts, limits on interest rates, and damdupat. The debtors' act was a far more radical measure. The local government could set up a Debt Settlement Board, which a debtor could approach. The board would then try to bring a debtor and his or her creditor(s) to an "amicable settlement" (section 19, (1).)[90] The reader will recall that the DARA had tried to reduce the incidence of the resolution of cases ex parte, that is, absent the borrower-defendant. Reversing roles, The Bengal Debtors' Act now made it possible for the creditor to have an ex parte judgment passed against him, if he did not respond to a notice within a month. The debt could then be "deemed to be the amount stated in the statement of debt submitted by the debtor."[91] Once the case proceeded the board would examine the documentation provided by both parties and decide what the correct amounts of debt and arrears of interest were. If the lender refused to accept a "fair" offer, the board would give the debtor a certificate, after which, if the lender went to civil court, he could not receive more than 6% per annum as interest.[92]

Civil justice reports from Bengal show that the creation of the Debt Settlement Boards led to further delays in an already slow legal system. Figure 4.2 first shows a declining trend in the number of cases pending for more than a year in the early 1930s. This was because of a decline in the number of suits, a change in reporting requirements (a suit could now be declared disposed

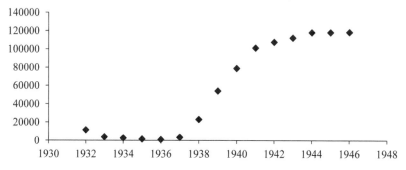

Figure 4.2. Number of suits pending for more than one year in Bengal subordinate courts. Source: The figures up to 1936 are from Bengal, High Court, *Report on the Administration of Civil Justice in the Presidency of Bengal* (Calcutta: Government Press) for the respective years. From 1937 onward they are from *Report on the Administration of Civil Justice in the Province of Bengal* (Calcutta: Government Press) for the respective years.

once a preliminary decree was passed), and quicker disposals. The act began to be implemented in 1937. We see that starting in 1937, there is a dramatic reversal of the trend and an increase in the number of pending cases.

The Bengal civil justice reports are very clear about why this happened. For every year from 1937 until 1944, the annual report, after listing the districts with the largest number of suits pending for over a year, includes the following sentence: "As compared with the figures of the previous year, the number of year-old suits shows a very considerable increase in all these districts, which is due mainly to the suits being stayed by the Debt Settlement Boards."[93]

The details of acts to regulate moneylenders and provide debt relief varied across regions, but they all seem to have led to a contraction of credit. In a landmark report in 1954 the Reserve Bank of India commented on the impact of these laws, drawing on reports from the colonial period as well as its own findings. The Punjab Civil Justice Report of 1936 had reported that (in contrast with Bengal) the act to provide debt relief had led to a decline in litigation, but also "lowered rural credit."[94] A 1946 report from Madras said that credit had contracted and the laws had been evaded. In the Central Provinces, according to a report in 1937, conciliation of debts had made it harder for farmers to get loans.[95]

The Reserve Bank of India also reported that the contraction of credit could be particularly severe for the debtor who had received relief from the court; "for him it was not so much a case of contraction as elimination of private credit." This was because "[t]he very process of adjustment involved so many restrictions on alienability of his property that no lending agencies could be expected to be favourably disposed towards him."[96] In response to the "plight" of the borrower the Bombay government had begun providing loans. Thus, it is abundantly clear that post-Depression legislation to help the borrower discouraged private lending.

Conclusion

In this and the previous chapter we have discussed three dimensions of land rights: the type of ownership, tenancy legislation (or lack thereof), and the transferability of rights. We found that studying transferability of land rights led to a discussion of credit. We then described legislation aiming to "protect" borrowers. We also addressed various dimensions of implementation of legislation: interpretation by courts, the speed and costs of adjudication, and difficulties in implementing court decisions. What have we learned about the origins of British-Indian law and its efficacy in dispute resolution? And did the structure of property rights and contract enforcement favor or inhibit economic growth?

Our conjectures depend on time and place. British-Indian land law and institutions, at one extreme, kept the state's role very limited: it outsourced tax collection and legislated on little else (Permanent Settlement in Bengal, ca. 1800). At the other extreme, it gave the tenant a permanent occupancy right, regulated the rent, and forbade the tenant to mortgage or sell the right (say, Santal Parganas ca. 1900). The functioning of courts varied. In the mid-nineteenth-century Bombay Deccan before the passing of the Deccan Agriculturists' Relief Act, courts perfunctorily passed ex parte decrees against borrowers, as many as sixty an hour according to the reminiscences of one judge.[97] In the mid-twentieth century in Bengal, court decisions on landlord-tenant disputes could take years. The attitude to credit market regulation varied enormously as well. In 1855 usury laws in the Deccan were repealed in imitation of British precedent, but by the 1930s, across British India, not only were usury laws in place, but debt relief boards were also using their discretion to reduce the amounts owed by debtors. In all of this there was indeed borrowing of doctrines from Britain, but elements of Hindu law were retained, and the practical exigencies of administration, the limits of knowledge, and, above all, the political fears of the Raj played important roles. By the 1930s administrators had a far more interventionist mind-set, influenced by nationalist and peasant movements, more than by British legal precedent.

Given this diversity of influences and administrative/legal choices, it is difficult to generalize regarding the impact of British-Indian law on the potential for agricultural growth. If we were to consider a Bengal zamindar in 1850, there might be nothing in law and institutional structure to inhibit investment. The tenants might hold their land at the zamindar's will, and his or her stronger position in court and even coercive power would permit rent increases. Like Jaykrishna Mukherjee (chapter 3), the zamindar might bring more land under cultivation and even introduce new varieties of crops. Given that this zamindari right was freely transferable, it was easy to borrow. By 1935, the same zamindari was occupied by tenants who were protected by law from eviction and rent increases. Zamindar-tenant conflict and courts' inability to resolve disputes quickly undermined investment incentives for all parties. And with debt relief boards looming large, a potential investor who did want to borrow would have found it difficult to obtain credit. In contrast, in central Punjab in 1915, a large landowner was able to lease land to a tenant-at-will and have the support of a relatively quick judicial system in the case of disputes. Credit was readily available from other agriculturist lenders, whose transactions, including seizure of land following default, were supported by law. If investment did not occur, the causes for this would have to be sought elsewhere, not in the structure of property rights or contract enforcement.

In this chapter, and the one preceding, we have discussed land rights at length. But whose rights were these? Were they the rights of individuals or the rights of families? What were the rules governing succession, inheritance, and alienation of family land and other forms of property? How different were the rights of men and women? We address this large class of questions in the next chapter.

FIVE

Succession of Property:
Joint versus Individual Right

The student who wishes to understand the Hindu system of property, must begin by freeing his mind from all previous notions drawn from English law. . . . Individual property is the rule in the West. Corporate property is the rule in the East.

—John Mayne, *A Treatise on Hindu Law and Usage*, 1880

In 1792, the chief civil court of Calcutta settled a dispute between two branches of a family over the control of a banking firm's assets. The founder of the firm, Amirchand, is a legend in Indian history. One of the wealthiest and most powerful men of his time, he was a secret ally of the East India Company and helped the British defeat the ruler of Bengal Sirajuddaula in 1757, an event that laid the foundation of the British Empire in India. Later, his friendship with the British soured because of rumors that he had double-crossed them. The huge inheritance he had left behind was the cause of a dispute between the sons of his brother-in-law Hazarimal, who managed the business after Amirchand died, and the descendants of Dayalchand, the founder's son, who was a minor when his father died. Hazarimal was in effect the surviving partner of the firm. But Hindu law favored the direct male descendant. And Hazarimal's own sons, being born of slave women, had a weak claim by religious law. To add to the confusion, Amirchand had scribbled his last wishes on a piece of paper that seemingly recognized the claims of both parties.[1]

The case was dismissed, on what grounds we do not know. But it illustrates the three types of issues that a number of property disputes at the turn of the nineteenth century needed to resolve. In a family firm, who had a stronger claim to inherit property, the partner or the son? When religious law privileged the claim of an heir on spiritual grounds whereas others' claims could be justified on grounds of equity or efficiency, what should the judges do? By what law would testaments be prepared and accepted in the courts?

The history of legislation in property rights (excluding agricultural land) is a history, first, of anomalies that came up in an assertion of religious custom, which sanctioned collective ownership, and second, of a gradual strengthening of testamentary powers of individuals.[2] The transition from one regime to another was begun by the judges and in the courtroom. The Transfer of Property Act (1882), among other new laws, was the response by the jurists to a recognized failure of indigenous doctrine.

The chapter proceeds in the following stages. The next section looks at property legislation in India in a comparative history context. In the next two we describe the ideological basis of the company's original plan, and why the plan unraveled. Two subsequent sections deal with case proceedings and judgments in chronological order; and the two sections that follow discuss the reforms, again in chronological order. The last section describes the evolution of Islamic law of property in India.

Economic History and Property Legislation in India

Institutional economic history assigns an important role to effective private property rights. The decision to do so comes from the intuition that in the real world property rights are usually not perfectly defined or costlessly enforced. In turn, secure property rights are preconditions for markets to operate without frictions, among other reasons, because security guaranteed by law limits prospects of expropriation and risks in trade.[3] These implications of security of property right can lead to one mode of doing comparative economic history, where societies are compared on how well they define private property in law and deliver security. This accent on definition and security of private property is not very useful in understanding either the distinctness of Indian institutions or the innovation that the British introduced to Indian institutions.

As far as we can gather, pre-British states took private property and the security of property quite seriously, so that there was little the British could add to this dimension. The Mughals maintained detailed revenue records, conducted cadastral surveys, and offered incentives to old settlers—these and other measures suggest that they valued private property. A large literature recognizes that the European settlers in many colonies often appropriated secure and well-defined rights for the benefit of the settlers (see chapter 1 for more discussion). In colonial India, in land and liquid wealth, law did not discriminate between people by the ethnicity of the right-holder. If anything, expatriate landholding rights were weaker than Indian rights until well into the nineteenth century (see below). Europeans could not own or purchase farmlands, for example, which is one of the reasons why the first tea estates in the 1830s necessitated special legislation. Nor was there a fundamental difference between England and India in the degree of private ownership of assets and the extent of entitlement to receiving protection from the state.

It was not private ownership or security of private property where the difference between the two cultures rested. Indian institutions of property were distinct from the European ones in that they defined the right of the collective, the family, in more detail than the rights of individual members within it. The British innovation was to strengthen that distinctness. The implications of the move can be seen in inheritance rules. English law accepted two distinct principles of succession, one which followed custom, or a more or less uniform convention sanctioned by the courts, and the other the will of the owner. Custom ruled by default, but custom could be superseded by a duly drawn-up will. There was little freedom available to anyone to claim a distinct family custom if it conflicted either with the will or with the court-sanctioned convention. In contrast, there was neither an established tradition nor procedures in precolonial India concerning wills. Therefore, any legal system that claimed to follow Indian tradition would in effect follow a custom-bound succession rule alone.

Given the cultural diversity of the Indian population, and the fact that the empire formed out of territories formerly ruled by many different regimes, a rule by custom would mean a rule by many customs. It would be practically unworkable. The British hoped to simplify the operation of the rule by custom by defining custom with reference to religion. Since classical Hinduism and Islam upheld the sanctity of the family or kin, British Indian law upheld the property rights of the family or kin (the citation above of an advocate general of Madras explains the perceived difference between England and India neatly). In the beginning, testamentary laws were left undeveloped or applicable to the Europeans alone.

Thus emerged the most important feature of British Indian law of succession and inheritance—property was jointly owned, and therefore it should pass on to a collective body. Any individual member of the collective body had restricted right to alienate property. Let us explore this idea a bit further.

Joint Inheritance

Chapter 2 showed that the Hastings project that began in 1772 established the official policy that all disputes among Indians should be settled with reference to religious codes. Although law derived of religion or custom was in principle applicable to contracts and debts, the main field of application of this principle was in the sphere of inheritance of property. In lower Bengal, where British colonization started, two religions, Hinduism and Islam, were predominant. Muslim law was officially the state law applicable to all Muslims. Hindu law was not a state law in a significant sense anywhere in India. In any case, a broad similarity was believed to exist across religions in the matter of property ownership. Jurists believed that property in India was held jointly by the members of an extended family or joint family. Each member who had a right to family property was called a coparcener.[4] The implications of this choice were significant. A legal theory that upholds joint ownership should also uphold joint inheritance, that is, the principle that after the death of a head of estate, the property passes on to the surviving coparceners, who should hold it jointly. The principle of partible inheritance was in theory allowed but in practice restrained by rules that made it difficult to partition a property into parcels. The weak testamentary powers of the head of the family acted as a restraint.

Why should a state, let alone one that is British and mercantile in origin, decide that protecting religion or family ought to be its fundamental duty? One answer to this question is that colonial law, while admitting exceptions for indigenous capitalists by placing kinship-based firms under personal law, upheld "universal models of modern market practice" for the Europeans.[5] In other words, the decision to uphold personal law and make it equivalent to universal law was simultaneously an act of legitimizing Indian business organization, which was thought to be personal, and a step toward making it inferior to the public law where impersonal contract ruled. It was an act to justify colonial rule. The idea of a hierarchical dualism in law comes naturally in a colonial society and is led by the assumption that law stems from a desire of foreigners to control Indian society.[6]

For the late eighteenth-century company state, this assumption may seem overdrawn. In the beginning, the state was politically and militarily quite weak. The decision to build a property right system around Indian religion or social organization can be seen as a response to the weaknesses of the Europeans in an Indian-dominated political world. There were three factors at work. First, politically speaking, institutional continuity would have seemed the safer option for the company state. Second, to the early codifiers of Indian law, the Hindu Dharmashastra and the Hanafi code books already available and in wide circulation would have seemed similar to a *Corpus Juris* (see also chapter 2). And third, the decision was consistent with the indigenous rule of law that the British encountered. The status of

Islamic law, established in large parts of India, was that of law revealed or divine in origin. British rulers gave the Hindus a chance to establish a parallel claim.

A similar set of arguments can be advanced to suggest why, in the 1770s, it would have been rational for a ruler to protect the "joint family." The term was not indigenous but an English borrowing. But the use made of it was Indian. It referred to a legal entity like a joint tenancy or a partnership, in which membership depended on religion and birth, and, more disputably, on gender and caste. Corporate ownership of property, the right of family members to use but not to sell or divide property, and legal obstacles to subdivision of joint property such as the "entail," were all common in the milieu that the British came from. Furthermore, in a region where productive capital was scarce, making subdivision of property difficult made sense from the point of economic efficiency. For example, agricultural land, when fragmented, would lose productive power because all the fragments could lose access to private commons like water and pasture. It was thought that primogeniture was rare in India. The best alternative rule, consistent with the texts, was the joint family. This was a partnership or joint tenancy that did not terminate with the death of one member.

Upholding the right of the family was also consistent with eighteenth-century European understanding of Indian history and society. Hindu Dharmasastras make an emphatic claim that the duty of the king was to protect caste and kinship.[7] The legislators reading these books absorbed this emphasis. The impression of Indian society as a collection of endogamous guild-like formations that called themselves *jatis* (the Portuguese used their term *casta* to refer to these formations) partly originated in Indo-European trade. European visitors to Indian port towns in the seventeenth century observed that in India, significant social interaction with other communities was forbidden to merchants, bankers, and skilled artisans. Merchants lived in an insular social world, and mercantile law existed as social conventions of endogamous guilds. Members of the group not only shared a trade but also married within the trade and ate together with people who belonged in the same trade. Such rules were not peculiar to India. But in India, such rules were accompanied with an unusually powerful moral force, an act of breach being deemed to bring disgrace and pollution on the community, inviting severe punishment, excommunication, disgrace, even death. Civil jurisdiction, it seemed, was decentralized into these jatis.

Despite such a neat ideological foundation, joint inheritance created more problems than it solved.

The Problem with Joint Inheritance

Joint inheritance created four types of problem—uncertainty over what the classical law really said, exclusion of women, a confusion between two roles of the head of an estate, as owner and as manager, and confusion over the religious identities of disputant parties.

A Hindu person's entitlement to property derived from a principle known as "spiritual benefit."[8] The principle stated that certain descendants were entitled to perform rites dedicated to the ancestors, and others not. This is how religion and family became interrelated—for it followed that all those individuals who could confer spiritual benefit also deserved coparcenary rights. Not all relations could deliver spiritual benefit. Agnates held superior rights (known as *sapinda*) in this respect over cognates, men held superior rights over women, a category of cognates known as *bandhus* and linked to the daughter's family had superior rights over other cognates but inferior to those of the agnates, and brothers of "full blood" had superior rights to brothers of "half blood." The typical property dispute in the colonial times entailed partition of, succession to, and inheritance of a joint family estate. These disputes frequently required the judges to decide what a joint family was, to distinguish cognate from agnate lines, to distinguish male from female agnates, since the classical texts were confusing with respect to women's property rights, and to compare and frame rights and obligations of different generations.[9] These matters were initially settled by consulting scholars appointed by the courts, pandits in the case of the Hindus and maulvi for the Muslims.

A fundamental problem with the approach was to decide what classical law really said. There were, by a conservative count, five major schools of thought on Hindu law (Maharashtra, Benares, Mithila, Gaudiya, and Dravida), and thirty-four main texts and compilations that represented these schools. These authorities displayed substantial agreement on the importance of the family as property owner, but significant differences on women's right to inherit and sell their husband's property. A single source text, Mitakshara, changed contents between Mithila and Benares. In practice, the application of Hindu law and the adoption of regional custom often converged. These authorities differed not only on the codes themselves but also on the doctrine of property, one school (Jimutavahana) holding that the notion of property derived from codes, and another (Vijnaneswara and his followers) that the notion of property evolved out of common usage. In pamphlets and books published in Bengal in the mid-nineteenth century, attempts were made to systematize the hierarchy of claims and propose orders of succession consistent with religion. A book by Prasanna Kumar Tagore, a leader of the conservative Hindu landholders, and a spokesperson for legal reform, was the most famous of these.[10] But, then, quite a different hierarchy was advocated by another leading interpreter of the time, Shama Churn Sircar. Even one hundred years after Hindu law was adopted as a code in Bengal, the judges functioned in an atmosphere of uncertainty over what Hindu law really meant to say about succession.

Further, the principle of "spiritual benefit" was Brahminic in spirit and excluded lower-caste persons from inheriting or receiving property from a higher-caste person—even when the two were related by marriage. It also excluded women from inheriting joint property in the same way as the men could. This was so because women did not usually have any right to confer spiritual benefit. Other elements in Hindu social practice reinforced the importance of the son. The average age at marriage of girls was very low (below thirteen in the late nineteenth century) in several regions of India where Hindus predominated. With average life expectancy in the twenties, the second feature would mean that many women became widows at a young age. If they were to remarry and were entitled to the same share of property as were the male relations, the dead husband's property would be threatened by a division. Such a prospect faced two obstacles in certain interpretations of Hindu law: prohibition on the remarriage of widows and prohibition on widows inheriting ancestral property, both subject to some exceptions.

Women had an escape route from this law: adoption of a son, provided there was documentary evidence showing the husband's consent to adoption. The Sudder Dewany Adawlut between 1800 and 1850 decided a number of cases where a young girl produced a document purportedly signed by her dying husband sanctioning adoption, which document was challenged by the husband's family. In the 1830s and 1840s, such claims had a reasonable hope to succeed; in the 1890s, these challenges were often dismissed.

The classical texts allowed for considerable latitude on the question of women's inheritance rather than disfavoring women outright. What was not allowed women in any of the texts was the right to mortgage, sell, and transfer property at will. What was left ambiguous or contradictory was the nature of their coparcener right, whether it was absolute and equal to that of the sons or not. The Dharmashastras did not speak in one voice on this issue. There was yet a third condition—in order to be worthy of coparcener right the widow would have to "keep unsullied her husband's bed." Words to that effect figured in almost all major classical texts. It was probably a benign provision, but no doubt left open the prospect of a nasty counterattack by the husband's distant male relations.[11]

A third general class of problem involved confusion of roles of the head of an estate. No individual was in effect an "owner" of a property; the head of the family was at best a manager, a custodian, or a trustee. The heads of some merchant families made sure that their sons understood this by gifting away the whole property to the family deity. It was generally accepted by the jurists that the wish to keep a commercial or zamindari estate intact was a reasonable one, so much so that it almost suggested a legal principle: "The law which regulates the descent of property must not be confounded with the power which arises from having dominion over the estate."[12] The rule was applied in numerous instances, most commonly in deciding the sons' right to demand a partition of a deceased father's estate.

The principle of separating ownership (vested in the male agnates of a family) and management (vested in the head of the family) faced challenges in case laws in five different ways. First, the rule worked by weakening the testamentary powers of the head of the family, even though this was not only inconsistent with other types of law in force in India (European and Parsi for example), but also inconsistent with parallel developments in the sphere of laws pertaining to wills and probates, which admitted the right of Hindus to make a will. Second, it was iniquitous in respect of that part of the family wealth that had been accumulated by the head of the family. Classical law weakened the head's testamentary powers. Some of the earliest cases of partition of commercial assets upheld the head's prerogative to decide future succession.[13] Third, it was iniquitous with respect to the female and/or cognate members of the family. Fourth, it made contracting debts and mortgaging assets by the head of the family difficult and exposed to challenges by others. A large number of cases in the middle of the nineteenth century decided what should prevail in succession and inheritance—the will of an individual or the classical rule favoring the collective body. And fifth, high-profile property cases in merchant firms in the nineteenth century revolved around rival claims between the real managers, sometimes called "managing coparceners," and distant relations with a theoretically stronger entitlement to inherit.[14]

These claims of the distant kinsmen were settled with tenuous, sometimes fantastic, references to the Hindu law code. Whether they were upheld or not, the judges invariably pored over Hindu code books and quoted from these at great length. Reference to religious code was becoming a waste of time. And yet, after all this scholarship, the actual outcome of the process was becoming uncertain. In the first half of the nineteenth century, few higher court cases disputed this issue. In the second half, a number of suits came to the high courts, in itself suggesting that a core principle of Hindu law (*Dayabhaga* in this case) was no longer held to be either realistic or sacrosanct. In some of these, the claim of the cognate sapinda was held to be more credible than a category now called the "distant kinsman" (*Moti Lal Bundopadhya v. Digumber Roy Chowdhry and Others*, Calcutta, 1883). Others took the opposing view (for example, *Bama Churn Chattopadhya and another v. Huri Das Bundopadhya*, Calcutta, 1888). Judges who expressed a more conservative view in the matter cited an influential judgment that was followed in Bengal in a number of similar suits (*Gobind Pershad Talookdar v. Woomesh Chunder Surmah Ghuttack*, Calcutta, 1870).

A fourth general issue was the difficulty settling who was a Hindu and who was a Muslim in India. Religious identity was not as fixed in the region as the jurists presumed, so that a religious theory of law made it possible for disputants to choose between laws: "A customary law of inheritance may, it appears, be changed at his election by the person subject to it attaching himself to a class of the community on which the custom does not operate and subject to a different law."[15] An example of this problem was the Indo-European population. A European merchant who married or lived with a Hindu woman could claim to be a Hindu joint family.[16] Such people were either treated as "after the manner of the Hindus" or placed in another category. The Allahabad High Court in a judgment held that Hindu law could be applied to those who, though not Hindus, had followed Hindu law. Prominent trading groups, notably Kachchi Memons, made use of this provision. Disputes between parties who followed different religions were another difficult area.

Facing these problems, the judges were left with little guidance. For example, the ambiguity in classical texts over women's property rights meant that the classical scholars who were consulted by the courts were not always neutral arbiters. In a high-profile dispute, there were charges of bribery. "In recent times," wrote one judge, "the nefarious practice of the males of the family seizing all the property of it, and reducing the females to a state little short of slavery, . . . the present race of Pundits are sufficiently inclined to support."[17] The middle decades of the nineteenth century reveal a tension on the status of expert opinion. The lower-court judges, who were mainly Indians, were repeatedly instructed that they were not to apply anything other than Hindu and Islamic law in matters of property, whereas in the appeals courts and in legislation, the judges and jurists often departed from a strict interpretation of religious codes. In the case of one expert, Ramcharan Sharma, all of his opinions that went against the material interest of a woman litigant were overturned by the judges or referred to other pundits until an opposing view was found. Where the validity of an inheritance was disputed by the pundit purely on ritual grounds, the view was usually overruled.

The judges did not seriously believe in spiritual benefit. They did not trust the scholars. Could they trust their instincts instead? Famously, a provision was added (1781) that where no explicit guidelines were available from Hindu and Islamic codes, the judges would act according to "justice, equity and good conscience." But judges could not get away by simply citing "equity." Whose equity were they entitled to protect? Equity in the eyes of religious belief and a humanist conception of equity did not meet. Given the force of the belief that only the son could secure salvation, empowering the widows or daughters at the expense of the son might serve a humanist definition of equity but compromised the believer's definition of equity, namely, the equitable right of the parent to enjoy a peaceful afterlife.

Court cases illustrate the dilemmas the judges faced more clearly.

Cases, 1785–1860: Right to Alienate Joint Family Property

The first cluster we draw upon comes from a publication of 1853, which collected cases of Hindu law settled in the Supreme Court of Calcutta between 1772 and 1801.[18] If a few cases on the negotiability of financial instruments are ignored, all were concerned with succession, partition, mortgage, and probate. The only exception was a business contract suit.[19] Then and later, most Hindu law cases involved one major point—where property was vested in a joint family, did the property right include the right to alienate by sale or partition or mortgage?

The judges had clear instruction that on such matters they must consult the Hindu classical scholars, pundits, but that religious codes and precedence could be invoked in settling procedural issues (*Sorropchand Adie v. Rogonath Chand and Kistnomonee*, 1796). In wills cases the two sides joined together, because there was no Hindu law on wills procedure. Almost all wills cases involved handwritten letters or bits of paper, often unsigned by witnesses. The substantial legal process involved framing a precise question that could be theoretically settled with reference to the classical texts. This question was forwarded to the in-house scholar. For a considerable length of time, the preeminent Sanskrit scholar of the sudder court was Ramcharan Sharma, who was later joined by Govardhan Kaul, a Kashmiri Brahmin well versed in Persian in addition to Sanskrit. The judges complained that the reference caused delay and, on several occasions, dispensed with it for no other reason. After Kaul joined the service, the two pundits often gave contradictory opinions. On a few occasions, the opinion of the pundit was overruled apparently because it violated equity.

In 1785 a property case came to the court. Two brothers of Hindu Khatri caste, Kaival Krishan and Ganga Bishnu, had jointly owned a property near Calcutta. The brothers were moneylenders, and very wealthy. On the former's death, the property was divided between Kaival's son Jaikrishna and the uncle Ganga Bishnu. Ganga Bishnu died without a male heir but made a will. The plaintiff in the case was one Munnulal Babu, the sole heir and manager of Ganga Bishnu's estate according to the will. The will was neither registered nor signed by all the witnesses, but the defendant, Jaikrishna, did not dispute the will on these grounds. The ground, rather, was that Munnulal was of low caste, bought by Ganga Bishnu as a slave when a boy. Ganga Bishnu "bred him up as a child of the family, and treated him as tenderly as if he had been his own son." But could an outcaste inherit the property? On this question, Sharma's verdict was disputed by Kaul, leading the court to seek the views of other scholars, including William Jones. In the end, the case was settled for the plaintiff, because this "seemed to be the better opinion of the pundits" (*Munoololl Baboo v. Gopee Dutt and others*). The opinion of the pundits was far from unanimous; the judges seem to have accepted the version of religious law that suited their own sensibility.

A number of suits in the 1780s and 1790s involved widows claiming shares in the family estate. The pundits proved that women did have right to property according to the classical texts, but a limited one. The rule was that the widows could demand a maintenance, the amount of which would vary according to the size of the estate. In theory, the allowance was the annuity of a share of the property rather than a subsistence allowance, which was often the practice. "The widow takes a moiety, but her interest is qualified—i.e. she has absolute power of disposal over the produce and profits whilst she lives, and she may, in pios usus [pious uses], encroach upon the corpus of her moiety, but under sanction and control of the heir" (*Dayalchandra Addy v. Kishori Dasi*). Some rich widows had the resources to enforce this right, their economic power derived from the capacity to spend in religious charity, and also from moneylending. A small number of suits involved the widow as a creditor.

Many widows' suits built around three questions. Could this share be gifted? Would the gift become void upon the death of the widow? Could the gift become void if the widow separated or, on rare occasions, remarried? A dispute broke out between the recipient of such a gift and other branches of the family on the first point. The plaintiff placed much emphasis on the fact that he, and not the beneficiary of the gift, performed the last rites of Parameshwari, the widow in question. Absent detailed views of the pundits, the judge dismissed the case with the "laconic comment" that performing the last rite was "no effect" (*Tilluckchand Doss v. Ramhurry Doss*).

A group of Hindu law cases on property settled in the chief civil court (the Sudder Dewanny Adawlut) were republished with annotations by the judge and jurist Thomas Strange. These cases came mainly from the provinces and were dated 1805–10. They, too, involved much the same issues as in the Supreme Court, namely, the status of a will made by a head of family, when the will disinherited a son, and the rights of a widow when an estate was partitioned. Women's property was again a subject, and the pundits reiterated the view that women had a right to a share, but only to enjoy, not to alienate.[20] This was so, provided the woman proved herself loyal to the husband. But disinheritance upon suspicion of infidelity could be a ground for disputation, as in a Madras case where a wife, who had been turned out of her home by a husband and never returned during his lifetime, was declared a rightful claimant to property.[21] Partition of a family estate by mutual agreement was allowed and would be easy if the estate was ancestral, but if it was acquired by the father of the coparceners, the will should take precedence.[22] This rule, however, was found to be difficult to apply in practice because common estate was almost always employed for private enterprise by members of the joint family.

A further collection of Hindu law judgments, dated ca. 1820–40, can be found in the famous reference work of the early nineteenth century known as Moore's Indian Appeals. The original compilation was reproduced in parts in several other sources, one of which we cite from.[23] By these years, joint family suits were more numerous, and the judgments relied upon precedence rather than consultation with the court-appointed expert. From time to time the judges would attempt to formulate and restate a synthetic concept of what the joint family was (commensality, common funds, and cohabitation), and what individual rights its members had or could assert. The two common subjects of disputation—partition of an estate during the lifetime of the head of a family, and inheritance of the estate by the surviving members—were closely connected in Hindu law because both actions were conditional on agreement between coparceners and on meeting certain guidelines.[24] When the members of a family actually satisfied the conditions of commensality, cohabitation, and so on, it was not too difficult to meet these guidelines. But an estranged son, a brother marrying out of caste, the widow of a brother, and uncertainty over whether or not a brother ever enjoyed the common funds all carried a very unclear form of right.

In the 1830s, a strange incident in the Dewanny Adawlut revealed the unreliability of the authority of Hindu law. Ramchandra Sharma, a professor of law in the Sanskrit College and the in-house authority on Hindu law in the court, was asked to deliver his opinion on a succession case involving a Brahmin landholding family of Benares. The original family consisted of five brothers and one sister. The sister's grandsons claimed succession, all other members except two widows having died. The question of religious law was: could these male survivors confer spiritual benefit? The government in its turn believed that the estate should revert to the state. Sharma gave his verdict in favor of the sister's grandsons. Six months later, he was dismissed from his job. The stated ground was that he had made an error of judgment. Sharma was influential among the Brahmin scholars and the Europeans of Calcutta, who campaigned for his reinstatement. The petition did not succeed, however, because subsequent enquiry brought up the real charge against him, that of bribery or "corrupt motives." The case exposed two issues, that trust between the classical scholar and the judges had broken down, and that classical scholarship failed to supply unambiguous verdicts.[25]

Disputes "between the relatives of a Hindu widow and of the deceased husband, as to the enjoyment of the property left by the latter," formed perhaps the most "numerous class" of property-related disputes in the cities.[26] Going by the length of the discussion on a widow's right, one appellate case in 1861 (*Gobindmani Dasi v. Anandamayi and 46 others*, original suit in the Dacca court) was a landmark judgment. Gobindmani was the daughter-in-law of Anandamayi, the widow in this case, and stated in her plaint that the latter, with the collusion of two servants, Nim Chand Das and Sarup Chand Das, one George Lamb, and forty-three other individuals had been auctioning a zamindari estate part by part to repay debts contracted by her, thus reducing ancestral property to waste, and acting against the rights allowable a widow. Anandamayi and her comrades were doing this on the assumption that her inheritance was absolute (that is, it could not be challenged by potential claimants) and included all of the estate. But the deceased had sons, and there could be an argument whether or not, according to Hindu law, the widow's rights could exceed that of the son. The discussion revealed the differences of opinion among texts, and the construction placed on the texts by the former judge and "a very great authority," Francis Macnaghten, led to a decision favoring Anandamayi.[27] The judgment also cited a number of previous civil court and Privy Council cases that had settled for the right of inheritance for the widow.

In *Narrayen Bhau v. Ganpat Hurrichund*, the property was acquired with the private enterprise of one individual, devolved on his widow, and upon the widow gifting it to her grandson, the brother of the original owner filed a suit claiming that she had no right by Hindu law to alienate the estate.[28] Neither scripture nor common sense seemed to suggest an undisputed right to the brother. "On a point of Hindu succession, where there was a conflict between the authorities, and the Shastrees of the Sudr Adalut, on a reference to them, also differed; the Supreme Court decided the case, in conformity to what the English law, and the rule of natural succession would seem to dictate."[29] In other words, the widow won.

The cases we have discussed in this section show that reliance on religious law led, in practice, to ad hoc or arbitrary decision making. A second large area of disputation was the division of roles of the head of a family between owner and manager.

Cases, 1770–1860: Managers versus Owners in Merchant Families

Some of the most famous and long-drawn cases of disputes in merchant firms involved a conflict between the rights of the family and the rights of the manager. The unstated assumption behind the wish to protect joint inheritance in a business firm was that the extended family would somehow supply managerial talent as well. Frequently, this was not the case, and in the interest of business, partnerships formed between merchants bound by a distant or notional kind of kinship not protected by joint inheritance. In such cases, inheritance would become a contested issue.

One of the earliest examples of the contest was discussed at the start of the chapter: succession to the estate of the banker and merchant, Amirchand. The case ended as a "nonsuit," showing how difficult it could be to settle who had a stronger claim to a merchant firm's assets, the partner or the male descendants.

About 1800, the large trading firm of Abdul Latif Sayed of Calcutta started a branch of the business in Bombay. Of the two chief clerks in the Calcutta office, Mahomed Khan and Mahomed Shustri, Khan followed Latif to Bombay. Latif, before his death, appointed Khan the heir to a third of the property and "called him partner." Khan married one of the widows, Mariam Begum, and until his death in 1820 was a major figure in Bombay, but less as a merchant and more as "a political agent" in negotiations between the company and the rulers of Muscat and Egypt. He was a leader of the Ismaili Khoja community. The firm, however, was managed by Shustri, who had moved in to Bombay in 1808. He was the executor of the property on behalf of Khan when he died. Shustri, in the name of his master, ran the firm but invested large sums of money in the European agency house Bruce, Fawcett in his own name. Indeed, the firm's reputation depended on his name.

Trouble began after Shustri's death in 1834, when the management of the trading firm was taken over by his son-in-law Mahomed Rahim, who received a third of the property via Shustri's will and controlled the rest. The widow and the son of Khan claimed the property to be their own, a claim challenged by Rahim. The point of religious law in this case was one that forbade a gift of more than a third of the personal property to someone who was not "a natural heir." Real succession in a merchant firm, however, did not follow these rules and occurred "by virtue of some arrangement tacitly understood between the parties, and therefore never brought into question." Neither family custom nor Islamic law supplied sufficient guidance on how succession *in management* was to take place. Rahim's case was dismissed, to his ruin, and almost certainly to the detriment of the firm.

In 1776, the Gujarati merchant Manohardas Rupji and his five sons owned a trading firm in Bombay. In that year, two of his sons formed a partnership called Ramdas, Harjivandas. In 1782, Harjivandas died, leaving a one-year-old son, Devidas. The brother Ramdas carried on the partnership in the old name. When he was older, Devidas tried to enter the firm as a partner, but his uncle Ramdas resisted. On his deathbed in 1808, the uncle called in four male relations, and in their presence persuaded Devidas to sign an agreement relinquishing all claims to the firm for a consideration. In turn, Devidas was appointed the executor of his uncle's will. He came to manage the firm, but without formal sanction. In 1832, the widow and son of Ramdas sued Devidas, claiming that the accumulated profits of business were owed to them and not to Devidas.

The argument for the defendant was the point of Hindu law that Devidas was the legitimate heir to the partnership, with or without the letter. Devidas claimed that his uncle did not disclose the real accounts of the firm, and that his claim exceeded the money he had agreed to receive. Mysteriously, key parts of the accounts were eaten by white ants between 1832, when the case began, and 1852, when it was settled in the Supreme Court. The plaintiff claimed that the letter was a statement to dissolve the partnership. But there was neither any record of nor procedure for a formal dissolution. In cases like these, much depended on the construction the judges and the lawyers placed on the conversations that occurred between the individuals concerned. In this case, the crucial conversation was held behind closed doors over a few days in 1808, and the case was tried forty years later. There was neither Hindu law nor European law to tell the judges whose secret intentions should be privileged in a family dispute. Devidas lost the case. By then he was advanced in years and the management was distributed among members of the extended family. The decision may not have been a loss for the firm.

The rights of the family versus the rights of the manager turned into a conflict between religious law and family custom in the case of three families, *Hirbai v. Sonabai, Gangbai v. Sonabai,* and *Rahimatbai v. Haji Yusuf.* The first two cases arose in the context of a large trading firm of Bombay managed by the brothers and partners Haji Mir Ali and Sajun Mir Ali, and after the former's death by the latter alone. When Sajun Mir Ali died in 1843, his brother's daughters filed a suit claiming inheritance of their father's share according to Koranic law. The defendants argued that their community, the Ismaili Khojas, formed "an exclusive sect or cast" who had converted from Hinduism four hundred years ago and therefore retained Hindu succession practices. These practices allowed a maintenance allowance to the women until marriage and some part of their marriage expenses, but nothing more. The third suit was almost exactly similar, except that the history of conversion of the Kutchi Memon community, involved in this case, was even murkier.

Sectarian problems of this kind posed a significant challenge to the application of Hanafi law to the courts. Meeting these challenges required a definition of who was a Muslim. In the twentieth century, the courts were said to have adopted the opinion of the late nineteenth-century jurist Syed Ameer Ali in defining "Muslim" as one who believed in two fundamental dogmas, that there was one God, and that Muhammad was His Prophet.[30] The application of this principle reduced the scope for admitting claims to distinctive customs among Muslim sects and simplified procedures for disputes stemming from apostasy and conversion when a family member, or even a husband, disavowed one sect and accepted another, and for certain religious disputes that involved settling who was a "true Muslim."[31]

In the early nineteenth century, however, the whole question of who was a Hindu in spirit and who was a Muslim in a cosmopolitan port city like Bombay appeared too vexatious and too risky to a British Indian judge to be allowed to become material. In a very broad sense, many communities could claim to be Hindus in spirit. Settlers like "Parsis, Moguls, Afghans, Israelites, and Christians . . . are seen to have exchanged much of their ancient patrimony of ideas for Hindu tones of thought." On the other hand, against the nineteenth-century backdrop, many communities were actively engaged in redefining their religious identities. Individual members of the Khojas, like many other sects, expressed the "intention to incorporate themselves with the general body of Mussalmans" in the nineteenth century.[32] In these cases, the women's claim to their father's share was sometimes rejected because the judge ruled in favor of family custom against religion. One could as well read the judgment to favor the manager over the asserted owner of a merchant firm.

For many judges and jurists, then, joint inheritance and its religious justification failed to supply adequate guidance. New laws were needed.

Reformist Legislation I: 1830–1865

It seems that before British Indian law began, succession of some landlord estates could follow either primogeniture or a partible-inheritance rule. In British Indian law, an exception to primogeniture was allowed to the Chota Nagpur and adjoining upland areas, though it was effectively removed in successive legislation. Succession by nomination—the nearest equivalent to a will in customary law—was allowed among some religious communities (*gossain*).[33] Among communities in which the remarriage of widows was common, the spiritual benefit rule broke down automatically.[34]

In the 1830s, a series of apparently isolated pieces of legislation tried to achieve equality in law. There were two major areas of judicial activism in this respect, equality between Indians and Europeans, and equality among castes. The regulations of 1793 made it necessary for all Crown subjects to seek the permission of the company to come to India. The company, in turn, forbade any European resident of its territories from buying or leasing land outside Calcutta without a license from the Board of Revenue. The former restriction ended in 1813 with the end of the company's charter, and the latter was removed with the Property in Land Act of 1837.

Until 1832, "loss of caste" through conversion and excommunication could entail loss of property for a Hindu. In 1832, Regulation VII passed in the presidency of Fort William announced the principle that religion could not be a ground for dispossession of property or civil rights. The Caste Disabilities Removal Act of 1850 generalized the principle to all company territories. The 1832 regulation expressly stated that the provision should not be construed to mean an introduction of European law of property. If Hindu law had no obligatory force on a person who underwent a religious conversion, what law of property was such a person subject to? In order to plug loopholes of this nature, the Indian Succession Act, applicable to all property matters other than those of Hindus and Muslims, was introduced in 1865.

A different type of departure from religion took shape in newly acquired territories. One of these was Punjab (annexed 1849), where Hindus and Muslims shared space alongside Sikhs. Instead of adopting a religious foundation for law, the Punjab administrators framed a Punjab Civil Code, which combined religious law with a number of principles and practices that can be read as local or customary. This principle became the policy with the Punjab Laws Act (1872). "From this time custom became the first rule of decision in all the Punjab Courts upon questions relating to [property]" (see chapter 4).[35] When upper Burma came into British possession (1885), with its large Buddhist population, a similar problem arose and a similar solution was endorsed. Other areas where custom was legally privileged were Central Province and the North-West Frontier Province. The privileging of custom had the backing of an authority. Henry Maine, the law adviser to the government, believed that law, especially law of property, evolved from customary and communitarian relationships in a village. Maine went further and advocated that future legislation in India should in fact build on local practices and extend to all of India after a local norm was tried for some time in the shape of a provincial law.[36]

This still left the question of legislative reform in the older provinces open. What was one to do with joint inheritance?

Reformist Legislation II: The Indian Succession Act (1865) and the Transfer of Property Act (1882)

Between 1800 and 1860, nearly every higher court civil suit dealing with property and involving a Hindu would refer to Hindu law. In the earliest of these, reference to the expert on scriptures was also routine. By contrast, in the twenty years since the enactment of the Transfer of Property Act, of the eight-hundred-odd suits settled with reference to the act, only twenty mentioned Hindu law. New legislation in the late nineteenth century, therefore, allowed the judges and the disputants to bypass the sanctity of the joint family altogether. In effect, the element of private choice in successions was allowed freer play (see table 5.1 for a list of the major laws passed).

The Indian Succession Act (1865) was the first piece of substantive law designed by the Law Commission and dealt with the devolution of rights on intestacy in the case of all groups domiciled in India other than Hindus, Muslims, and Buddhists. In fact, the scope of the law proved to be quite variable. It was applicable to Europeans by birth or descent domiciled in

Table 5.1 Major enactments on property

Major Acts	Explanation
Property in Land Act, 1837	"Made it lawful for any subject of His Majesty to acquire and hold in perpetuity, or for any term of years, property in land, or in any emoluments issuing out of land in any part of British India"[a]
Caste Disabilities Removal Act, 1850	"Enacts that law or usage which inflicts forfeiture of, or affects rights on change of religion or loss of caste should cease to be enforced"[a]
Indian Succession Act, 1865	Jurisdiction, all Indian subjects other than Hindus, Muslims, and Buddhists; discussed and recommended by Third Law Commission; regulations passed in 1841 and 1842 made for protection of property from wrongful possession in course of succession
The Parsi Intestate Succession Act, 1865	Codified succession procedures of Parsis, partially based on community practices.
Hindu Wills Act, 1870	A previous enactment (Madras Regulation V of 1829) *denied* testamentary powers to Hindus
Probate and Administration Act, 1881	Discussed and recommended by Fourth Law Commission, 1879
Transfer of Property Act, 1882	Jurisdiction whole of British India except certain territories including Punjab and British Burma; by 1914, whole of India; discussed and recommended by Fourth Law Commission, 1879
Trusts Act, 1882	Applies to all trusts, except religious charities, including wakf; these were partly covered under the Religious Endowments Act 1863, and Charitable Endowments Act 1890
Indian Registration Act, 1886	Treated as a part of procedural legislation; see also chapter 9
The Mussalman Wakf Validating Act, 1913	Set out procedures for settlement of property as wakf.

[a] B. K. Acharya, *Codification in British India* (Calcutta: S. K. Banerji and Sons, 1914), 228.

British India, the "East Indians" or persons of mixed descent, the Jews, the Armenians, and the Parsis. Testamentary succession among the Parsis was governed by a different law. The Indian Christians were taken off the list in 1901, whereas the Brahmos and Sikhs were classified as Hindus for the purpose of succession. Later amendments of the act excluded other smaller groups from its scope. The excluded groups included large "tribes" of Assam and the Jews of Aden. The law was framed with reference to the English counterpart but also deviated from it on important points of detail. A point in common was that the widow had the same right to property as a widow in England. The Hindu counterpart of the Indian Succession Act was the Hindu Wills Act of 1870, which copied the text of the former. It is necessary to emphasize the fact that, except Muslims, none of the communities that were indigenous to India had a formal tradition of writing wills. For all of them, except the Muslims, testament was a British import.

A large number of succession cases concerned terms of will and the validation of will. Mixed, uncertain, or altered religious identity presented a frequent occasion for litigation. For example, the death of individuals who had converted from one religion to another could make a subsequent dispute among the successors over division of property boil down to the choice of the appropriate religious law. In the event of mixed marriages, the proceedings considered the validity of the marriage. A fascinating succession case that brought in a number of these points together involved the estate of Thomas Skinner, probably one of the sons of the famous mercenary commander James Skinner, himself born of mixed parents. Thomas's will attracted disputation not only because the mixed-marriage heritage in the family made the reference to law particularly confusing, but also because he had himself married a Muslim woman by rites that were deemed invalid in personal law (*Richard Ross Skinner v. Durga Prasad, Thomas William Skinner v. Richard Ross Skinner, Thomas William Skinner v. Durga Prasad*, Allahabad, 1904).

The Probate and Administration Act (1881) was an afterthought and a response to a peculiar gap left in the Hindu, Muslim, and Buddhist succession laws. These laws left no explicit provision for conferring the right to own or manage the property of a deceased person. The Hindu Wills Act dealt with testamentary succession, but it was in force only in the presidency towns and lower Bengal. Outside this area, letters of administration could not be issued according to any directly available law for individuals dying intestate. On the other hand, the very institution of the new law also made it possible to challenge an existing probate on the ground that the will was a forgery; in that case, the suit would be filed with reference to this law rather than the Succession Act. Most suits in fact did concern revocation of probates, and a number of these also had to decide the validity of interreligious marriages, for the challenge often came from an alleged successor who had been expelled from the immediate family on account of the religion of the mother. Whereas nearly all succession and probate suits were filed by members of family or designated administrators, "claiming to have an interest in the property left by the deceased," one offbeat case was brought in by a creditor on the ground that were there a will to get a probate, debts owed him by the deceased would be dishonored by the successor. The argument was accepted by the Calcutta High Court (*Kishen Dai v. Satyendra Nath Dutt*).

The Transfer of Property Act (1882) decided the validity of gift, sale, and exchange of property. It covered transfer of land, the sale, mortgage, and lease of immovable assets, exchange and gift of property and the assignment of contractual rights. It was the federal counterpart of a large class of provincial laws dealing with tenancy and sale of agricultural land (see chapter 9). Where a suit was not explicitly covered by these provincial laws, the Transfer of Property Act became the active point of reference. Nevertheless, the two spheres—federal and provincial—needlessly overlapped and were at times in contradiction.[37] Also, the act did not supersede religious or family law already in force. In fact it was often combined with the provisions of the latter. For example, sale of a share of a joint estate involved the right of preemption (the other cosharers had to be offered the sale first), which was a legacy of Muslim law. The chapter on mortgages recognized forms of security admissible in Hindu law.[38]

Since its ambit included redemption of an outstanding mortgage or resumption of a leased estate by the owner, the act was the one most used in suits concerning agricultural land and extrafamily transactions in business assets. A common point of dispute was conflict between the landlord's interest and the mortgagee's interest in a property. The mortgagee's interest was upheld usually on the point of whether or not the property was alienable. This was a serious point in jointly held estates where a loan had been taken without the agreement of all holders, or when the mortgagor extracted an agreement that the mortgagee could take possession but not sell the estate (*Faiyaz Husain Khan v. Nilkanth*, 1901). In another case of a business, the court deemed part repayment of a mortgage an undue favor to one creditor among several, since the business soon filed for bankruptcy (*Malukchand Amirchand v. Manilal Nansha*, Bombay).

The landlord's interest was defended on a variety of grounds. In one case over a mortgaged zamindari estate, transfer was refused by the Madras High Court "on grounds of public policy" (*Rama Sami Naik v. Rama Sami Chetty*, 1907). The act laid down conditions when collusive deals could be suspected. In one suit involving a business estate, the lower court judge decided that a sale of a property was invalid on the ground that "the mortgagees or their agents so conducted themselves with reference to the sale that would-be-bidders at it were induced to leave," suggesting a collusion between the buyer and the mortgagees (*Chabildas Laloobhai v. Dayal Mowji*, 1897). When interest on a loan was expressed not as a percentage but as a lump sum "bonus," the judged needed to decide "whether the mortgage was so unconscionable as to be unenforceable in its integrity" (*Hari v. Ramji*, Bombay).

A particular problem arose in respect of debts incurred by a father and inherited by a son. A strict application of joint inheritance would make any mortgage by an individual member difficult, at least exposed to challenge by inheritors. The Transfer of Property Act (along with the Code of Civil Procedures of 1859 and the Indian Registration Act of 1886) eased the situation, by clarifying the right to sale of land and defining categories of mortgage.[39] In a landmark case, the son's right to repudiate debts of the father and reject the validity of a sale of property in discharge of debt by the father was overturned by the Privy Council (*Girdharee Lall and others v. Kuntoo Lall and others*, 1876). This issue of the sons' right to challenge a transfer owing to a mortgage taken out by the father was again raised, and settled in favor of the creditor in an 1882 high court case (*Ambica Pershad Tewari and Others v. Ram Sahai Lal and Others*).

A major case concerning the Hindu Wills Act in Madras High Court in 1906 (*Subba Reddi v. Doraisami*; also referred to *Bhaba Tarini v. Peary*, 1897, Calcutta High Court) again revealed how religion complicated the interpretation of "equity." By then the Hindu Wills Act had made it possible for a daughter to unconditionally inherit her father's property. However, if a son was born after a will was prepared, and given that the son alone could perform the last rites, should the equitable right of the parent to these rituals require that the earlier will be automatically revoked? This was the construction placed on "equity" by one of the two judges in a bench. The decision, however, was rejected on appeal, which stated that on matters like these, the Hindu Wills Act needed to be compatible with the Indian Successions Act.

The last major development in property legislation took place in the area of Islamic law.

Islamic Law

Although in principle Muslim law in India had Arabic roots, in practice, as we have seen in chapter 2, it had already been modified and adapted even before the British arrived. British Indian courts further diluted it via the "infiltration of common law doctrines such as equity."[40] The bias for joint inheritance was present, in a weaker form, in Islamic law in India. Islamic law had a more explicit testamentary provision than Hindu law but circumscribed the freedom with restrictions on what proportion of the property could be gifted at will. Like Hindu law, Islamic law privileged agnate descendants, males among the descendants, and carried an institutional bias against division of family property.

Recent scholarship suggests that Islamic inheritance practices, which were more conducive to division of family estates than Hindu law, were often avoided by means of the wealth-preservation instrument *wakf*, and that the use of the instrument imparted a bias for informality and against expansion of scale upon Muslim businesses.[41] It is certainly plausible that a Hindu-Muslim contrast in business organization and a distinctive quality of Muslim business organization both derived from law, but the material we explore here is not rich enough to evaluate these conjectures. One legal historian suggests that Muslim inheritance law in India did not operate as an independent body of law at all, until the so-called Wakf Act of 1913 and the Shariat Act of 1937. From much before 1913, "custom had eaten into the body of the Islamic law," and so did English law, which had on balance "a healthy effect on Muhammadan law in India."[42] This expert defines Islamic law in twentieth-century India as possessing some unique features, but falling short of being "a discrete system." All of this points at the difficulty of distinguishing Islamic law as a separate domain. But, as we have seen, Muslim inheritance practices did create problems of a particular kind, at times pushing jurists even to define who was a Muslim in Indian society.

The Indian law of wakf was enacted in 1913, even though the instrument came down from precolonial law. The lateness of legislation owed to the fact that the distinct nature of the charitable trust under Muslim law was lost on the judges. The particular notion of charity implicated in a wakf was providing for descendants in perpetuity, and not the notion of charity at large, namely, providing for the poor. The two appeared to be conflated in a landmark judgment by the Privy Council in 1894 (*Abul Fata Mahomed Ishak v. Russomoy Dhur Chowdrey*) that disallowed the formation of a wakf. This negative judgment indirectly paved the way for legislation in the matter.[43] In addition to the definition of charity, in both trust and wakf, the right to exist in perpetuity and the issue of oversight over corrupt trustees or managers led to suits which took longer than the usual time to settle.[44] The 1913 act was partly a response to the encroachment of the trust law into what was a traditional Muslim institution, and partly a response to the disputes entailed in the management of any trust with poor oversight.

A similar move, the Shariat Act (1937), was created in response to the perception that "custom had eaten into the body of the Islamic law" especially in matters of women's property rights and inheritance. The act allowed the application of the sharia to inheritance, except in the presence of a will, and except in charities other than wakf.[45]

Conclusion

This chapter has shown that the British innovation in property law consisted in upholding joint ownership of property, supposedly sanctioned by religion. Among Hindus, the religious principle became known as "spiritual benefit." Joint ownership entailed joint inheritance. The head of a family had questionable authority to bequeath, mortgage, and partition estates. The spiritual-benefit argument to justify joint inheritance was by and large anti-women. Reference to religious codes wasted time because the codes disagreed on many rules. The legal system had made property rights secure but weakened the right of the individual.

The legislative response to the problem at first took shape in the courtroom, and later was formed of new laws. But these new laws did not actually nullify any existing arrangement. Personal law proved remarkably resilient among both Hindus and Muslims. In fact, attempts to reform personal law after 1947 invited political backlash. Personal law persisted even as escape routes from it were added. Legal reformers after independence (1947) could look back, with some justification, at the mid-nineteenth century as "a chaotic state" without a proper framework of law and a "fragmentary" property law at best.[46] This chapter has shown why the chaos arose, and the legislative reforms that it led to.

In the late nineteenth century, a major focus of legislation was modern industry and trade. New laws targeted enforcement of contract. In this field, the bias for preserving social order gave way to a bias for securing market exchange. The drive, however, took very different forms in the three main fields that it changed—labor, sale of goods, and the business firm. The next three chapters tell the stories in this order.

SIX

Labor Law: From "Slavery" to Trade Union

Introduction

Two authoritative sources, the reports of the Royal Commission on Labour (1931) and the Royal Commission on Agriculture (1928), provide snapshots of the conditions of workers in late colonial India.[1] They show huge variation in the (apparent) status of different types of workers. The Royal Commission on Labour, on one hand, describes a number of protections for industrial workers, in factory acts and other legislation. These protections drew heavily on British precedents: limits on hours of work, regulation of employment of women and children, workmen's compensation (for injuries), and the like. Perhaps most significantly, the commission discusses the boost to union activity provided by Indian Trade Unions Act of 1926, and notes that the "importance of developing healthy trade unions is denied by practically none."[2] On the other hand, the same report notes the disempowerment of the plantation worker, especially in the tea districts of Assam. Penal contracting under British-Indian law (whereby a worker could be jailed for breach of contract) had been largely abolished only as late as in 1926.[3] Many plantation workers still did not know this; some were still beaten, and some were housed in jail-like conditions. The Royal Commission on Agriculture revealed worse. It reported on *kamiauti*, a system of debt bondage in rural parts of Bihar and Orissa, noting that this was often a "life sentence," and equivalent to slavery. The borrower could even be sold for the amount of debt. Legislation to protect the *kamia* (bonded laborer) had been ineffectual.[4]

Thus, we see the Raj in three very different roles: ineffectually protecting rural workers, undermining worker freedom via the legal recognition of penal contracting, and proactively promoting worker welfare in the factory sector. This chapter asks why legislation on the worker was so fragmented.

The short answer is that labor laws emerged at different times and locations in response to particular problems and issues. Protecting rural workers was simply beyond the practical capacity of the colonial state and may have also run counter to its predilection for favoring the landed classes (see chapter 4). Factory legislation was subject to many influences, including liberal critics in India and Britain, British industrial interests, workers' and nationalist movements, and pressure from the International Labour Organization (ILO). One of the key puzzles is the survival of penal contracting right up to 1926, long after "welfarist" approaches had come to the fore elsewhere and in India. We explain this anomaly by interpreting penal contracting as a (cruel) solution to a contractual problem: it was a means for an employer to recoup up-front expenses incurred in hiring workers from a distance. This is why the law, favored by well-organized employers in industries like tea, survived in the face of intense criticism.

Colonial Law and "Indigenous" Unfree Labor

It is difficult to define and distinguish different types of "unfreedom," in India and elsewhere, either in theory or in practice. We will primarily use two terms: "slave" and "bonded laborer" (or, equivalently, "debt bondage"). We use the former term as meaning the person in question was the salable personal property of his or her owner, without legal means of escape from this status. Debt bondage, in contrast, is a status terminable (in principle) upon repayment of a specified sum of money.

The classic economic analysis of labor servitude focuses on the labor/land ratio.[5] When this is low, wealth resides in the control of labor. Unfree labor is a likely outcome, though this does not follow automatically. The state plays a critical role by enacting supportive legislation. For instance in England, given labor scarcity following the Black Death, compulsory work laws, violation of which could lead to imprisonment, were passed under the Statute of Laborers.[6] In India, the land frontier was not reached until well into the colonial period. Since labor was the scarce factor, we expect to see servitude, and indeed there is ample evidence of this in both precolonial and colonial periods.[7] The desire to control labor was enhanced by caste norms. In some regions high-caste status was, in part, demonstrated by nonparticipation in agricultural work, so it was all the more important to control labor to work the land.

But unfree labor can emerge even when the labor/land ratio is high. A large initial borrowing can lead to a debt trap. The worker and his or her descendants cannot repay the money, and they owe labor services in compensation, an obligation which can extend across generations. Such an arrangement can also have a "patron-client" dimension, providing insurance to both parties.[8] On the one hand the lender-patron is assured that labor will be available when really needed, for instance, during the harvesting season. On the other hand, for the borrower-client, the arrangement guarantees subsistence at times when the demand for labor is low. Bonded labor of this kind remained widespread even after population density increased in colonial India and is present even now.[9]

During the transition to colonialism (the second half of the eighteenth century), the East India Company's approach to labor contracting was driven by the compelling need to obtain labor services, by whatever means. One historian of Madras reports that workers were needed for domestic chores, for transportation services, and for the army.[10] The company drew on indigenous labor mores as well as created newer coercive institutions when necessary. Workers were subject to corporal punishment, and domestic workers were often slaves. The company also extensively drew on existing practices of forced labor known as *vetti* or *Al-Amanji*, especially in times of military conflict.[11] One important feature of labor recruiting, which continues to the present day, was the use of an intermediary, a "headman" whose caste and community connections helped in both locating and managing the workers.

The most discussed labor policy problem in the early nineteenth century was, of course, slavery. Slavery seems to have especially emerged in times of war or famine. The company's attitude to slavery was cautious and varied across time and space. There were numerous factors at play.[12] These included the intention to uphold Hindu and Muslim law, which led to the conclusion that slavery was permitted; early court decisions that translated this into legal practice; the concern that tax collection might be undermined if landowners' rights to slaves' labor were eliminated; some commentary that slaves were not necessarily worse off than other workers; and the various moral sentiments and reactions of different officials. The company even owned slaves in Malabar.[13] It is safe to say that the company in India was not, in itself, either eager or proactive in seeking to eliminate slavery.

But there was a powerful external pressure at work. This was the movement against slavery in Britain, where legislation was passed in 1807 to prohibit the slave trade, and participation in the slave trade was declared a felony in 1811. The abolition of slavery was discussed when the East India Company's charter was renewed in 1833. The Slavery Abolition Act was passed in 1843. This was a limited measure in that the slaveholder could not now approach the state to uphold his ownership right. Owning a slave became punishable in law only later, after the Penal Code was passed in

1860. Despite the legal changes, slaveholders had many means to retain control, including the threat of eviction of slaves from their homes.[14] The attitudes of Indian employees of the company were also not conducive to the abolition of slavery, in part, because many were themselves slaveholders. Ironically, the slaves may have gained by escaping to coffee plantations in South India.[15] As we will see below, plantations became notorious for treating workers harshly.

It is difficult to comment on the impact of slavery abolition, in part because a slave's status could be redefined as that of a bonded laborer.[16] Official documents make few references to slavery from the later nineteenth century onward. For instance, in 1879 in the Madras Presidency, where the incidence of slavery had been the greatest, there was only one offense reported under the categories of "buying or selling of slaves" and none under "habitual dealing in slaves."[17] There was, however, clear evidence regarding debt bondage. For instance, government statistics in the late nineteenth century reported that 56% of agricultural laborers and 11% of the total rural population of Gaya, in South Bihar, were bonded laborers.[18] There was little legislation to regulate the bonded labor relationship. It was only in 1920, by which point welfarist attitudes to workers had come to the fore (see below), that the Bihar and Orissa Kamiauti Agreements Act was passed. The act declared that period of the contract of the kamia could not extend beyond a year. In 1932 the government of Madras passed an order to terminate bonded labor under the name *vetti*.[19] However, because workers were driven into these contracts by economic desperation, and these contracts served the lender-employer's interests, it was, and remains to this day, difficult for the state to enforce such regulations. The Royal Commission on Agriculture noted that the Bihar and Orissa Kamiauti Agreements Act had been "ineffective."[20]

As the brevity of this section suggests, the colonial state intervened to a very limited extent in rural labor relations. Chapters 2, 3, and 4 have demonstrated that its preoccupation was with land, in relation to which it legislated extensively. However, in the mid-nineteenth century a new form of organization, the plantation, which often recruited workers from a distance, emerged. This required new legislation, the subject of the next section.

Penal Legislation

Recent research has shown that imprisonment of workers for breach of contract, far from being a deviation from the norm, was quite common in England until late in the nineteenth century. The long history of the relevant legislation has been traced from the Statute of Laborers, following the

Black Death, to the Master and Servant Act of 1823.[21] Under the Master and Servant Act a worker in breach of contract could be imprisoned for three months of hard labor.[22] The act was repealed only in 1875, in response to political pressure from the labor movement. Given this background, we would expect British-Indian law to contain similar legislation. It did. The Employers and Workmen (Disputes) Act of 1860 was passed after a violent dispute between European railway contractors and their workers in Bombay. The act allowed magistrates to summarily decide cases, and also allowed for imprisonment of the workers for up to two months.[23] It is interesting to note, though, that the Employers and Workmen (Disputes) Act was limited to railways, canals, and other public works. "It was only extended to certain districts and was seldom used" before its repeal in 1932.[24] The act that *was* widely used in India was the Workman's Breach of Contract Act (1859, hereafter WBOC). It was similar to the Master and Servant Act in allowing three months of imprisonment, but it was different in one important respect. It applied only when the worker had received an advance. The WBOC was extended to a wide range of locations in colonial India and was extensively used in the plantations. It was repealed only in 1926.[25]

Why did penal contracting in India last fifty years longer than in England? The obvious answer is that British-Indian capital was well organized, whereas Indian labor was not; hence legislation that favored capital survived. But if British-Indian capital was so powerful, why did it settle for the WBOC, when an act with a broader scope (the Employers and Workmen [Disputes] Act), with precedent in English law (the Master and Servant Act) was available? More generally, why didn't employers obtain broad powers to have workers imprisoned for breach of contract *even absent an advance*? We conjecture as follows. By the late nineteenth century, labor law and practices in India were under scrutiny by British critics as well as Indian nationalists, a countervailing force to British-Indian capital. The Raj was not eager to expose itself to criticism. However, it succumbed to the pressure to retain the WBOC because it solved a specific contractual problem.

A transaction that begins with an advance to a worker has a built-in risk for the employer. If the worker does not fulfill the terms of the contract, the employer will lose his or her up-front payment. Unless there is a mechanism to prevent this, the transaction may not occur at all.[26] The WBOC was such a mechanism. Could this be why it was retained for so long? One way of evaluating this conjecture is to see when the WBOC was used. If our explanation is correct, industries in which workers were given significant advances would lobby for its introduction. If there was no need for an advance, or the advance was small, employers would not lobby for a harsh penal contract that might discourage workers from seeking employment with them. And if the advance was very large, it is conceivable that the employer would want an even stronger protection than that offered by the WBOC. Ideally we want an "experiment," in which other factors are held constant, and the need for an advance is varied.

Historians usually do not expect to find perfect experiments. However, in this instance a reasonable approximation can be found in the history of cultivation of tea in northeastern India. There were three main regions in which tea was grown, with different recruitment costs. Tea gardens in all regions were largely owned by European companies managed by the same small group of managing agencies. Also, planters had formed local associations in all regions. So, political factors were roughly similar. Arranged in ascending order of recruiting costs (hence higher up-front expenditures by employers), the regions were: the Dooars in North Bengal, the Surma Valley in Lower Assam, and the Brahmaputra Valley in Upper Assam (see map 6.1). We find that the Dooars never used the WBOC or indeed any penal contracting. The Surma Valley favored the WBOC. The Brahmaputra Valley used a form of penal contract significantly harsher than the WBOC—these were permitted by "Special Acts" passed for Assam. Thus, the cross-region variation in the use of the WBOC is consistent with our explanation of the purpose it served. We flesh out this argument in the remainder of this section.[27]

In the early nineteenth century the company was keen to find alternative sources of tea, to reduce its dependence on China. Tea was "discovered" in Assam, and systematic efforts to introduce and expand cultivation began with the Assam Tea Company, which began its operation in 1839. After some initial experimentation with varieties and even hiring of Chinese workers who were expected to have the requisite skills, the tea industry, funded by British capital, began to expand rapidly in the second half of the nineteenth century. The state greatly aided this effort by providing land leases at low rates. But the forests had to be cleared, and plantations set up, tasks that were labor intensive. Assam was relatively sparsely populated, and the local peasant population did not find plantation work attractive. The plantations needed to hire workers from other parts of India where labor was more abundant.

Even though migration to Assam was "internal," in the sense of not crossing international borders, the costs and distances could be substantial. There was the cost of travel itself—depending on the time period, some combination of railroad, boat, or steamer was required. Also, potential migrants had to be found. The Assam planters could rely on professional recruiters ("contractors"), or they could send their own workers "home" to find potential

Map 6.1. Tea-growing regions in the northeast. Adapted from India, *Report of the Royal Commission on Labour in India* (London: HMSO, 1931).

migrants. In either case the costs could be large, more than a year's wages.[28] Planters complained that a worker whom they had paid to recruit might, on his or her way to the plantation (a long journey), or after arrival, be "enticed" by another employer.[29] The would-be employer would then have lost his initial investment. To prevent this, they argued, legislation was required to tie the worker to his or her initial employer for a period of time and make "desertion" a crime for which the worker could be jailed. The WBOC had both these features. It was first passed in 1859 at the request of the Calcutta Trades Association and was meant to apply only to the presidency towns, but it was "almost at once" extended to the tea districts in Assam.[30]

We have argued that if the recruitments costs were very high, employers might want legislation that gave them more power than the WBOC. This is what happened in Assam. In 1865, Bengal Act VI was passed, and its statement of objects clearly articulates the planters' argument that the WBOC was not adequate: "The planter declares that he imports laborers into the province at a very great expense and that as soon as they arrive they refuse to work or leave service; that the punishment for desertion [WBOC] is slight and carries with it release from all engagements and that therefore the laborer willingly incurs the liability to punishment in the hope of being set free from the contract."[31] In response to this complaint, Bengal Act VI, one in a series of Special Acts applicable only in Assam, included the provision that the employer could privately arrest the worker and only subsequently approach a magistrate. In part this was also justified on the grounds that, in this sparsely populated area, magistrates were not close at hand.[32] This extraordinary privilege for the Assam tea planter was withdrawn only in 1908.

The Assam plantations became notorious for their harsh treatment of workers. The nationalist newspaper the *Bengalee* published a series of articles in 1886 describing the conditions of workers as a "qualified form of slavery," with planters "kicking and cuffing" workers and locking deserters in "dungeons."[33] A missionary, Charles Dowding, published articles in a similar vein in a publication called *The Churchman*.[34] Planters' own memoirs report violence. One noted in his diary in 1903: "Sent for Behari [a plantation worker] and gave him a bottle of rum. It is the best way to deal with a coolie: half kill him when he plays the fool and then show him how kind you can be if you like."[35] Other planters' memoirs contain similar descriptions.[36]

But all this criticism was not sufficient to eliminate the right to private arrest, which was retained through several revisions of the Special Act, including a major overhaul in 1882. By 1900 some officials like Sir Henry Cotton argued that penal contracting was counterproductive: it was discouraging migration to Assam, in which the rapidly growing tea industry was facing labor shortages.[37] Percival Griffiths, who was closely associated with the tea industry, is somewhat dismissive, arguing that Cotton's "heart was always apt to overrule his head."[38] The administration had the same reaction, and the right of private arrest was included yet again in another substantial revision of the Special Act in 1901. Still, the controversy continued. After the report of a committee to investigate labor conditions, the Assam government administration commented on the "unpopularity of service in Assam, which obliged the tea industry to obtain its labor at high cost to the detriment of wages and dividends." It attributed this unpopularity "most of all to the penal contract and the right of private arrest by the employer."[39] The Assam

Labour Enquiry Committee (1906) was appointed to look into the working of the Special Act, with the right of private arrest without warrant being of particular interest.

If the primary purpose of the Special Act, especially the unpopular right to private arrest without warrant, was to protect the up-front investment in recruiting, we might expect that the regions where recruiting costs were low would be more willing to abandon the Special Act. This is exactly what we find. The Surma Valley planters had initially used the Special Act. But improvements in transportation had eased problems of labor supply. The climate and disease environment of the Surma Valley was also more suitable for workers from closer by. So the Surma Valley had transitioned away from the Special Act and used the WBOC instead. The planters of the Brahmaputra Valley, farther away from the regions from which they recruited their preferred workers, faced higher recruitment costs and relied more on the Special Acts.[40] The 1905 gazetteer of Sylhet, a district in the Surma Valley, explains the thinking of Surma Valley planters and contrasts their situation with that of Brahmaputra Valley planters. It is worth quoting at some length.

> The climate of Sylhet is not unsuited to the natives of the United Provinces and planters are thus enabled to work their gardens with labourers who in Assam [Brahmaputra Valley] would quickly sicken and die. The coolies who are most difficult to procure, and who cannot, as a rule, be imported for less than a hundred rupees a head, are Sonthals and other jungly tribes from the Chota Nagpur plateau. Of them there are comparatively few and one of the most important assets in the planter's favour in Sylhet is the fact that he can obtain his own labour at fairly moderate rates. The gross cost of importation is, however, large and few people would be willing to spend considerable sums of money in bringing coolies to the district, without some guarantee that, for a time at any rate, they would be able to retain their services. This guarantee is offered by Act XIII of 1859 [WBOC].[41]

Consistent with this analysis, planters in Brahmaputra Valley who relied heavily on workers from Chota Nagpur and Santal Parganas were not satisfied with the WBOC, arguing that "the power of private arrest was not commonly abused, and was necessary to guarantee the importing employer against loss by desertion of new coolies, and to protect him from entice-ment."[42] A compromise solution was arrived at in 1908. The right to private arrest was eliminated in all of Assam, but penal contracting under the Special Acts was only eliminated in the Surma Valley and the two districts in Brahmaputra Valley that were close to their recruiting regions. In 1915 the penal provisions of the Special Act were removed in Brahmaputra Valley as well, and planters resorted to the WBOC. Proposals for repeal by Indian nationalists led to dilution of the WBOC in 1920.[43] After protests and riots by tea garden workers in 1920–22, it was again proposed that the WBOC be repealed. Unsurprisingly, the Assam planters opposed this.[44] The central government also had its own reasons for wanting the WBOC in place. Large public works could require workers brought from a distance, and the up-front investment had to be protected.[45] Still, the WBOC was repealed in 1926.

This story, in which the Surma Valley, which was closer to its recruiting regions, favored the WBOC, whereas the Brahmaputra Valley, farther away from its recruiting regions, wanted an even harsher contract, is consistent with our interpretation of the WBOC as a solution to a contractual problem. So is the history of tea cultivation in the Dooars region in North Bengal. Like the Brahmaputra Valley, the Dooars recruited heavily from Chota Nagpur and Santal Parganas, but these regions were much closer by. And there was a train line straight to Jalpaiguri, close to the tea gardens in Dooars. We have computed, using figures provided by the Duars Committee of 1910, that the gross outlay per recruited adult worker was only twenty rupees; and the net figure (accounting for repayment of advance by the worker) was only eight rupees.[46] By way of comparison, the reader will recall the recruiting cost figure of one hundred rupees to "import" a worker from Chhota Nagpur and Santal Parganas into Assam. The Dooars planters never used any kind of penal contracting, and the planters interviewed by the Duars Committee (1910) were sure that their "free labor" system was a better alternative. G. W. Stoddart, manager of New Glencoe Tea Estate in the Dooars, who had also been a manager in Cachar (Surma Valley, Assam) told the committee: "I think the Duars system preferable to the system of working coolies through the penal contract which was in force in Cachar, both for the employer and the coolie."[47] Other managers had similar comments.[48] The Duars Committee concluded: "We are emphatically of the opinion that any legislation providing for penal labour contracts, or the regulation of recruitment is most undesirable and would likely prove fatal to the interests of the tea industry in the Duars, of the labour it employs, and of the district."[49] Thus, the region with low recruitment costs did not favor the WBOC, or any other penal contract.

Finally, comments by various planters, and by the Duars Committee itself, suggest that one of the reasons they were opposed to introducing Assam's Special Acts was that the acts incorporated measures for the protection of workers. Dislike of these regulations also could have played a role in the

Surma Valley planters' preference for the WBOC. Provisions in the Special Acts tried to ensure that would-be emigrants understood where they would be going, and what a Special Act contract entailed.[50] Labor contractors had to be licensed and could be punished for fraud. The 1882 version of the act even required that the plantation guarantee workers a maximum price for food grains.[51] Working conditions on the plantations were liable to be inspected, even if irregularly. For the Brahmaputra Valley planters, with high recruitment costs, these regulations, though irksome, were a price they were willing to pay to get the extraordinary powers to prevent "enticement."[52]

Before concluding this section we should recognize the distinction between the de jure and de facto status of workers. Legal changes did not easily change facts on the ground. Plantation workers were often from very impoverished backgrounds, from diverse locations, and unable to organize effectively. Planters were better organized. Though penal contracting was eventually abolished, planters agreed on "labor rules" preventing entice-ment. According to the Brahmaputra and Surma Valley Local Recruiting Agreement of 1939, a plantation which "enticed" a worker who had been assisted in migration by another had to pay the latter one hundred rupees for the first year, seventy-five for the second, and fifty for the third. Also, in the Brahmaputra Valley managers controlled access to workers' residential areas, preventing the entry of people they considered undesirable.[53] Thus, the workers' mobility could be restricted in practice, even without the help of the law.

We have argued in this section that the WBOC and even harsher pe-nal legislation survived in the face of nationalist and missionary criticism and workers' protests for a substantial period of time because they solved a contractual problem. The political power of British-Indian capital was no doubt influential in passing and retaining these laws. Political factors are even more prominent in the next section of this chapter.

Factory Legislation

In the second half of the nineteenth century, two major modern factory-based industries emerged in India, producing cotton and jute textiles. What wages and working conditions would they need to offer to motivate work-ers to move from nearby rural areas to the city? A typical analysis of migra-tion (say, the famous Lewis model) would take the wage or living condi-tions in rural India as the benchmark, or "reservation wage." The urban industrial employer would then need to pay a bit more (W. Arthur Lewis's guess was 30%) to persuade the worker to migrate.[54] However, it appears that a "dual labor market," with wages substantially higher in the factory sector than in nearby rural areas, began to emerge in the colonial period. Susan Wolcott finds that the ratio of the Bombay cotton mills' wage to the nearby agricultural wage is always above 2 from 1920 until 1938.[55] A similar ratio for jute varies between roughly 2.5 and slightly more than 1, but is usually above 1.5.[56] These figures cannot be easily interpreted as differentials in living standards because rural and urban areas varied in terms of other "disamenities"—poor housing, disease, and caste oppression—but it is not obvious that the urban areas come off worse in these nonwage comparisons. And it is striking to note that in cotton textiles, real wages in both Bombay and Ahmedabad more than doubled from 1900–1904 to 1940–44 at a time when agricultural wages were flat.[57] Real wages in jute, on the other hand, show a much smaller increase of about 16% in the same period. Thus, it appears that a dual labor market was emerging, at least in some locations. What was the role of legislation?

The modern factory was a British import to India (the machinery and technical knowledge and supervisory staff were imported from Britain).[58] It was inevitable that a range of issues that had arisen in the British context— child labor, women's work, safety, and working hours—would need to be addressed in India as well.[59] Missionaries, humanitarians, and nationalists pushed for better treatment of workers. Perhaps the most prominent supporter of factory legislation was Mary Carpenter, a Bristol-born social Christian social worker, who first visited India in 1866. She supported and influenced Sasipada Banerjee, who is considered the first Bengali *bhadralok* ("respectable" middle-class) advocate of factory legislation.[60] But, compared to plantation-related legislation, there was an additional factor at play now. Both jute and cotton had rivals in Britain: Indian jute was eating into the market share of Dundee, whereas Indian cotton's competition was the more formidable Lancashire. Both Dundee and Lancashire were threatened by lower labor costs in Indian industry and favored worker protections that would raise these costs. For the same reason, the India-based industrialists, Indian and British, opposed such legislation.

The legislative process appears to have begun with a question posed in the House of Commons in 1875. The secretary of state was asked whether he was aware that women and children were being worked sixteen hours a day in factories in India, and whether "the Indian government will adopt some such Factory Legislation as we have in this country for the prevention of such evils, before they attain greater proportions."[61] In response to this question, which raised humanitarian concerns, the secretary of state asked the government of Bombay to investigate the matter, following which a commission of enquiry was set up. However, the interests of British industry were part of the discussion from the very beginning. The Earl of Shaftesbury, though a social reformer and philanthropist in the British context, argued in an address before the House of Commons in 1875: "There is also a commercial view of this question. We must bear in mind that India has the raw material and the cheap labor and if we allow the manufacturers there to work their operatives 16 or 17 hours and put them under no restrictions, we are giving them a very unfair advantage against the manufacturers of our own country, and we might be undersold, even in Manchester itself, by manufactured goods imported from the East."[62] The Bombay Commission voted against passing legislation, but the lobbying continued. A Bombay-based Parsi businessman and philanthropist, Sorabjee Shapoorjee Bengallee, drafted a factory bill in 1878 and sent one hundred copies to an influential friend, John Croft, in Manchester. The issue was then taken up by the *London Times*.[63] Mill owners in Bombay and elsewhere strongly opposed legislation. A modest Factory Act was eventually passed in 1881, focusing on working hours for women and children and some safety provisions to prevent work injury. But the provisions were steadily strengthened in factory acts and amendments in 1891, 1911, 1922, 1923, 1923, 1926, 1931, and 1934, which reduced hours for women and children, placed limits on the working hours for men, and provided for breaks during work, and holidays.

The trend toward increasing worker protection was reinforced by the Washington Convention of the ILO in 1919, which established international standards. Because India was one of the larger industrial producers in the world, the government of India was under some pressure to meet these standards. A Workmen's Compensation Act was introduced in 1923. The Royal Commission on Labour in India (1931), whose perspective has been described as "reformist,"[64] produced a thorough and massively documented report recommending further modifications to legislation and also better means for implementation. Its recommendations influenced the last of the colonial-era factory acts, that of 1934. The royal commission's tone and commentary are worth discussing, for the "model" of economic development that was implicit. The commission did not take the rural wage as a benchmark for the factory wage. On the contrary, for the commission, industry would grow only if workers were treated well: "But, in the experience of India, there is abundant evidence to show that a generous policy in respect of labour is a wise policy in respect of industry. . . . In the views submitted to us, the suggestion that cheap labour is a national asset was seldom made. On the contrary, there is widespread recognition of the fact that industrial activity finds its strength and much of its justification in the

Table 6.1 Number of inspections of registered factories, 1939

Province	Factories	Number of Times Inspected (%)				
		Never	Once	Twice	Thrice	More Than Three Times
Bombay	3,120	12	34	29	12	13
Madras	1,811	3	24	40	26	7
Bengal	1,725	19	52	14	8	7

Source: India, *Report of the Labour Investigation Committee* (Delhi: Government Press, 1946), 43.

Table 6.2 Cases filed under Factories Act and number of convictions, 1939

Province	Factories	Number of Workers	Cases	Convictions	Fine per Conviction (Rupees)
Bombay	3,120	466,040	322	311	29.3
Madras	1,811	197,266	—	542	14
Bengal	1,725	571,539	102	95	—

Source: India, *Report of the Labour Investigation Committee*, 45.

prosperity of all who contribute to it."[65] This is what we might call an efficiency wage model—well-paid workers are more productive and therefore, in effective terms, cheaper.[66]

We might be tempted to believe that the legislation that emerged from this thinking helped create a special category of well-protected industrial workers. But that might be true if it had been enforced. The government of India's (1946) report on labor conditions showed that while many of the larger factories were obeying the provisions of the Factory Act, overall, enforcement was weak.[67] The report provided data on the number of inspections, cases filed, and prosecutions of employers. These are summarized in tables 6.1 and 6.2. As we can see in 1939, 19% of factories in Bengal were never inspected and half were inspected only once. Also, the fines were fairly small, so it was profitable to break the law and absorb the fine as a cost of doing business.[68]

A different criticism of the impact of factory legislation focuses on the type of information collected by the government of Bengal, arguing that it shared the employers' interest in an adequate supply of labor, rather than the welfare of workers.[69] So, with respect to health, it was primarily concerned with epidemics, not with chronic nutritional deficiencies. Dipesh Chakrabarty describes the findings of an investigation into the health of women mill workers in 1931–32, ordered by the Royal Commission on

Labour in India. The investigating doctor found that women and children were suffering diseases such as rickets and venereal disease which the mill doctors who accompanied them were unaware of. On the whole, it seems factory legislation provided the workers modest benefits.

A different explanation for the relatively high status of the factory workers, compared to their rural counterparts, is their bargaining strength, in particular the ability to strike. Between 1921 and 1938, the cotton and woolen textile industry in India lost 10.5 days per worker per year due to strikes.[70] The corresponding figure for jute mill workers was 3.5. In contrast, in the same period the textile industry in the UK lost 1.75 days per worker per year. Worker militancy in Bombay seems to have begun even earlier. While the royal commission claimed that strikes were "rare" before 1918–19, Morris David Morris notes that they had occurred at least since 1874 and quotes an official report to the effect that by the early 1890s strikes were a "frequent occurrence in every one of the mills in this city."[71] In 1919 a general strike broke out in Bombay cotton mills, and there were seven other general strikes up to 1940.[72] It seems plausible that the high wage gains of Bombay workers were a consequence of their bargaining power. What was the role of legislation? Did it facilitate or undermine the bargaining power of labor?

The evidence on this is ambiguous. In 1926 the Indian Trade Unions Act was passed. The act allowed seven workers to form a registered union and provided protections to them from criminal and civil prosecution. In particular, a civil suit could not be brought, in the context of a trade dispute, "on the ground only that such act induces some other person to break a contract of employment, or that it is interference with the trade, business or employment of some other person or with the right of some other person to dispose of his capital or of his labour as he wills."[73] On the one hand, legalization of trade union activity could have facilitated labor organization. On the other hand, Indian workers appear to have often had a loose relationship with their unions—they might be active during a strike but drift away subsequently. They paid dues irregularly.[74] The Indian Trade Unions Act appears to have been a response to worker militancy, part of a broader effort to create a more predictable and reliable labor force.[75] The Royal Commission on Labour spelled out this perspective: "Some form of organization is inevitable, since the need is acute and is bound to evoke a response. If that response does not take the form of a properly organized trade union movement, it may assume a more dangerous form. Some employers have already suffered from the lack of responsible trade unions."[76] Legislation was also passed to limit workers' militancy. The Trade Disputes Act (1929) made "lightning" strikes illegal in public utilities. Thus, the Raj's legislative efforts were aimed at regulating the labor force and making its behavior more predictable, rather than strengthening its bargaining power.

The impetus toward legislation to curb the militancy of workers also came from two other sources. The first had to do with the "jobber," the ubiquitous intermediary in Indian labor recruiting from mine to plantation to factory.[77] The jobber played several roles in the factory. His (or her, in some cases) caste or community connections facilitated recruiting. He might provide workers credit, and command respect as a local *dada* (tough). He could bring workers' concerns to management's attention, and help maintain workers' discipline. But the jobber might also exploit his position to ill-treat workers, extract payments from them, or even physically abuse or sexually harass them. He or she also had no reason to hire the best worker, and could simply go with the one most beholden to him or her. The jobber might gain from a larger-than-necessary labor force, or one with high rates of turnover, because he or she earned commissions from new recruits. The government of Bombay reported to the Royal Commission on Labour in India that the jobber system led to "intensive 'graft.'"[78] The situation was similar in other regions.[79] Given these tensions between jobber and worker, and the increasing availability of workers at the factory gate itself, it is not surprising that employers began to question the jobbers' utility. The increasing incidence of strikes in Bombay led employers to conclude, by the 1930s, that jobbers could no longer be relied on to maintain labor discipline.[80] This motivated them to find other means of labor control, including, presumably, new legislation.

The growing strength of the communist movement, especially in the form of the Girni Kamgar Union in Bombay, was also a concern to mill owners, and to the Congress, because it needed workers' political and electoral support. In its turn the Raj was worried about the rise of "Bolshevism." The government of Bombay pushed the government of India to crack down on communist leaders for their alleged responsibility for violence during the strike of 1928, though the evidence against them was weak. Eventually, in 1929, thirty-six communists were charged with conspiracy to overthrow the king, which led to the famous Meerut Conspiracy Trial. After legislation was passed in Bombay in 1934, a worker could take a concern to a labour officer instead of the union, thereby reducing its relevance. The Government of India Act of 1935 allowed for "provincial autonomy," and elected Indian governments came to power in provinces. As the Congress gained power in Bombay it was, if anything, more willing to crack down on labor militancy than was the Raj. In 1938 the Congress ministry in Bombay passed legislation requiring that a union have at least a quarter of the workers as members to be considered representative and to engage in mandatory conciliation and negotiation procedures before it could legally declare a strike.[81] The motivation for this legislation partly came from competition between the ATLA (Ahmedabad Textile Labour Association), a union with close ties with the Congress, and a communist union, the Mill Mazdoor Sangh. The goal was to use legislation to suppress the communists.[82]

The spirit of the 1938 Bombay legislation was also reflected by the Congress Working Committee in 1946 when it wrote that "avoidable strikes cannot have the backing of public opinion, and in view of the dire need of the country for more goods and services, hasty or ill-conceived stoppages . . . constitute a distinct disservice to the community."[83] We can now summarize our response to the question with which we began this section: To what extent can the creation of a dual labor market be traced back to the colonial era legislation? On the one hand, as we have seen above, none of the participants in debates on legislation pertaining to labor conditions took the rural and informal sectors as their benchmark. In that sense, discursively at least, factory workers were treated as a distinctive segment of the labor force from very early on. On the other hand, enforcement of protective legislation was weak, and its substantive significance is open to question. Worker militancy may have led to higher wages, but legislation on capital-labor disputes was a consequence, not a cause, of this militancy. And, as we have seen, some legislation was aimed at reducing the incidence of strikes.[84] The dual labor market emerged in the colonial period, but legislation probably made only a modest contribution to this process.

Recent research shows that factory legislation affected men and women differently.[85] Legislation intended to "protect" women could hurt them as well: by making them more costly to employers and hence less worth hiring, by giving employers excuses for retrenchment when they wanted to eliminate workers for other reasons, by simply banning them from some kinds of work (e.g., underground mining), by creating structures (e.g., trade unions) that might be dominated by men, and by reinforcing patriarchal norms pertaining to women's behavior.

There is no evidence that early factory legislation reduced the employment of women. Indeed, between 1892 and 1928 the number of women employed in factories increased 480%, compared to 378% for men.[86] The decline in women's participation seems to have begun after 1931. While the percentage of women in the labor force in Bombay Cotton Mills was 22% in 1931, it fell to 15% by 1939 and 11% by 1947.[87] Morris David Morris partly attributes this to the fact that night-shift work was extensively used after 1931, and women were prohibited from working at night.[88] The proportion of women employed in Calcutta's jute mills began to fall at roughly the same time as in Bombay, 1932.[89] The percentage of women in the labor force fell from 15.8% at that date to 12.8% by 1940 but stayed fairly steady after that and was 13% in 1947.[90] Samita Sen argues that in the 1930s, when the jute industry was under financial pressure and wanted to reduce the size of its labor force, the concern for working-class motherhood provided convenient justification to let women go.[91] The ban on underground work by women seems to have reduced their employment in mines, though it is hard to quantify. In one instance, in the Lodna Colliery in Bihar, where 698 women were employed underground in 1929, after underground work was banned, only 361 women were able to find work on the surface in 1938.[92]

The decline in women's presence in Calcutta's jute mills is far more striking after independence. Women were 12.4% of the jute mill labor force in 1950, 4% in 1960, and 2.5% in 1971.[93] While trade unionists and managers attributed this decline to the cost of maternity benefits mandated by law, this argument is not consistent with the timing of the maternity benefits legislation in Bengal, which was passed in 1939. The more persuasive argument is that the growing strength of the male-dominated trade union movement led to the exclusion of women: "The process of *organisation* thus went hand in hand with *masculinisation*."[94] The power of social norms regarding the fragility and vulnerability of women, as opposed to legislation itself, is reflected in the comments by a historian of Kanpur, that the percentage of women employed was high only when demand for labor was high: "Given the more limited scale of industrialisation in Kanpur, pressures to employ women workers were weaker."[95] In Kanpur textile factories, the percentage of women in the labor force was never very high (5% in 1906) and fell (1% by 1944).[96] If legislation contributed to the decline of women's work in factories, it was in conjunction with powerful patriarchal norms.

Conclusion

The colonial state's attitude to labor varied greatly across time and space. Protections for rural workers were limited and ineffectual. Penal contracting was highly consequential and controversial when in place but was entirely eliminated, and morally repudiated, by the end of the colonial period. Factory legislation initiated by the Raj had a modest impact, in part because enforcement was limited. The marginalization of women in factory work, which began in the colonial period and intensified in independent India, was influenced by factory legislation but had deeper determinants in social norms. One important trend toward the end of the colonial period was the

Congress adopting a role as referee between capital and labor, giving the government extensive rights to intervene in disputes. This was one element of a broader set of economic policies involving a larger role for the state, adopted after independence.

One of the principal drivers of economic change in colonial India was the expansion of trade, within and outside the subcontinent. But trade needs to be supported by methods for enforcing contracts. What methods did the company find prevalent in India? How did British Indian law evolve to support growing and changing forms of exchange? We explore these issues in the next chapter.

SEVEN

Contract: Late Westernization

Early in April 1859, administrative officers feared that an uprising was imminent in the southern Bengal countryside. Peasants refused to sell indigo leaves to the European owners of indigo factories, violating written agreements. The indigo export business, once lucrative, had run into rough weather for a few years past. The immediate reason for the dispute was this recession. But there was another, long-running, reason: the absence of adequate mechanisms for drawing up sale contracts and for enforcing these. The factory owners did not hesitate to use coercion to enforce sale contracts with the peasants. But they had also repeatedly demanded a contract law of the government. In April 1859, when many peasants refused to fulfill contracts, the planters filed a large number of suits in the local courts. As if to confirm their claim that their legal position had been weak all along, they lost these cases. The episode exposed the propensity of the trade to generate violence. It underscored something else too: that the subject of contract had been left too long to local conventions, and that oversight could end up killing capitalist enterprise.

For business firms in the early nineteenth century, indigenous commercial law was either invisible or an obstacle. Traditional religious law was not good enough to meet the needs of modern business and was rarely used. The idea of a contract law did exist in India, and jurists tried to revive these laws. But the revived laws were never actively used. If buying and selling were done by spot trades, exchange without contract law was unlikely to become problematic. But if buying and selling were done by long-period contract, laws were needed to deal with breach of contract, and these laws needed to be secular. Impersonal and secular laws of business could not be found written down anywhere; no courts existed where such laws had been recently applied, whereas at the same time, the scope of business transactions between parties that did not share similar customs expanded enormously.

The decisive response to this uncertainty was the Indian Contract Act of 1872, which broke with indigenous law and custom explicitly. The act drew upon Western models, even though it was caught up in a debate over Indian practice. At the turn of the twentieth century, imperialist historiography explained the triumph of Western law as embodied in the contract act as an instance of the civilizational superiority of the English. More recently, historians have explained it as a step toward the establishment of British dominance over Indian society.[1] Both these perspectives overlook the functions of a contract law. It is an instrument of trade. We need to consider how well law served the needs of trade before the act came in place.

The chapter shows that until 1872, three potential remedies to the absence of a contract law had been tried, and each had failed. These were the revival of Indian codes, a series of specific laws covering particular types of transaction, and reliance on agents and middlemen. The chapter then traces the story of the tortuous journey toward the Contract Act. The first two sections deal with the failure of the Hindu law of contract, and the response of the courts to this failure. The next two sections discuss how the subject of contract was addressed informally by trade and formally by legislators before 1872. The following two sections describe the politically explosive episode of contract failure in the Bengal indigo trade in 1859–1860. The last section deals with the outcome of the indigo crisis: the Indian Contract Act.

1796: An Artificial Discourse

In 1796, a compilation of the Hindu law of contract was published in Bengal. It was compiled by Jagannath Tarkapanchanan, and translated and extensively annotated by H. T. Colebrooke. Tarkapanchanan (?–1806) was possibly the most famous Sanskrit scholar, or pandit, of his time. Hailing from Tribeni, a center of learning, he was reputed to be nearly a hundred years old when Colebrooke and others started consulting him on points of law. His legendary memory and skills as logician helped the others produce a connected account of Hindu law of contracts. Colebrooke was a man of many accomplishments. Sent to India as a civil officer, he learned Sanskrit as part of his training to be a senior judge and then started writing treatises on Hindu law based on his readings of the original. Tarkapanchanan helped him in this task.[2] The product of their collaboration was an impressive work of scholarship by any benchmark. The one-thousand-page book was divided into the two principal parts dealing with contracts and successions. Contracts were divided into four subjects: loans and payments, deposits and partnerships, nonperformance of agreements, and duties of man and wife. Successions consisted of one major subject, inheritance. Even if we confine ourselves to the first three of these five subjects, this was a minutely detailed work, comprehensive in the range of issues covered, and with commentaries added to adapt the ancient laws to modern usage. In a later publication, Colebrooke set out the Hindu law of contract, occasionally drawing parallels between Hindu law and English law.[3]

For the scale of the project, the erudition, and good intention it embodied, the book was a failure. It was not known to be frequently consulted in a higher civil court. The cases of debt or sale contracts that came to the appellate courts did not refer to occasions when this work had been followed in the lower court. Why was the Hindu law of commercial contracts so thoroughly abandoned during the golden age of Hindu law?

The solution to the puzzle is that, whereas the digest was a work of textual scholarship, it was a difficult book to use as a practical guide. It purported to be a code book, but did not clearly specify whether it was a codification of common law or codification embodying a legal theory. It made no credible reference to historical usage, and, therefore, it was unreliable as a codification of common law. The issues addressed had a real-life counterpart. And yet, each one of the cited textual authorities borrowed words and ideas from one or more previous authorities, to such an extent that it was difficult to tell if a specific proposition was a mere copy, a record of an existing convention, or an original injunction. The texts themselves sometimes referred to law in "actual usage," but usage was not specified by time or provenance.

Could this compilation be seen as codification based on a common principle? It is indeed possible to discern a principle, but one that was quite alien to the world of commercial transactions. The propositions are sprinkled with assertions of the superiority of the Brahmin, and the priestly prerogative to interpret law. But, then, the Brahmins were asked to mind their own profession, which, of course, was not trading. And likewise, "the king should compel a man of the mercantile class to practise trade . . . and a man of the servile class to act in the service of the twice-born [spiritually reborn, usually refers to a Brahmin]."[4] If in real life occupations were indeed so segregated, Brahmins would not be a reliable authority on commercial law, classes engaged in trade would devise strong conventions that neither the priests nor the king could possibly know in full, let alone improve upon, whereas the king would have no obligation to enforce commercial contracts involving the "servile classes." Numerous other rules displayed the same general sentiment behind these codifications—the king should give forfeited property to the Brahmin, should never tax a Brahmin, should feed him in famines, should make a perpetual land grant only to the Brahmin, and so on. The discussion on commercial partnership contains a large subsection on partnership between the priests and the traders, with detailed instructions on fees payable to the priests (and curiously, another on partnership between "robbers" and kings).

There were other anomalies. Although the translation contained provision for written contracts endorsed by officers, "it is . . . remarkable," Colebrooke added in a footnote, "that the ordinary modern words for books, paper, ink, writing, &c., are said not to be discovered in any *Sanskrit* work of genuine antiquity."[5] There were references to revealed knowledge (the Vedas) and interpretations thereof (Smritis), but no word for books and documents. There was great uncertainty over interest rates. Different authorities prescribed different rates as those stipulated by law. The correspondence between "contract" as understood by Colebrooke and his contemporaries and contracts in the field of trade was far from close. Both Tarkapanchanan and Colebrooke understood by the term obligations in general. On the one hand, in works on so general a meaning of contract, it was not necessary to investigate common law conventions, for surely no common convention could be found when the word "contract" encompassed marriage, succession, loans, and sales. On the other hand, there were too many implicit or explicit exclusions from commercial codes. From the injunction that a partner unwilling to carry on in business is succeeded by an heir, we can conclude that the case the legislators had in mind was a firm consisting of kinsmen.[6] One needed to be born into the partnership. But this would restrict the scope of partnership too narrowly. Like the servile classes, women were expressly excluded from the scope of the law. The grammarian Katyayana (ca. 140 BCE) settled the matter bluntly: "Nothing should be lent to women, because they are unable to repay it."[7]

It should be clear that this code could not have any utility whatever as commercial law. It did not arise out of commercial practice, was written by people who did not do commerce, and might even have looked down on it. The dominant sentiment behind these codes was the establishment of Brahminic authority over the written word. Colebrooke had taken on the heroic task of reconstructing a codebook based on texts that were not credible as usage, and outlandish as principle. Jurists thought too that the Hindu law of contract was unworkable. Thomas Strange, a justice of the Madras High Court (1830) and author of a major treatise on Hindu law, recognized areas of overlap between Indian texts on sale and debt contracts and European usage but believed also that the Indian texts incorporated many subjects that were "irrelevant matter, some, not in general classed under this title."[8] He described the manual as "the best law-book for a counsel, and the worst for a judge."[9] The only guidelines that it was possible to draw from the ancient texts were "dependent upon ethics alone," but the particular conception of ethics embodied in this text was unrelated to the ethics in business.[10]

Much later, when jurists reconstructed the history of the Indian law of contract, there was a discussion on the Indian counterpart to the *lex mercatoria* acceptable to the judges in British Indian courts.[11] Three specific Indian usages seemed to be acceptable as widely understood custom—these were a debt rule called damdupat (see chapter 4), the remittance instrument known as hundi (chapter 8), and the Hindu joint family, legally defined as a partnership in which the members joined by right of birth (see also chapters 5 and 8). By default, almost everything else, from sale of goods to insurance to banking to partnership, was delivered to equity or more rarely to English common law.

In this legal vacuum, how were contracts written and enforced?

1796–1872: Contract Cases and Informal Enforcement

In contract cases that arose in the port cities—involving auctions of commodities, damaged freights, insolvency, marine insurance, and trading accounts with banks—neither religion nor tradition was an issue. English common law was referred to with no questions asked. The one small exception was a series of cases in the 1830s and 1840s involving opium sales in Bombay. The idea of tradition came up in these cases of forward contracts, and there was a strong suspicion of betting on more than one occasion. Opium was sold by government auction, and merchants and bankers were routinely suspected of trying to combine and corner the whole lot, to bid up prices for everyone else. The bettors were the defendants in the cases, and the plaintiffs were the brokers who had entered wagering contracts with the former, promising to buy opium at relatively high prices.[12] Nothing illegal had been done in the opium case. Wagering contracts were legal in English law, and wager was extensively practiced in India. For collusion to be proved, the courts had to be shown that the bettors by their action had brought about the event which had been wagered on, but this was not easy. Judges, therefore, ruled differently. In the end, the majority view was that a contract had to be performed and settled the cases for the defendants, with a strongly worded cautionary note for legislators to regulate wagering contracts.

"In practice, the English law, as far as applicable, is adopted by the Courts."[13] Indeed, from the eighteenth century, the company's city courts (mayors' courts) had found that, on matters of contract, Indian disputants preferred to let cases be decided according to English law.[14] Our browsing of dewanny court proceedings between 1835 and 1857, which are available in print in Bengali, partly confirms the above statement—partly, in that in most contract cases, the borrowed doctrine of "equity" seemed to take precedence over particular English usage.

In general, commercial disputes were rare in the first place. Nearly all suits were land related, and a few related to debt, succession, and defamation. One such exception was a principal-agent dispute of 1855. This was a case between a banker in Bengal who had sued his agent. The agent was instructed to buy company stock for a certain sum of money and lost the money on account of a fraudulent transaction in Calcutta. The judges settled the appeal (for the plaintiff) with reference to English law.[15] A second exceptional case was a dispute over a banker's draft that was wrongly refused payment.[16] In one curious case, between a landholder and his family priest who was dismissed from priestly service, Colebrooke's authority was cited in respect of the discussion on employment of priests.[17] Perhaps the most significant cluster of cases concerned sale of commercial assets with disputed liabilities. One such sale of an indigo factory (*Kearne v. McDonald*, 1857) made a reference to a number of other dewanny cases of a similar nature.[18] It was this last category of cases that drew on English law in an obvious way.

The Dewanny Adawluts were absorbed in the high court system after 1862. Between 1862 and 1872, when the Indian Contract Act was drafted, there was somewhat greater activity in the Calcutta High Court on this subject. Of the 185 suits decided by the court in these ten years (criminal and civil), only five referred to Hindu law, one to Islamic law, fourteen to English law (eight of these were criminal proceedings), and four to contracts. Of these four, two were debt transactions, one was the sale of the indigo factory mentioned above, and one involved sale of goods. The indigo factory case began as a dewanny suit and ended as a high court one. These four cases paid an unusual degree of attention to the word "contract," discussed distinctions between types of contract, the difference between quasi contract and implicit contract, and appropriate design for a contract. The discussions on these points of law were sometimes extensive, suggesting that outside the court, contracts were then becoming a debated subject. A particularly significant example of the debate was *Rambux Chittangeo v. Modoosoodhun Paul Chowdhry*, from 1867, where the issue in dispute was the obligations of cosharers of a landed estate, a topic that often came up in partnership firms.[19]

The other courts were no different. J. D. M. Derrett mentions sixteen cases that cited the Hindu law of contract between 1839 and 1872, of which only two were decided before the high courts came up in 1862.[20] The remaining fourteen would form a small proportion of the civil suits settled in these ten years. By contrast, between 1872 and 1910, 409 cases referred explicitly to the Contract Act of 1872, and if we include contractual disputes that referred to the Code of Civil Procedures, the number should exceed one thousand.

If businesses did not rely either on indigenous law or on the British Indian courts, what did they rely on? In trades in silk, salt, hides, cloth, and indigo, the universal practice was for the buyer to advance a sum of money against delivery of finished goods. The risk that the suppliers, once they "worked up the amount they really had received, . . . ran away," was pervasive in these other trades.[21] In order to minimize that risk, buyers hired intermediaries who exercised some degree of social control over the sellers. In the eighteenth century, the private European merchants and company officers purchased cotton textiles through the intermediation of the headmen of local weaving communities. The privilege commonly granted to them was that the principal would not buy from others when there was excess supply in the market.

The middleman was hardly the ideal solution, however (see also discussion in chapter 2). The result was that contractual disputes exploded in Indo-European trade and often took on a violent character. Transactions in cotton, wheat, textiles, silk, opium, and indigo involved serious disagreements. The discord turned political in the indigo case, as we shall see.

1823–1859: Specific Legislation

For an administration reluctant to legislate on civil matters, the default policy was to deal with breach of contract by means of existing criminal laws. This was evident in labor contract (see chapter 6). In the business of the sale of indigo leaves by Bengal peasants to European "planters" (factory owners), Regulation VI of 1823 granted powers to the magistrate to order summary redress to a planter injured by the evasion of a peasant who had taken an advance against the promise to supply indigo; Regulation XV of 1824 gave the magistrate powers to enquire into proprietary rights to land and crop; and Regulation V of 1830 made evasion of a contract by a peasant a criminal offence inviting imprisonment. This last law was repealed by Act X of 1836, though the general principle was reaffirmed in 1839, when the Law Commission reiterated the position that the matter of "affrays" resulting from indigo contracts should be dealt with by means of penal laws.

The policy of dealing with breach of contract by poor peasants, artisans, and laborers with penal law was seen by many to be harsh as well as inefficient. Criminal intent was inapplicable in a situation where breach of contract could happen due to bad weather. The criminal courts cost money. The indigo planter and the tea plantation owner could afford to employ lawyers, bribe court officials, hire witnesses, and pay the stamp tax. Without any one of these steps, the disputant in criminal cases had little chance of receiving a fair hearing. The police report played a crucial role in criminal cases. The police tilted to the side which could pay more money. A lower Bengal landlord explained that "when the darogah [chief of police] sees that the magistrate is in the habit of going and remaining in planters' houses, and racing and hunting with them," it was suicidal to stay impartial.[22]

A powerful opinion, therefore, was that breach-of-contract suits needed to shift from the domain of criminal law to that of civil law. Criminal law entailed the threat of imprisonment; a civil law entailed performance. The key problem, however, was that "the ordinary process of the civil courts is inoperative and powerless to compel specific performance if prayed for."[23] In the absence of adequate laws, civil courts were, for the capitalist, useless.

The question of a contract law was debated twice by the law commissions, but on both occasions the discussion ended without resolution. On the first occasion, an intermediate legal step was proposed by some officers of district administration, involving registration of contracts together with penal law. Registration in principle, by insisting on a format, would make the contents of the contract more transparent, while it would also indicate the peasant's consent to the contract. In 1835, a proposal that indigo contracts be registered before a magistrate was rejected by Thomas Macaulay as being too intrusive and impracticable. The winter of 1839 again saw parlays among members of the Law Commission, senior officers of the government of Bengal, and judicial officers arguing for an act that would be applicable to cases of contract enforcement by coercive means. The draft act was reviewed by the governor general and returned to the commission with the polite message that the matter needed further consultation. The years between 1854 and 1859 saw a burst of complaints on behalf of the Bengal planters. The executive branch of the administration saw the indigo situation as one of "errors of law," a combination of "unrighteous dealing" and unenforceable decrees, rather than criminal conduct.[24]

How did the indigo trade end up in such a mess?

The Blue Mutiny

From the last quarter of the eighteenth century, the East India Company began to purchase indigo from India for export, the Caribbean sources of supply of the dye having become unreliable.[25] Indigo was purchased from northern India and Bengal, but the practice of setting up large factories in villages developed only in Bengal. In the last decade of the eighteenth century, total British import of indigo increased from nine hundred to eighteen hundred tons, Bengal's share rising from well below one-third to about three-fourths. In the rise of Bengal, a small transit duty imposed on the northern rival was helpful. But the more important factor was the established position of Calcutta as a financial center, as a port, as a point of information exchange, and as the political center. The company's servants deposited their savings for remittance in Indo-British partnership firms known as the agency houses. This money was invested in indigo. Demand, however, was unstable. Raising money at low rates of interest was not easy, especially since government bonds competed with indigo investments. And despite efforts to induce the government to create a lender of last resort, no such institution came into being. Any recession, therefore, could induce contagious bankruptcy, the biggest of these having hit the industry in 1833 and 1846–47.

There were three methods commonly used by the manufacturers to obtain indigo. The first method was to contract with peasants for growing the crop on lands on which the latter had tenant rights, the second was to purchase estates and cultivate with hired labor, and the third was to lease land from the tenant or the zamindar and induce the peasants already settled on such lands to grow the crop. Before 1829, almost all land held by the planter was on leasehold, but usually not in the name of the planter. In 1829, direct leasehold was made possible by a new law, though numerous restrictions on Europeans owning or leasing land continued. In 1837, all Crown subjects were made equivalent on the right to acquire or hold land in perpetuity. Thereafter, some planters bought estates, and many took land on secure lease signed with a zamindar or with a tenant.

The make-or-buy choice involved a choice between two contract regimes, hiring wage workers and directly organizing cultivation, or making deals with peasants. It was not necessary for planters to buy estates (they could lease in land instead) in order to organize direct cultivation, but some planters thought that step would help. Buying estates was expensive in the densely populated districts of lower Bengal. The best lands for growing indigo were sandbanks, or *chars*, that formed out of alluvial deposits in the middle of the rivers of the Ganges delta. Property rights on char lands were ambiguous. Planters did not want to become full-fledged farmers. Hiring labor was not easy in Bengal. Some planters tried to address the labor problem by recruiting migrants from the Chota Nagpur hills, but this solution never took root and presented its own difficulties. The job not only needed labor; it also needed large amounts of money, often borrowed from the local moneylenders at high interest. Contracting with peasants who would grow the crop kept the rates within established convention but required close monitoring. The zamindars were wary of planter power, had a share in the profits of rice trade, and exerted overt or covert influence on the peasants' crop choices. There were many points of negotiation—price, seed and weeding costs, quantity, weather, soil quality, and the opportunity cost of using land for growing indigo.

Some planters owned zamindari estates. Whether they did own estates or did not, the planters needed to make individual agreements with peasants cultivating land on the sale of crops grown on each farm. The standard agreement specified not the quantity of the crop to be delivered, but the extent of land to be sown with it. The yield of land was implicitly assumed to be constant. The same delivery price per bundle of leaves appeared in the records year after year, suggesting that this factor too was believed to be immaterial. In a normal year, the business was profitable for the factory and no less profitable than competing crops for the peasant. Peasants did not usually grumble about the contract. The advances were given in October so as to tie in the peasant in March. The money came in handy when rent was due and the festival season near. Still, every indigo season planters were anxious that some peasants would run away with the money advanced them. Peasants could and did try to run away. They could overreport the extent of cultivation and underreport the yield. And they could, on the three days when the sowing had to be completed, make themselves scarce.

As in many other industries, the indigo contract tied debt with sale. The contractor advanced a sum of money and did not fully clear the credit account when the crops came in. A loan account was created. It showed debit when money was left unpaid, and credit in the case of bad debt. The sign of the balance was immaterial. The creditor knew these were irrecoverable debts, and the debtor was not too worried about repayment. All that the loan account did was to make the relationship as permanent as possible. After Act V (1830) made breach of contract on the part of the peasants a criminal offence, a stamp paper agreement between the cultivator and the factory began to be prepared. The requirement was repealed three years later, and reintroduced in 1859. Although these documents were a gesture toward the law, even the planters admitted that they amounted to no more than "keeping up appearances." "Any intelligent judge would with half a dozen questions, see the hollowness of the contract."[26] The stamp papers on which the peasants signed were left blank at the time of signing. Some of these were never filled in. When they were filled in, details of compensation for breach of contract were not entered.

Not surprisingly, then, force was sometimes applied to ensure indigo contracts were respected. How extensive the application of violence was cannot be ascertained. A business that lasted for sixty years over a large area could not have been sustained mainly by violence. But, then, many acts of coercion or threat in rural Bengal went unreported or were treated as a way of life. It was not necessarily clear who coerced whom. It might seem that the planter, by virtue of being a European, with influence over the European magistrates, would be the agent of oppression. While there is plenty of evidence of coercion perpetrated by indigo planters, there is perhaps an even stronger case to be made with regard to the Bengali factory officer.[27] The planters were outsiders, and not friendly with the zamindars, the real bosses of the countryside. In this hostile scenario, they laid much hope on the *amin*, or the chief clerk of the factory, and other local supervisors and security personnel. These individuals built secure friendships with the peasant headmen, and, depending on their influence upon the peasants, the headmen and the officers shared some part of the advance payments and gained from mild doctoring of the accounts. This game of complicity was as common as direct extortion by factory officers from the contracting peasants, by using the threat of breach of contract. The planter in good or bad faith did not interfere with the work of the subordinates.[28]

If these problems were everyday in nature, what happened in the indigo season of 1859–60 was quite special. As mentioned before, the contract did not involve negotiation on price. From the early 1850s, rice prices had been increasing, and indigo export profits had become unstable. The planters were more determined than ever to obtain performance of the contracts and the peasants equally determined to defy them. Some planters thought the law must be on their side, since the peasants had unpaid debts in the books. They filed a number of suits for breach of contract, on the basis of the stamp paper agreements and books of account. Most of these suits were rejected by the judges, and the rest were withdrawn. Complaints of illegal confinement of peasants and of torture became more common than usual, and the peasants' case was taken up by influential urban publicists. This was the Blue Mutiny.

In popular perception in contemporary Bengal, as well as in present-day historical research, the Mutiny is seen to be caused by "the planters' unceasing greed and atrocity," their "plainly exploitative purposes," "a contract system not far from slavery," "the rapacious tenacity of the white planters," and their fashioning "a mechanism that efficiently and relentlessly attached unpaid labour."[29] The concept of the predatory European takes different forms. Nearly all authors agree that the planter could "terrorize ignorant ryots" with the connivance of the magistrates.[30] A recent study argues that the planters' power to oppress the peasant had increased after new laws allowed them to buy zamindaries.[31] In one work, the planter-peasant transactions are interpreted within a framework of unequal exchange between the metropolis and its satellites.[32] In another, the Blue Mutiny is interpreted as a peasant rebellion, one of many that the nineteenth century witnessed.[33]

There are, however, difficulties with a mainly political explanation of the episode. First, at the time of the Blue Mutiny, planter power was in decline. Second, neither were the planters a homogenous class nor did they act in concert. And third, the argument that the episode reflected nothing more than an exercise of racialist power ignores not only the whole context of trade and contract enforcement, but also the most important legacy of the episode, the Contract Act of 1872.

The Indian Contract Act

An administrative note prepared in 1862 by Secretary of State Charles Wood initiated the proceedings for the creation of a breach-of-contract law in India. The third paragraph of this note mentions the circumstances that led the India Office to take this step. "From the date of the commencement of the differences between the indigo planters and the ryots in some of the districts of Lower Bengal," it stated, "your Government has, on various occasions, considered the expediency of providing some more stringent measures than the ordinary process by civil action for the enforcement of contracts."[34]

Against the anarchy of the courtroom, a commission of enquiry was instituted in 1860. The members were more or less unanimous on the point that the solution was an equitable and efficient law. The prevailing sentiment was clearly against a penal law. But they did not all speak in one voice on the alternative. The two important proposals that emerged were registration of contracts, and empowering the civil courts to try contract cases quickly. The latter course would need legislation without being seen as a special favor to the planter. A proposal to quickly produce a breach-of-contract act appeared well beyond the capabilities of the Legislative Council. Dithering, therefore, continued, at considerable cost. In the first half of the 1860s, the Bengal industry was practically destroyed, many agency houses went under, others changed businesses, and indigo moved on a much diminished scale to north Bihar.

Administrative opinion was divided over the course of action. The administration in Bengal was reluctant to adopt measures that could be construed as protecting the planters' interest. The Bengal view received support from the secretary of state in London. Wood, in a note to the governor general, sympathized with the planters that their capital was not protected but concluded that the administration was not ready yet for a new law. The lawmaker in this case was the council that advised the governor general, who expressed unhappiness over the axis between London and Calcutta and the tendency to mix politics with law. The little protection that the planters received in the past had come from the council. The intellectual resources of the council were enhanced by the induction of Henry Maine as the law member in 1862. Shortly after joining, he voiced an apprehension that the absence of a contract law would kill this business and perhaps others too.

This became the official position in the mid-1860s, when the Indian Law Commission took up the subject of contract. In 1866, a six-member committee headed by the judge and parliamentarian John Romilly produced a draft Indian contract act. The draft was partly an abridgment of English laws on the subject, and partly adapted from the New York state civil code. The state that framed the act "freely availed itself of its supreme power to define what shall henceforth be the law of the land in regard to a large part of the civil rights of the population of India which do not affect religious usages or institutions."[35] It appeared a foregone conclusion that indigenous common law supplied no model for a law "applicable to the whole population." Colebrooke's scholarship on contract law was quietly buried. Contract was seen as one of those "great chapters of law on which in India there was no indigenous system of rules of any sort."[36]

The draft act was caught up in debate, because, fearing peasant unrest in the future, five sections of the act exempted contracts governing cultivation of crops from specific performance of the contract.[37] Maine argued against these qualifications on the grounds that they would discourage the nonofficial Europeans from doing business in India, that they were unnecessary because the planters had declined as a political class, and that it would be a mistake to deny a civil law to "contracts with the ryot . . . on the a priori assumption that all such contracts are from the nature of the case unjust."[38] Maine then supplied an ingenious additional point. The majority of court judgments on unpaid debts in rural India remained unexecuted, for the average rural debtor had little property other than land, and land titles were not easy to transfer. "The result is that these decrees are *hoarded*. They are divided, bequeathed, inherited, and sold in the open market," until these were purchased by a capitalist or a "neighbour of the debtor" who had the money and the patience to get it executed, at great cost to both the original debtor and the creditor. The indigo planter had been doing just this, hoarding a set of agreements that were individually doubtful and releasing them at the opportune moment. In this scenario, a strong rather than a weak contract law was in the best interest of the peasants themselves.

In 1859, the second Law Commission had designed a uniform code of civil procedure to govern the functioning of the courts. Sections 93 and 192 of the Code of Civil Procedures laid out broad rules for the judges who might want to try a contractual suit. The proposed contract act would have superseded these rules with more restricted powers. An earlier proposal to revise the code to simplify the specific performance rules had been denied by the secretary of state and the Indian Law Commission, on the ground that the new contract act would supersede these provisions of the code anyway. When the draft act became ready and did not live up to the expectations, Maine was not giving in. The manner of application of specific performance, he reminded the lawmakers, was a matter of "procedure" and not "law"; statutes needed to be broad rather than restrictive.[39] Maine was debating with nervous politicians but won in the end. The draft was kept on hold for six years, during which the architects of the draft resigned their positions. Eventually, the final version of the contract act dropped the controversial clauses.

The act defined different types of contract, classified types of contract failure, and ordered performance in the case of willful breach. Although modeled on English common law, the Indian Contract Act departed from its English counterpart in some respects, especially in rules concerning contracts agreed remotely (when the parties were physically far apart), revocation, consideration (a consideration is an agreement to perform a desired action, without a reference to which contracts became void), and the rule that an act performed in ignorance of a proposal but consistent with it could count as acceptance of the proposal. In a case judgment, an Indian judge discarded the rule, on the ground that the underlying reasoning was open to question.[40] Section 16 of the act stated that a contract would not be valid if drawn under "undue influence." The phrase "undue influence" derived from the discourse on unconscionable bargains in the English law of contracts and addressed the problem that the precise context in which a contract was negotiated was usually hard to assess.[41] Its specific application in this case was very likely to have been influenced by the memory of the indigo disputes.

As mentioned before, the act led to an upsurge in contractual cases. What were these cases about?

Contract Cases after 1872

The introduction of the Contract Act did not immediately mean either that all commercial contract failures were settled with reference to this act or that suits under this act were necessarily commercial in nature. Between 1872 and 1910, the majority of the contract cases displayed a mix between the personal (family, marriage, private circumstances) and the public (fairness of a formal agreement).

Although the Contract Act emerged in the specific context of sale of goods, about one in ten suits under the act in 1901–8 concerned liability of the members of a joint family. This was an effect partly of the fact that the partnership law was incorporated within the contract act in India, unlike in England, where the law was codified into a separate act (1890).[42] The joint family business represented a particular context for confusion over the form of liability it entailed. In a partnership, liability (whether "joint" or "joint and several") fell on the designated partners. In a family business, there were notional partners, but who they were and their responsibilities in the firm were matters internal to the family and invisible to others. Furthermore, in Indian law, it was implied that liability was joint and several, unlike English law of 1890, so that individual members were technically competent to sign agreements to borrow money or lend money. These two features together made for a huge field of disputation. Other members of the family could dispute the partner status of the said individual, and contracting parties could dispute their liability to the individual as well (see also chapter 5 for examples of debt cases tried under the Transfer of Property Act).

For example, a debt suit was settled in a lower court in favor of the defendant, who had borrowed money. The argument was that the plaintiff had no authority to receive money in repayment, being only one member of a joint family business. The decision was reversed in this case, and apparently in almost all the appeal cases of a similar nature that came up before the high courts (*Gopal Das v. Badri Nath*, Allahabad, 1909). There was one case of a member of a family firm who contracted a loan after his "retirement" from the business, giving the impression that he was still in a position of authority within it. The judge held that neither would the liability cease to be effective on account of the retirement nor could the debtor pass the liability to the other members because he was once one of them (*Mian Amar Singh v. Seth Chand*, Madras). On the other hand, a plaintiff's claim to a family property on the plea that the property had been acquired through the operations of the family business when the plaintiff was a part of it was not accepted by the court, both on limitation and on the point that the division was not part of a preagreed contract (*Sudarsanam Maistri v. Narasimhulu Maistri*, Madras, 1901).

These cases were common enough for the judges to attempt to define the coincidence between partners and members of a family business, the test being the degree of control over property, profits, and liability for losses (*Haji Noor Mahomed v. Macleod Russell, J.*, Calcutta, 1909; *Vadilal Lallubhai v. Shah Khushal Dalpatram*, Bombay, 1904). But these exegeses were of limited value. For those characteristics that made a family member a deemed partner and "the real intentions" behind a debt contract drawn in the name of an individual were invisible to those transacting with a family firm (*D. Maclaren Morrison v. S. Versychole*, Calcutta, 1901).

A parallel set of conflicts occurred in the context of marriage with an element of implicit contract in it. These contracts usually entailed agreement to pay bride-price or dowry in the form of a stream of payments. The cases for recovery of the money were often started by the woman when the marriage failed but was not dissolved. The point was that in the English tradition, she would not enjoy "privity," which prevented third parties from the right to sue. The woman herself was the third party in a dowry contract between prospective parents-in-law. In the American tradition, on the other hand, she would enjoy that right. The latter principle was upheld in one of several cases of this kind (*Mussammat Daropti v. Jaspat Rai*, 1905).

A cluster of cases dealt with "undue influence," "immoral" and "illicit" contracts, "inequitable condition," "unconscionable bargain," and, more rarely, champerty (the case when a third party finances a contractual dispute expecting personal gain). The shadow of indigo fell on a few cases where undue influence exercised by merchant creditors upon peasant debtors was suspected but could not be proved (*Hemraj v. Khuda Bakhsh*). Undue influence was also a point in disputes over deeds signed by married women, and in the case of "gifts" or payments made by weaker parties or under duress. These situations arose often in disputes between guardian and ward, father and son, patient and medical adviser, solicitor and client, trustee and cestui que (beneficiary) trust (for a gift from a son to a father in a business family, *Lakshmi Dass v. Roop Laul*, 1906). These cases could be concluded either way, as influence not proved or refusal to give "relief from a transaction or contract merely on the ground that it was a hard bargain" (*Dhanipal Das v. Raja Maneshar Bakhsh Singh*, 1906), or by the argument that the nature of the case warranted that "strictest proof of good faith and fair dealing was necessary and the plaintiff had failed to adduce it" (*Hoti Lal v. Musammat Ram Piari*).

In a number of debt cases, where the defendant alleged undue influence, the court made a distinction between influence and duress. As we show in other contexts (for example, the Usurious Loans Act, discussed in chapter 4), judges tended to be sensitive to the borderline between an unconscionable bargain and an agreement involving difficult, but justifiable, terms. The presence of a great need for money as such became inadmissible as evidence of influence exercised by the creditor upon the debtor (*Rani Sunder Koer v. Rai Sham Krishen*, 1906). A related category dealt with the situation when "a contracting party, who cannot read, has a written contract falsely read over to him and the contract written differs from that pretended to be read" (*Dagdu v. Bhana*, 1904). The high court rarely heard such cases, which were possibly quite common in the lower courts and in such fields as indentured labor. Agreements for cohabitation outside marriage, when the partnership ended, led to claims for monetary compensation. A surprising number of such cases came up before the high court and involved deeds executed on stamp paper between a man and a woman. The words often employed by the courts to dismiss cases of this kind were "the interest of public policy," meaning equity, presumably. These words came up in many other situations as well, such as wagering contracts (see below).

Only about one-tenth of the suits dealt with business-to-business disputes. The failure of voluntary trade restraint among members of an informal cartel came up in a series of cases (for example, *S. B. Fraser & Co. v. The Bombay Ice Manufacturing Co. Ltd.*, 1904). Specific performance was sought in a series of cases where delivery or construction was not completed within the stipulated time (for example, *Narainaswamy Reddiar v. The Madras Railway Co. Ltd.*, Madras). Other cases between corporate firms included disputes between a company and its managing agent, and those between partners of a firm. Some of these suits, settled with reference to the Contract Act, and yet dealing with the issue of division of authority between owners, directors, and managing agents, are discussed in chapter 8 on corporation.

Wagering contracts placed the court in a moral dilemma at times, especially when an agent had borrowed money from a principal for gambling, and lost. The majority of the wagering contracts occurred in the context of commodity trade. Sometimes these were in the nature of disputes between a cotton mill and a cotton broker or trader, when an actual delivery of goods was involved (for example *Sir E. Sassoon v. Tokersey Jadhawjee*, 1904). More commonly, disputes broke out when parties bet on future prices without an explicit agreement to transact in the commodities. Such betting was extremely common in commodity and stock markets, and known as *badni*, *tezi-mandi*, *nazrana* or *nichrawal*. These were principal-agent disputes. When a commodity trader had made money by trading in inventory held for the principal, wager was again at stake, but now without a wagering contract. In an interesting case, a colliery manager borrowed money at 150% per annum interest from a neighboring colliery to save the business, but the interest obligation drove the firm to bankruptcy. The manager had acted in the interest of the principal, but the owner, who did not take much interest in management at all, had no knowledge of the cost of the loan. Who was liable? Would good intention of the manager count more than the daftness of his action (*Heramba Chandra Pal Chowdhury v. Kasi Nath Sukul* and *Kasi Nath Sukul v. Heramba Chandra Pal Chowdhury*, Calcutta, 1905)?

These cases formed the murky borderline of contract. Some of these invited the broad maxim on "turpitude" stated in the Indian Contract Act (1872), namely, that all suits arising from contracts would be void before law if the purpose was illegal, immoral, or against public policy. This broad rule could be seen to encompass wagers and a variety of marriage broking, especially where the bride was a minor. But the actual disputation often discriminated between cases. For example, different high courts in India held different views on marriage contracts.[43] Another cluster of borderline cases consisted of those where the meaning of illegality was open to disputation, for example, in the colliery case above, where the agent had acted in good faith but against the interest of the principal.

Conclusion

The Indian Contract Act emerged from trade disputes rather than from either European or Indian legal tradition. Trade disputes had an older and broader history. But the Blue Mutiny supplied the immediate impetus to the making of the act. Why did these other disputes fail to have legislative effect, whereas the Blue Mutiny had such an impact? The answer is that the political repercussions of trade disputes varied, and the indigo episode had serious political repercussions. The fact that it was about peasants, whom the Raj felt obliged to help, that it was a dispute between Europeans and Indians, and that it followed so soon after the great Mutiny of 1857 made for a serious commitment to institutional reform. But the demand for a contract act did not just arise at the time of the Blue Mutiny; it was an old demand that had arisen in Indo-European trade much earlier.

Although the Contract Act was extensively used, against a trading world that was growing rapidly between 1870 and 1930, the number of suits that referred to the act might seem too few. Like general legislation of property (see chapter 5), the act created an option to draw up a legally recognized form of a contract that would be protected by courts. But the act did not insist on it, nor did law suggest that any other form of a contract would not be admissible in court. Informal and extralegal mediation continued to rule, and a number of contractual disputes continued to refer to acts other than the Contract Act.

If the Contract Act represented a case of a Westernization that occurred late, corporate law represented Westernization that was incomplete and flawed from early on. This is the subject of our next chapter.

EIGHT

Corporate Law: Flawed Westernization

One of the unfortunate results of reproducing English legislation in the entirely different industrial conditions of India is the lack of control over the managing agency system.

—P. S. Lokanathan, *Industrial Organisation in India.*

In 1882, a judgment of the Bombay High Court settled a long running case between the managing agent of a company and a director of the company (*Nusserwanji Merwanji Panday v. Gordon*). The managing agent was technically hired by the board of directors to manage the firm but frequently allowed to exercise overall control, especially when the agent was also a majority shareholder. This authority was challenged on the impression that the board alone was the rightful representative of the shareholders at large. The court settled the case in favor of the agent and thus upheld the practical rule that the agent had the last word on management. The judgment opened up, or at least failed to address, a source of persistent conflict in Indian companies.

The managing-agency contract was mainly a South and Southeast Asian innovation, and its form changed between places within this broad region. Company law, which followed British precedent closely, was a poor guide to dealing with the formal contract and these variations in its usage.[1] In effect, the law left subjects such as the division of authority between the board and the agent, or protection of minority shareholders, to be decided by convention and sometimes case law. Managing agency was not the only example of a situation where Westernization would create judicial oversight. Partnership was another field where neither Indian nor Western legal precedent offered complete guidance. In turn, these issues arose because the large firm was not a Western transplantation but evolved out of a mix of indigenous and expatriate enterprise in the port cities. The law governing the firm tried to keep in step with the evolution and often fell behind. Faithful Westernization was a flawed procedure from start.

The first two sections of the chapter present a chronological account of the evolution of the Partnership Act and the Companies Act. The third section focuses on important cases concerning these. The fourth section deals with managing agency, and the fifth with other commercial laws, in particular, negotiable instruments. A good starting point is partnership, which was commonly used until 1882, when the first comprehensive company law was framed.

Toward the Partnership Act, 1932

As opposed to the company, which was a legal entity distinct from the individuals who owned it, partnership was defined as a contract between individuals. In practice, this concept implied that a firm could not sue or be sued in its name. The partners were individually liable. The flexibility enabled individuals with diverse capability to associate as partners. But it was inconvenient for those transacting with the firm, and unnecessary for the partners themselves in a large number of cases. The Code of Civil Procedure 1908 admitted the possibility of the firm being sued in its name, though formally the partnership firm continued to be defined as an association of individuals without its own distinct identity.

In the sphere of European trading firms, the first informal partnerships involved officers of the East India Company as associates of the private merchants. Little is known about the legal status of the agreements they entered into and the available means of dispute settlement. The first registered partnerships in Calcutta were the agency houses that served the expatriate population in a variety of ways, chiefly by supplying banking services. Their main business was commodity trade, but several had also a banking branch. Financial service needed to be integrated with trade apparently because the company government was reluctant to offer licenses to banks. This informality of the banking operation made insider lending likely, and made these firms particularly vulnerable to commodity market risks.

How were business disputes settled before 1850? From the few cases involving partnerships, it is clear that, if the plaintiff was in Britain, the suit was tried by jury in an English court. One such dispute (*Hart v. Alexander*) involved the famous Calcutta firm Alexander, which went bankrupt in 1832. The risks of the indigo export market were transferred to the firm's own banking operations, leading to episodes of contagious crisis. In this case, the plaintiff, who was a merchant and an officer of the company dealing with Alexander for twenty years, sued a retired partner of the firm after Alexander closed operations. The suit was rejected on the ground that the retired partner was not liable.[2] There may be more cases of this sort in the English case history compilations, but few that came to the Indian courts.

For nearly forty years after this case, partnership suits were covered by British law, though it is hard to be exact on the point. The Indian Contract Act (1872) had a number of clauses on partnership and was the major instrument for settling partnership disputes thereafter. These clauses were separated from the Contract Act in 1932, to form the Indian Partnership Act, modeled after its English counterpart instituted in 1890.

Why was a new law needed? The likely explanation can be found in the codification program and attendant debates in other countries that followed the English common law in such matters, especially the United States. The American Uniform Partnership Act of 1914 was a direct influence on Indian legislation together with the 1890 English act, even though the war and political instability delayed the revision. When the Indian Contract Act departed from the English precedence earlier, the new act retained these differences. For example, the Indian act insisted on neither a written agreement nor compulsory registration of agreements.[3]

It is obvious that partnership occupies a rather minor place in the legislative history of India. The reason for this is that the Hindu coparcenary firm governed by the Mitakshara law was not only completely different from the partnership and copartnership of the English type, but also governed by property law (such as the Transfer of Property Act of 1882) rather than the contract and partnership acts. Most Indian large firms were governed by the former, whereas most European and Indo-European firms fell in the latter category. The former law was a law of property and succession of the Hindu joint family. The latter category was covered mainly by procedural and contractual law.

The Mitakshara, in force in Bombay, Bihar, and Benares, technically defined a partnership firm wherein the right to be a partner was acquired by birth. The right accrued to the male heirs of the legally recognized male head of the family. The Dayabhaga in force in Bengal differed from this model on a few minor points; in effect this text too defined the partnership as a firm into which ordinarily male partners were born. Whereas a synthetic partnership was dissolved when a partner died, the Hindu coparcenary firm continued as long as the family line continued. Like synthetic partnership, the association in this case was not a legal person separate from the persons of the partners. In this respect, the organic partnership of the family and the synthetic partnership between associates were both different from the company. Unlike synthetic partnerships, the joint family of Mitakshara was expected to be the representation of a real indigenous tradition. More likely, it was a legal fiction; but we can never know for sure what it represented. In compilations of high court cases we have been unable to find a single example pertaining to a Hindu business family between 1800 and 1860, even though several instances of landlord property disputes probably entailed business assets as well.

If the Hindu partnership was an extension of the family in a legal sense, industrial firms started by the Indians displayed a marked preference for the joint-stock company form.

Toward the Companies Acts, 1850–1936

The origin of the idea that a corporation is a fictitious person—the embodiment of the rights and powers of many individuals "amalgamated and reconstituted for their more efficient and effective utilisation" and made substantial by means of law—is probably very old.[4] The evolution of a separate jurisdiction for the business corporation, however, is a much more recent phenomenon. The constitution and operation of the East India Company, for example, influenced the evolution of English company law. The "application of corporate personality to business associations, the concept of permanent joint stock, the practice of transferable shares . . . , separation of ownership and control," and several other features are owed directly or indirectly to the existence of the company.[5]

The idea of the joint-stock firm as a legal personality took shape in the Indian port cities less as a direct effect of the East India Company than as an effect of sustained contact with English law and the cosmopolitan commercialism of these cities. Compared with the situation in Britain, among industrial firms in Bombay and Calcutta, limited liability became unusually popular, much more so than partnership. The fact that many of the port city firms were global in reach would have required them to adopt a legal framework compatible with that of Britain and the empire. Also, the joint-stock company form made raising money either from banks or from the public easier. In fact, one historian attributes this popularity to the high cost of capital in India. Entrepreneurs did stake their personal wealth in new ventures in the mid-nineteenth century, but the joint-stock form reduced their liability to other investors.[6]

While thus addressing the scarcity of capital problem to some extent, the industrial firms created another problem. Most enterprises were family firms, and no matter the profile of the shareholders, the family still wanted to maintain close control of the company. The answer to this second problem was the managing-agency contract drawn up between a company and a managing agent firm. Because of these two elements—joint stock and managing agency—the structure of corporate law that evolved in British India acquired a distinct feature. On the one hand, limited liability allowed a company to raise money from the public, if on a very limited scale in the beginning (the Bombay Stock Exchange started in 1875). On the other hand, the managing-agency contract allowed one firm to control others by virtue of a contractual agreement. The typical industrial concern around 1900 was a company with shareholding of family and friends as well as the public, and managed by another firm, which was either a partnership or a company closely held by the same family or, on rarer occasions, a trust. The company had a legal identity as a public body, but it was managed like personal property.

That a personal element was thus embedded in the corporate is a well-known feature of Indian business history, and surely not special to India. Historians tend to read this combination in terms of an attempt to distinguish Indians (wedded to personal law) from Europeans (modern in their choices).[7] But a model of ethnic segmentation can be overdrawn. In fact, most large business houses, whether Indian or European, made use of both the impersonal and the personal provisions though this combination of a managing-agency firm and a public company. Indian personal law was effective only on questions of succession and inheritance of control, say, of the managing-agency firm. In public dealings in the market, especially in raising capital from the market, the company advertised itself as an independent entity. In short, the legal system gave many firms the choice to hide some aspects of management while revealing other aspects to the public. In effect, law made management and control less transparent to the shareholders than it needed to be.

Because of the early and sustained popularity of the company, legislation in the nineteenth century followed a distinct pattern; almost every new company act instituted in England induced the framing of a new Indian counterpart about four years later. This practice continued in the early twentieth century. The Indian version used English law as a guide. Important areas of revision—such as the power of auditors, rules regarding financial companies (chit funds), and, most important of all, managing agency—reflected Indian realities.[8] Still, the availability of an English corporate-law framework made for resistance to legislating on specifically Indianized institutions, such as the managing agency.

The principle of joint stock, like that of partnership, was not unknown in India. In a very unusual partnership dispute from 1843, a joint-stock company formed to receive and dispose of goods stolen from ships in Bombay harbor was sued by one of its shareholders for a breach of trust. The court heard that the company followed Indian customary law, had existed for decades, and performed its task diligently for the benefit of the owners. Nevertheless, the suit led to the undoing of both the plaintiff and the defendants, who were together transported to a penal colony for ten years.[9]

The Joint Stock Companies Act of 1844 was the first English legislation on the joint-stock company, excluding the East India Company charter. A series of Indian acts came soon after. Act 43 of 1850, an act for the regulation of joint-stock companies, Act 19 of 1857, an act for the incorporation and regulation of joint-stock companies, and Act 7 of 1860, an act to enable joint-stock banking companies, were the earliest laws subsumed and automatically repealed by the Indian Companies Act of 1866. The 1866 Indian Companies Act followed closely the text of the English Companies Act 1862.

The operation of the company acts between 1850 and 1900 has been studied in the existing scholarship.[10] There are four points to note. First, before the Companies Act of 1850 was passed, English common law applied by default to the European firms in India. But there was inconsistency in how these were applied, and the absence of insolvency procedures caused a great many problems. Second, after a spate of business and bank failure in 1846 in Calcutta, a new pattern of European entry began in the trading world of the city. These firms were larger in scale than before, with shareholding, and they were occasionally manufacturers. They needed legal innovations to reduce risks and raise capital and used two key institutions, the managing-agency contract and the law of the joint-stock company. Shareholding was usually confined within small groups of people known to each other. The shares were ordinary shares with high face value. In Bombay in the 1850s, a similar pattern of company formation had begun among Indian firms. Third, there was a shared understanding in the Indian legislature that an English law on the company would be appropriate for India. And fourth, while this was the case, within India sharp disagreements were present—influenced by the many instances of bank failure—on the desirability of limited liability. Some banks themselves argued against unlimited liability to the law commissions, whereas provincial administrators believed that limited liability would compromise the creditors' interests. Limited liability was permitted by law in 1857.

The acts of 1850, 1857, and 1866 made little practical difference. The 1850 act made a provision for registration of a company by the then Supreme Courts of Bombay and Calcutta, which were to be merged into the high courts in the 1862 reforms. The design of the "deed of settlement" resembled the memorandum of association of a company. The 1857 act, as mentioned, allowed limited liability. Subsequent acts can be seen as further elaboration of the joint-stock principle (table 8.1). Limited liability and registration under the Companies Act became mandatory only when the number of shareholders exceeded twenty. In practice, an unregistered joint-stock company with fewer than twenty shareholders and unlimited liability did not differ very much from a copartnership. The only material difference seems to have been that the shares in a company were transferable without the consent of all shareholders. This could not have been easy when the shares had high face value. And therefore, actual recourse to law did not frequently refer to the Companies Act until well after 1882. In 1882, five-hundred-odd cotton, jute, and tea firms appeared in a list of working companies, but this was a combined list of registered and unregistered firms.[11]

So much can be derived directly from legal history and business history. Yet the standard historiography of corporate law has not discussed case proceedings in India in much detail. By doing so we will notice the gaps that legislation left open until 1882.

Cases: Partnership and Companies

A key stylized fact about corporate law around 1900 is the small number of cases tried under the Companies Act of 1882. Among more than a thousand suits in 1900–1908 in the area of contracts and agency, only forty came under the ambit of the Companies Act. Only a few of these (see below) involved disputes between the owners and managers, suggesting convergence between the two groups. Furthermore, disputes involving the business association were not only decided with reference to the Companies Act, but also with reference to the Indian Contract Act, 1872, by procedural laws, and occasionally, property laws.

The most common field of disputation in partnership firms was settlement of liability during liquidation. Because Indian trading firms in the late nineteenth century did not usually register themselves, loans taken on behalf of the firms carried the names of individual partners. When such firms came to an end, the creditors were likely to sue the individuals and the latter were likely to make the plea that the loans were taken on the firm's account. Such disputes were not easily settled not only because of the entanglement of the private interest with that of the firm but also because no ready reference was available in an existing act. These cases made extensive reference to English

Table 8.1 Evolution of corporate legislation in India, 1850–1936

Date of Passage of Indian Act	Indian Act	Date of Passage of Corresponding British Act	Significant Aspects
1850	Registration of joint-stock companies	1844	Enabled registration of unincorporated partnerships with transferable shares by the Supreme Courts of Bombay, Calcutta, and Madras; certain management rules set out; conflict of interest addressed via rules restricting deals by directors; company could sue in its own name, and be sued by shareholders; insolvency proceedings specified
1857	Incorporation and regulation of joint-stock companies		Recognized limited liability, but not for banking and insurance firms
1860	Amendment	1857	Limited liability extended to all companies
1866	Incorporation, regulation, and winding up of trading companies	1862	Defines directors and their power
1882	Companies Act	1882	"Consolidating" act
1887	Amendment		Provision for priority of debts during insolvency proceedings
1891	Amendment		Hundi (indigenous credit-cum-remittance instrument) formally acknowledged as a bill
1895	Amendment		Companies can alter their objectives with approval of court
1900	Amendment		Companies allowed to keep branch register of members in Britain
1910	Amendment		Authorizes payment of interest out of capital and reissue of redeemed debentures
1913	Companies Act	1908	"Consolidating" act—discusses the division and overlap of functions between directors and managing agents, but does not introduce comprehensive regulation of the managing agent
1936	Companies Act	1929	"Consolidating" act; also, significant for legislation on managing agency

precedence, and Indian precedence if available (*Durga Prosonno Bose v. Raghu Nath Dass and others*, 1898). This last-mentioned case was between two partners in a business formed on the expectation that both partners would contribute money, but at the start, the plaintiff extended a loan to cover the defendant's share, which he wanted repaid. Would that money be treated as investment in the firm or a personal loan? Two courts held different views on the question, but the high court settled in the plaintiff's favor.

Between 1866 and 1910, a few cases were settled in high courts with reference to the Indian Contract Act and dealt with the scope of the authority of the officers of a company. Directly or indirectly, they involved the appropriate division of authority, when shareholders, directors, managing agents, and brokers seemed to share interest, as they did in many small-size firms. "The agreement between a company and directors how far binding," was the issue in two of these. In one example the plaintiff was both a director of a mill and a *mutasuddi*, or broker for the firm, and in that capacity entered a contract with the managing agents to supply raw material for a fixed commission. The company's board terminated the contract, and the court upheld the board's authority over that of the managing agent (*Ram Chand v. Diamond Jubilee Flour Mills Company Ltd.*, 1903).

Another Calcutta suit that eventually went to the Privy Council settled a point of law, whether promissory notes (in this case, East India Company's notes) held as security for a loan (extended by the Bank of Bengal) could be used to discharge a different contract entered by the same debtor with the same bank.[12] The council decided it could not. Inheritance of the assets of a deceased partner in a Calcutta firm was the issue in another suit of uncertain date.[13] Between 1880 and 1910, about ten suits were heard in the Calcutta High Court on terms of long lease of mining land to leading Calcutta firms. At least one case involved a dispute between the large zamindari estate of Silda in Midnapur and Watson, one of the last surviving indigo planting companies of western Bengal. The tax liability of agents of British firms doing insurance or banking businesses in Calcutta was settled as well. The mining cases did not involve the newly instituted commercial laws like the Companies or the Contract Acts, possibly because their main business involved property issues.

By contrast, forty cases referred to the Indian Companies Act 1882. These cases referred to the act because they involved firms that had been registered under the act. No new principle was laid out or discussed in these suits. The majority of them were liquidation suits and involved claims of creditors and malfeasance by directors. As before, the liquidation proceedings of a company made loans contracted by the directors disputatious. In nearly all the cases examined, the appellate court judged these loans to be in effect loans on the firm's account (for one example, *The Ganges Steam Tug Company, Limited ex parte The Delhi and London Bank, Limited*, 1882).

One of the early corporate cases was *Jahangir Rastamji Modi v. Shamji Ladha* (1866–67), started in the wake of widespread bankruptcy in Bombay, and challenging the directors' right to trade in the companies' own shares.[14] The judgment said that any activity not stated or implied in the memorandum and articles of association should be treated as ultra vires, thus establishing the importance of these documents. Curiously, the judgment referred to English law and not the Indian Companies Act. Similar cases, where the directors of a manufacturing firm had used company funds to trade in goods, bullion, or shares and were taken to court by the shareholders, continued to come in before the high court (for example, *Kathiawar Trading Co. v. Virchand Dipchand*, 1894). These cases posed increasing difficulty and on one occasion saw judges taking sharply different positions (*Wamanlal Chhotalal Parekh v. Scindia Steam Navigation Co., Ltd.*, 1944), because the articles and the memoranda of many Indian companies tended to be all-encompassing in anticipation of ultra vires suits.[15]

Firms often ran into disputes with banks. In almost all of the cases that involved banks, the issue in question was the liability for unpaid loans contracted with one partner or one director. For example, the death of one of the copartners led to a dispute between a tea estate company and a bank in 1882 (*Harrison and another v. The Delhi and London Bank and another*). Twenty years later, a similar case came up, now in a joint-stock setup. When a bank sold goods taken as collateral to recover an unpaid loan, the Delhi Cotton Mills argued, unsuccessfully, that the loan had been drawn by the directors in excess of their power (*The National Bank of India v. The Delhi Cotton Mills Co. Ltd.*, 1902). Another management case settled by the Contract Act involved a dispute between two partnership firms when the same individual acted as partner in both, creating the legal anomaly that the defendant and the plaintiff became identical (*Rustomji v. Purshottamdas*, 1902). A purchase of shares by the head of a religious institution led to a dispute over whether the shares belonged to the head or the institution (*Mahant Kishobadassji V. The Coimbatore Spinning and Weaving Company*).

If reference to English law was somewhat adequate on some issues, a crucial gap concerned the managing agency. Managing agency was not covered by a comprehensive set of laws until as late as the Companies Act 1936.[16] It was not even clearly defined anywhere. The oversight had owed, in the view of the author cited at the head of the chapter, to the practice of blindly following British law, whereas the managing agency was an Asian institution. Be that as it may, if the company acts focused on the relationship between the owners and the directors, the relationship between the firm and its managers remained underlegislated. The next section explores this large anomaly at the heart of British Indian corporate law.

The Managing-Agency Contract and the Debate on Managing Agency

The managing-agency system began in European insurance business in early 1800s India. In this system, the directors or representatives of the shareholders contracted a firm to manage the company for a fee (or commission on sales) for a fixed term. In some cases, the entrepreneur who had started the company wrote a management contract between the company and himself. The idea of a management contract survived recessions in the 1840s. By the 1870s it had become established in large-scale industry, mining, and plantations. The system had two major advantages. First, the promoter and the manager being often identical firms or families, the agency contract enabled them to earn two types of income, dividend and commission, thus reducing their exposure to market shocks. Second, by having a reputation fixed on an established management firm, the promoters ensured interest from the wider public in start-ups. This second effect can be read as conservation of managerial resources, since the reputation of one manager was shared by old and new firms alike. In the case of the largest European managing agencies in tea, jute, or engineering, the agent had such a brand name that its involvement made it easier to raise capital from public issues.

Possibly because the managing agency was an Indo-European system, English law did not supply ready guidance on the contract, and because it was poorly regulated, distortions arose and persisted for a long time. The contract could be one-sided. The agent could gain almost complete and near-perpetual control (some contracts were valid for sixty years) over a cluster of companies with which it had management contracts. This was not a problem for the shareholders when ownership and management were vested in one family, but it was a problem after public shareholding expanded. Because the company law did not intervene in managing agency as much as it needed to, the broad outlines of an agency contract tended to be governed by the generic Contract Act. The upshot was that the shareholders could do little to stop the mismanagement of the firm they owned when the agency firm was in the hands of a bad manager, or when a predatory takeover of an agency firm transferred control of an entire cluster of firms in one sweep to a bad manager.

In practice, managing agency came in different forms. There were two types of principal-agent formations. In the first type, the principal company was loosely held but the agent company closely held. In the second type, both companies were closely held. The former was more common among the European firms in Calcutta.[17] These were satisfied with a small controlling stake and happy to spread dividends among a wide and diverse body of shareholders, raised a lot of capital from the market thanks to easy access to corporate banks, but retained control by means of the managing-agency contract, and the "special voting rights" that the shareholding of the managing agent enjoyed. Their reputation in effective management of the companies under their control allowed them access to bank loans and generally enhanced the credit of the companies themselves. Few traded on their own account. The board of directors was recruited from public figures. In principle the shareholder body could rally around the directors and question the agents, but this was not an easy thing to do. Individually, some of the directors of the Calcutta companies were decision makers in their own firms. But their presence on the boards of other firms fulfilled the role that P. G. Wodehouse attributed to "nodders." While technically equal to any other director, informally the nodder was a director whose principal duty in the board was to nod approvingly at anything the owners said in a board meeting. A small set of nodders, consisting of princes and landlords, populated a very large number of company boards in Calcutta, giving rise to the scenario of "multiple directorships" that was a major focus during the 1936 revision of the Companies Act, and caused much unease in enquiries on company management in the 1950s and 1960s.[18]

In Bombay, the system worked in a different way. The owner of an industrial company was typically an Indian trader or banker. The owner had a controlling stake in the company and appointed a board of directors from friends and relations. The board appointed an agent, which was a firm belonging to the owner. The owner, in short, exercised control over a company by three means, shareholding, a compliant board, and the agency contract. The situation gave rise to two common issues, conflict of interest as the trading firm transacted with the industrial firm and the agency firm earned commission on such transactions, and a tendency to make the term of the contract as long lasting as possible.

The managing-agency contract was made a legal document following the 1913 Company Act. But the act did not apply strict guidelines on the limits of the agent's power. Most cases involving agency related proximately to conflicts between the managing agent and the board of directors, and ultimately to the protection of shareholder interest. The landmark case cited at the start of the chapter (*Nusserwanji Merwanji Panday v. Gordon*, 1882) made the managing agent's authority more absolute than that of the board of directors. The judge ruled that in matters of direct conflict, where service to the company's interest was not in serious question, the agent's wish would prevail. Cases like these, however, were rare, because only on a few occasions did the directors represent a distinct interest and on even fewer occasions would they want to organize themselves. In an overwhelming majority of companies, the "directors of the managed company . . . [were] ex officio representatives or nominees of the managing agents themselves . . . [so that] conflict of authority between the directors and the managing agents rarely occurred in practice."[19] The asymmetry in the powers was acknowledged in the Companies Act of 1936 and reaffirmed as late as 1949 in *Rodier Textile Mills Ltd.*, where the agency agreement set out that the agents "shall not be under the control and directions of the directors."[20] By the turn of the century, an increasing number of cases settled with the Contract Act involved disputes between the managing agent and the company (*Anderson v. Delhi Cotton Mills Co.*, 1903). An important question was whether or not an old managing-agency contract remained valid after a company became a limited-liability firm (*S. B. Fraser & Co. v. The Bombay Ice Manufacturing Co. Ltd.*, 1904).

Some legal experts wanted more legislation to plug the gap; others resisted. The proponents of the status quo consistently argued that the directors, and not the agent, were in real control over a company, subject to sufficient checks and balances already present, and therefore separate provisions applying to the agent were not needed.[21] But, then, nothing prevented a company from setting out in its articles of association a division of duties between the directors and the agent, effectively turning the board of directors into a "board of dummies."[22]

The comment above was made by a leading expert on corporate law in the troubled interwar period. Early in the interwar period, with liquid savings earned during the World War I trade boom and protective tariffs fueling an industrial boom, "mushroom companies" appeared on the scene. That many of them had a rather short life seemingly exposed the weakness of law, which was seen as "a menace to the healthy evolution of business life in this country."[23] The European firms faced growing anxiety about the future control over their enterprises in the 1930s and the 1940s.

Soon after independence, a case of abuse of shareholder trust occurred in Calcutta. In the 1950s, there were hostile takeovers of a number of European firms. In Calcutta, commodity traders and stock market insiders had amassed considerable liquid wealth through speculation on real estate and commodities during World War II. For a few years after Indian independence, cash was poured in to inflate the value and induce a sale of the stocks of the European firms, which were purchased by individuals loyal to the speculator. The capture of one agency firm transferred control of an entire cluster of firms in one sweep, and the capture of one publicly traded company could be a way to rewrite the agency contract; in either case, the shareholders could do little to stop this.[24] The transfer of ownership was a traumatic event in Indian business history because most of the firms thus taken over went bankrupt or left their core businesses soon after. Nevertheless, the episode is poorly researched, because the families who gained control left little by way of a paper trail. Of course, corporate law was not a sufficient explanation of why the transfer happened. As the historian Maria Misra reminds us, the conservative style of the European firms made them poorly adaptable to the great changes unfolding in the business environment in the postindependence decades.[25] The Partition of India had already dealt a blow to the jute and tea companies under British ownership. In theory, the companies should have been able to survive these crises, since they had enough cash in hand, but for the fact that after the predatory capture the management went to inexperienced and in some instances unscrupulous individuals. In any case, shareholder response was unquestionably muted, because the managing-agency system did not give shareholders much voice in the first place.

The managing agency was abolished in 1970. Family firms found alternative ways of controlling companies, usually by means of a holding company that was not public, and, on occasion, a trust. A kind of legal "ring fence" similar to the managing agency was achieved by many Indian families by means of the Indian Trusts Act of 1882.[26] The act allowed a category of organization that it called private trusts, which were associations of individuals set up to serve a common purpose, whether commercial or noncommercial. Management of property, for example, could be delivered to a trust. Or a private trust could manage a temple or religious institution, which in turn owned property. Trusts were exempt from several measures of public scrutiny (such as registration) that applied to a joint-stock company. A trust was both more opaque and more secure as a mode of ownership of large property than was a firm. It was not easy for a member to divide a trust property. The trust owned a firm, which owned and managed other companies formed of public shareholding. Using the trust law for corporate control parallels with the Islamic wakf, which was a similar law in design but rarely used for corporate control (see chapter 5 on property for more discussion on the wakf). Not all large business groups followed this pattern, and some managed to retain control through intercompany shareholding. All of these modes of ownership were prominent in the 1950s while undergoing further changes on account of independent India's new industrialization policy.

Taking a long-term view, the history of legislation on managing agency mirrors fundamental shifts in Indian business history. The managing-agency contract solved one problem, which was to share and economize on business reputation, but created another, which was to expose shareholders to risk. The former should make it easier to raise capital, the latter should make it harder to raise capital. In the early stages of Indian industrialization, shareholding was restricted and reputation made it easier to raise capital from among a small set of wealthy people. Presumably, the system survived so long because the reputation benefit outweighed the risk aspect. But over time, the risk aspect became more important as shareholding became more dispersed. In keeping with these changes, legislation intervened relatively little in the managing-agency contract in the nineteenth century but turned relatively more interventionist from the 1936 Companies Act onward. A range of other business-related laws had a similar history to company law, in that they became subjects of specific legislation in the late nineteenth century, whereas earlier the generic contract or procedural law was expected to serve these.

Negotiable Instruments and Other Commercial Law

For Indian trading firms, the one commercial law that might have mattered most was the Negotiable Instruments Act (1881). In part, the act was a response to the growth of joint-stock banks and the use of checks. And in part, it wanted to standardize a group of instruments collectively known as hundi.[27] The common meaning of *hundi* was a banker's draft or promissory note, though sometimes merchants' bills of exchange were also called hundi. It was the standard instrument used to remit very large sums of money every harvest season from the ports to the interior agricultural trading zone. The act itself was probably more of an attempt to collect duties from registered contracts than a response to disputes. But a few disputes did come into the courts. The judges often had difficulty understanding hundi and had to call in experts. Nevertheless, the very presence of the act made the hundi more transparent and standardized in form, and more acceptable to the corporate banks.

Along with legislation, the reputation of the acceptors as banking houses, and the customary law and conventions that they followed, ensured that the hundis they issued were discounted by the corporate banks. These customs remain more or less invisible, at least in their details. But some of the chambers of commerce on occasion wrote down and published their rules and regulations. One example was a rule book issued in 1916 by the Marwari Chamber of Commerce of Bombay setting out rules on hundi, for sale of goods, and settlement of disputes around sale of goods.[28] The Chamber set up special committees for appeal, quotation, and arbitration. The rules dealt with the breach of sale contracts in detail and made distinctions among cotton, grain, and oilseeds. Few details are available on the actual process of settlement using these rules.

As for other commercial laws, the absence of a specific law to protect trademarks until 1940, when England had its law of registration of trademarks in 1876, has often surprised legal historians. This was not exactly an oversight. Indian law, both criminal and civil, covered the subject in several places. Act IV of the 1889 Merchandise Marks Act, and another passed in the previous year (the 1888 Design and Invention Act), dealt with related issues. The former concerned trade description specifically. The Specific Relief Act of 1877 was available to enforce copyright on trademarks, sometimes in perpetuity. The Indian Penal Code had sections sanctioning a penalty for fraudulent copying of trademarks. The elected legislature of 1937 started the proceedings to bring about a dedicated trademark law, which was passed in 1940.[29]

Conclusion

The chapter has shown that, because British Indian company law drew upon British precedence, vital areas of corporate governance, such as managing agency, remained poorly legislated. Paradoxically, even as legal experts blamed the agency contract for giving shareholders an unfair deal, court cases involving managing agency remained conspicuously rare. Quite simply, the litigants did not know which law they could refer to. The citation at the head of the chapter expresses that opinion.

Soon after independence, company law reformers saw their mandate as "to protect the majority of shareholders against the dominant minority."[30] In keeping with this sentiment the further amendment of the Companies Act in 1956 changed course and made many routine decisions subject to the discretion of the board. While the law did adapt to changes in the business environment, the process did not necessarily prevent abuses. The hostile takeover of European firms soon after independence was one example of a failure of law. There was another example. In the 1950s, an industrialization drive pushed by the state encouraged company formation. But businesses needed licenses to start new enterprises. Many licenses were cornered by a few families. This pattern of expansion came under scrutiny in separate en-quiries conducted during the 1960s.[31] The reports hinted that the history of law had a role in industrial concentration. For example, many large Indian companies were managed by an agency firm that was either directly owned by a "controlling interest" or indirectly owned by a trust.[32] The agency con-tract and trust made the diversification process opaque to the public. Over time, increasing government shareholding in some of the new private enter-prises enabled a different form of collusion, even corruption.[33]

The laws discussed in the previous three chapters on labor, contract, and corporation were products of judicial activism that began in the late nine-teenth century, led by procedural reform. The next chapter describes this turning point. It also revisits the judicial system more broadly, updating the discussion we began in chapter 2.

NINE

The Burden of Procedures

Crown rule began with reforms in the court system, its enlargement, and a legislative drive that ended the long-standing dualism between English and Indian law (chapters 2, 7). A break with Indian tradition occurred in trade, agency, corporate law, and wage employment, in keeping with expansion in the scale of trade and employment of wage labor. But there were elements of continuity as well. In property, personal law still supplied guidance. The reliance on religion and custom was never officially given up. "Hindus retain their law of marriage, of adoption, of the joint family, or partition, of succession. Mahommedans retain their law of marriage, of testamentary and intestate succession, and of *wakf*, or quasi-religious trusts."[1] In the field of land tenure, rent and revenue regulations in all regions showed "a struggle and compromise between English and Indian principles," and these struggles took on new forms, as we have seen in chapters 3 and 4.[2]

The focus of legislation during this phase of judicial activism fell at first upon codification of procedural law. The Code of Civil Procedure (1859, 1908) was of particular importance. This piece of legislation became a favorite with appellants who had earlier had a decision under a substantive law. We can guess that where the ambiguity in the contents of law was great, and therefore the outcome uncertain, references to procedural correctness would multiply. This is apparently what happened as a result of the late nineteenth-century legislative drive. A great number of cases "left over" from contract, property, and even personal law disputes ended up as appeals on points of procedure. This chapter will first set out the context, and then discuss procedural cases.

Rise and Fall of Judicial Activism, 1860–1940

If we track the number of federal laws passed between 1835 and 1910, we find a rise in the third quarter of the nineteenth century, and a point of inflexion in the series about 1880. Thereafter, the major drive to introduce new laws had passed (figure 9.1). Similarly, the legislative drive in the provinces peaked early in the last third of the nineteenth century and had spent itself by 1900 (figure 9.2).

Did legislation slow because the government decided that the existing framework had been sufficiently perfected? Such an inference is belied by the finding that there was an explosion of appellate cases in the early twentieth century. Cases were taking longer to settle than before. The reform in procedural law was expected to reduce the incidence of cases resulting from procedural uncertainty or contradiction. The Law Commission of 1856 expected that the framing of a Code of Civil Procedure would reduce the need for civil suits by one-fifth.[3] In fact, the opposite happened. Procedural cases proliferated after the reforms. Did the legislation drive slow from a realization that legislation had caused more problems than it had solved? The cost of accessing the courts may have fallen somewhat with the physical expansion of the system. Still, it is not very plausible that litigants went to the

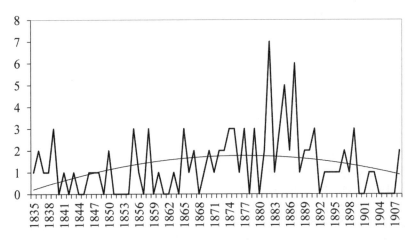

Figure 9.1. Number of supreme government acts (civil) passed every year, 1835–1910. This and the subsequent figures and tables in this chapter are based on data available from B. D. Bose, *Digest of Indian Law Cases Containing High Court Reports, 1862–1909; and Privy Council Reports of Appeals from India, 1836–1909, with an Index of Cases, Compiled under the Orders of the Government of India*, vols. 1–6 (Calcutta: Government Press, 1912), and other sources as explained in the text and endnotes.

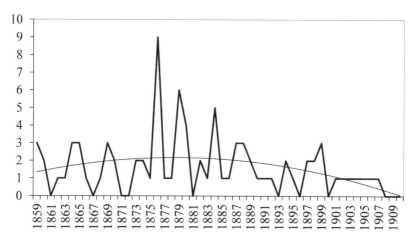

Figure 9.2. Provincial legislation (Bombay, Madras, and Bengal, in number of acts instituted).

appellate courts in greater numbers because the price of legal services fell. Surely the transaction costs in terms of time, transportation, and perhaps adverse publicity were still a deterrent. More likely, legislation slowed because the government started running out of money and ideas from around World War I.

The use of law, however, continued to rise after the legislative peak was over, and it was beginning to strain the system. Figure 9.3 tracks both criminal and civil cases in the chart. Both indices show a rise, but civil suits rose at a faster rate. The two types of cases seemed to move roughly together, which is a curious coincidence unless we assume that property disputes often involved a package of civil and criminal suits. These short-term changes could not be spuriously generated by population movements, because the population growth rate was small before 1921. The two lines enable interesting speculations about the short-term effects of economic fluctuations upon litigation. For example, an early spike at the turn of the twentieth century was possibly prolonged, if not started, because of the two great famines (1896 and 1898), and the resulting dislocation of lives and property. A later and smaller spike occurred in the immediate aftermath of the Depression.

There was no slowdown in the scale of the judicial infrastructure at any time. Figure 9.4 tracks the number of judges, in all courts combined, between 1810 and 1935. The graph shows acceleration, with an inflection occurring about 1880.[4] To some extent, the British Indian system was

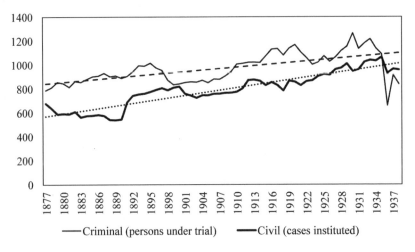

Figure 9.3. Civil and criminal cases per 100,000 population.

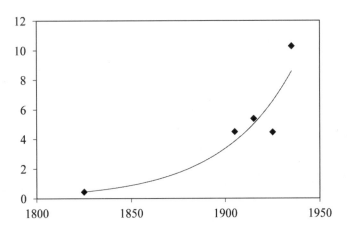

Figure 9.4. Judicial officers (judges) per 100,000 population.

replacing preexisting institutions in the early nineteenth century, whereas by the twentieth century the latter had largely melted away. Nevertheless, the growth in capacity was very large. The expansion of judicial personnel was relatively greater in regions annexed to British India in the mid-nineteenth century, including some of the most populous areas of northern India. In short, the capacity of the system to hear cases rose in keeping with territorial and demographic expansion.

But the capacity of the system to settle cases seemed to be in decline at the same time. Figure 9.5 shows that there was a significant increase in

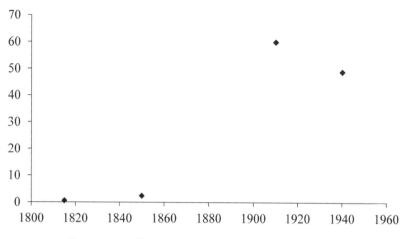

Figure 9.5. Appellate civil suits per 100,000 persons, 1814–1939.

appeals in the long run; and figure 9.6 shows that even after the growth in the number of judicial personnel, streamlining of the courts, and intense legislative activity for twenty years, the proportion of pending cases in total cases was increasing steadily. Cases were taking longer on average to settle. More laws and better laws seemingly increased the disputatious propensity of the population, suggesting a serious and mounting problem about the perceived quality of laws themselves. An exchange of letters between the Court of Directors and the governor general in council about 1815 revealed that there were a total of 139,271 civil suits pending in all courts of the Bengal Presidency in 1814, and the number of civil suits pending in the Suddur Dewanny in the same year was 318.[5] The total number of civil suits formed roughly 127 suits per 100,000 people in Bengal in 1814. The corresponding number for 1877 was 787. In order to strengthen its case for procedural codification, the Law Commission in 1856 quoted a similar set of statistics. There were 4,528 appeals cases before all courts in 1851. The figure was arrived at by adding pending cases from the previous year to the number of new cases instituted during the year. The report estimated that, were there high courts in 1851, there would have been 955 "regular or first appeals to the High Court. Supposing 20% to be deducted under the new system of procedure, there remains a balance of 764 cases."[6] The former actual number (4,528) would amount to 2.4 per 100,000 people, and the latter notional number (764) to 0.33 appellate suits per 100,000.[7]

The number of appellate suits for two later years are shown along with these nineteenth-century ones in figure 9.5. The comparison suggests that

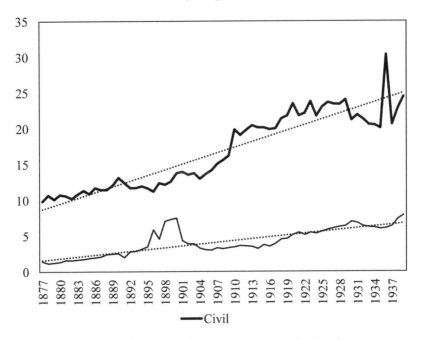

Figure 9.6. Pending cases at end of year as a percentage of instituted cases.

the relative incidence of litigation in fact increased by a factor of 30 between 1851 and 1910. The actual number of high court appeals was twenty times the notional number for 1851. The rise was relatively greater in the sixty years after the establishment of the high courts. Still, the huge rise in appeals cases must be explained. Were litigants going to the appeals courts in such large numbers because the courts were that good, or because they were unhappy with the lower courts?

The striking feature of the rise in appellate cases was that a large percentage of these related not to substantive law but to procedures. Provincial laws, as we see in table 9.2, followed a slightly different trend. Appeals cases were not uniformly distributed, but concentrated in a few major areas. Some civil laws attracted litigation more than others. Which were these laws? In table 9.1, a summary of the data for 1901–8, when the legislative drive was almost at an end, is shown. The table is based on appellate suits settled in the four high courts of British India (Calcutta, Bombay, Madras, and Allahabad). Ignoring the provincial acts, there were 7,628 cases settled with reference to acts passed by the Supreme Council. There were ninety-three acts in all, and all but fourteen of these were passed as separate acts after the Mutiny

Table 9.1 Appellate civil suits covered by principal acts, 1901–1908

	Property	Contract and Agency	Procedure
Names	Indian Succession Act, 1865 (50) Probate and Administration Act, 1881 (101) Transfer of Property Act, 1882 (808) Land Acquisition Act, 1894 (167) Guardian and Wards Act, 1890 (71)	Contract Act, 1872 (409) Specific Relief Act, 1877 (195) Negotiable Instruments Act, 1881 (55) Railways Act, 1890 (52)	Code of Civil Procedure, 1908 (3296) Court Fees Act, 1870 (150) Evidence Act, 1872 (302) Limitation Act, 1908 (1047) The Stamp Act, 1899 (97) Registration Act, 1877 (183)
Number of cases tried under these acts	1,197	711	5,075
Percentage of all cases	16	9	66
Percentage of all acts	5	4	6

Note: Acts are selected if fifty or more cases were tried with reference thereto. Numbers of cases are shown in parentheses.

(1857). Only fifteen of these acts accounted for more than 90% of the cases. And the four big ones (the Transfer of Property Act, the Indian Contract Act, the Code of Civil Procedure, and the Limitation Act) accounted for 66% of all appellate suits. The fifteen major acts can be divided into three broad classes: those dealing with property, such as definition of ownership, succession, inheritance, and transfer; acts dealing with trade, contract, and agency; and those relating to procedure. The division is somewhat artificial, because a few cases made cross-references to several acts. For example, one of the provisions of the Evidence Act 1872 was to privilege documentary over other forms of evidence, especially where terms of contracts were concerned. The issue of contract performance, therefore, was intricately related to forms of evidence. This overlap notwithstanding, the classification of cases is based on the law with reference to which the judgment is passed.

As in the central sphere, in the provinces too, only a few acts saw the most action in the courtroom (table 9.2). On the other hand, the contents

Table 9.2 Appellate civil suits covered by principal acts instituted in major provinces, 1901–1908

	Land Revenue and Rent	Local Administration
Names	Bengal Revenue Sale Law, 1859 (62)	City of Bombay Municipalities Act, 1888 (22)
	Bengal Tenancy Act, 1885 (356)	Madras City Municipalities Act, 1884 (34)
	Deccan Agriculturists Act, 1879 (24)	Calcutta Municipal Act, 1899 (27)
	Madras Rent Recovery Act, 1865 (93)	
Number of cases tried under these acts	535	83
Percentage of all cases	55	8
Percentage of all acts	5	2

Note: Number of cases shown in parentheses.

of laws varied between the two spheres. Almost all new laws aiming to regulate the relationship of the landlord, the cultivator (where diffferent from the landlord), and the governement were instituted in the provinces (see also chapters 3 and 4). In the Permanent Settlement areas, which included all of Bengal and a large part of coastal Madras, this general goal needed to be achieved with a whole array of laws covering encumbered landlord estates, partition of estates, and the court of wards. The largest act by far in this category, the Bengal Tenancy Act of 1885 (see chapter 3) dealt with the accrual of secure user rights after continuous possession, limits on increases in rents, suits about rent arrears, claims to fixed rent tenancy, and the legality of subleasing. The provinces also passed laws regarding urban administration and a variety of semipublic goods, including irrigation, roads cess, embankments, tramways, and policing. Conspicuously missing from the basket of provincial acts were business laws, contractual laws, and laws relating to judicial procedure. These statements are restricted to the three major provinces, because the others that were somewhat active in this time (Central Provinces with five acts, North-Western Provinces with 17, Oudh with 13, and Punjab with 13) fell in the same pattern as the older provinces but attracted many fewer appeals cases.

By far the most important dispute-enhancing law, and the greatest contributor by far to appeals, was the Code of Civil Procedure.

Procedural Law

The Code of Civil Procedure was not a new law, but a compilation. By its very nature, its application was not confined to a particular set of issues but was extended to all cases where a reasonable argument could be made by the plaintiff that a mistrial had taken place in a lower court on the ground of procedure, and a reasonable case could be made by the defendant for dismissal of the suit again on procedural ground.

A wide variety of cases was tried in reference to the Code of Civil Procedure. Needless to say, many of these were about the meaning of terms in an earlier suit, such as the meaning of "decree," and about jurisdiction. Under the jurisdictional type, a few cases (about thirty) concerned the conduct of public officers and the conduct of pleaders. In a very large number of suits involving cosharers of mortgaged property or joint holders of tenure on land, the right to sue an individual defendant was in question. On points of law, probably the largest coherent class (about four hundred) decided the validity of an appeal when the defense argued for the application of res judicata (a matter already judged cannot be retried on the same ground, with the same facts, and between the same parties as before). The next largest group (about sixty) related to the meaning of "contract."

When res judicata was deemed inapplicable, the contention was that the lower court judges had made an erroneous decision, or new facts were produced during further argument, or the lower court had refused to admit one point among several in disputation. An important judgment on lower court decisions held that "a decision in a previous suit on a question of law, even if erroneous, would operate as res-judicata in a subsequent suit" (*Bishnu Priya Chowdhurani v. Bhava Sundari Debya*, Calcutta). Where defendants formed a group, as was often the case, res judicata cases decided whether or not substantially the same case could be retried against an individual member of the group. A rare but fascinating category of disputes related to the right to worship in temples. In one judgment from 1908, an 1840 sudder court decision to bar one caste from entry into a temple was overturned by the Madras High Court rejecting the defense plea that such disputes could in principle employ res judicata at all (*Sadagopachariar v. Rama Rao*, Madras).

A number of land mortgage and tenancy contract suits tended to come up as procedural cases even when they concerned contractual issues. The apparent reason for this was that land mortgage deals almost invariably involved an implicit or informal contract. Index entries in a 1910 compilation of civil suits include the three phrases "implied authority," "implied contract," and "implied grant." These were only the cases where the object of the deal was well defined. In numerous instances the objects were multiple or vaguely defined as well as implied.

For example, a mortgagor and a mortgagee agreed to certain terms of use of the collateral, or the mortgagee took possession of the land but agreed not to resell to give the other party a chance to redeem the land. Such mutual understanding was extremely common and yet never written out. Similarly, a huge number of rent deals involved an understanding between the tenants and the landlords. For example, it was common practice to have a representative farmer pay rent on behalf of a group, even when there was no explicit cosharing of property. Disputes could break out within the group or between landlords and tenants if the arrangement broke down, say, due to the death of one member. The terms and the existence of these contracts needed to be proved before the validity of any subsequent transaction with the land could be deemed legal. The majority of the cases where the term "contract" or the phrase "contract act" was employed were of this kind. Although technically these cases decided the appropriate jurisdiction of the plea, the judgments usually contained definite directives and were final. In this sense, the Code of Civil Procedure filled in for a broad area of fuzziness in contracts resulting from implicit agreements between neighbors and relations.

Along with land-related disputes, a number of business disputes also came up under the rubric of contract. For example, when a business deal between a British Indian subject and a subject of a princely state failed, could the latter sue the former in a British court for breach of contract? The court decided, crucially, that the jurisdiction was valid (*Tadepalli Subbarao v. Gulam Allikhan of Banganapallai*). Several jurisdictional cases with contracts related to such mobile instruments of business as a long-distance sale agreement or hundi, a bankers' draft. A business deal between an import merchant in Lahore and an export merchant in Cochin fell through. Could the Lahore merchant sue in Lahore rather than having to travel two thousand miles down south? The court ruled, again with wide import, that the suit could be filed in the town of the plaintiff (*Premjit Khetsey v. Ghulam Sarwar Khan*).

Another class of contractual procedure related to promissory estoppel (the binding nature of promise made by word or conduct against a consideration). Estoppel cases came in a variety of forms, but one particular class consisted of disputes about temple land. The lands belonging to temples in South India were leased out to members of the community of priests connected with the temple, often without documentary evidence in a legal form. With the passage of time and generations, these contracts became disputatious (*Vythilinga Mudaliar v. Ramachandra Naicker*, Madras).

Another procedural law, a reformed version of an older regulation, attracted a large number of appeal cases. This was the law of limitation. Judicial regulations of 1772, the year when a Supreme Court was established in Calcutta by a parliamentary act, held that "complaints of so old a date as twelve years should not be actionable." The statement in effect applied to suits regarding recovery of debts and movable property, for in suits of landed property, claims as old as sixty years continued to be admitted long after this statement. It was believed then that whereas the Hindu codes had provisions for limitation, the Islamic codes did not, and that, therefore, the English statute should be adopted by default irrespective of religion. The choice of ten or twelve years was justified with reference to the Hindu codes.

Between 1772 and 1840, limitation was established as a general rule, but the Bengal codes had also led to great differentiation in actual practice. Whereas the Bengal Regulations of 1793 and 1832 reaffirmed the rules of limitation, the Madras Regulations of 1802 made exceptions in the case of recovery of mortgages, and the Bombay Regulations limited the scope even further. Courts within a presidency could interpret limitation rules in different ways. The reference to Hindu law effectively meant that in the "mofussils," judges adopted twelve years for the purpose of limitation, whereas in Calcutta, judges could be more flexible. The plea of limitation was sometimes raised only in an appeal, partly because the initial proceedings had taken a long time to settle. A great gap remained between cases concerning recovery of immovable property and those concerning movable property, the former still admitting claims as old as fifty-nine years, so that evidence of continuous use or occupation had to cover an impossibly long period. A law to bring provincial practices and land and nonland suits into uniformity had become necessary.

The first draft law of limitation for British India was prepared by a former judge of Hooghly, D. C. Smyth, and submitted to the Law Commission of 1842.[8] This was debated and elaborated upon, and alternative versions were proposed. The Law Commission settled for a limitation of twelve years in the case of claims to recover immovable property, six years for disputes on debt and contract, and one year for all other disputes. A final document was passed into law in 1859.[9] Differences in interpretation of limitation procedures had led to a proliferation of appeals cases before 1859. Some of the appeals cases instituted after 1859 revealed instances in which Indian practice deviated from the English law of limitation.

One of these instances concerned positive prescription. A positive prescription is a right defensible with reference to fundamental principles such as right to a life in comfort. The English term "easement," applicable to a right to the use of a road through another person's property, is a common form of positive prescription. In a number of cases dealing with limitation, the right to a running flow of water for irrigation was at stake. Were this flow interfered with within one's private lands, causing damages to a neighbor, was the neighbor's complaint bound by the statute of limitations? In one case from 1864 (*Bandhoo Sookoolaney v. Joy Prokash Singh*), the plaintiff claimed rights to irrigation works located in a neighboring property, which claim was denied on the ground that continued use of the works for twelve years could not be proved. The appellate court reversed the decision on the ground that "the proof of ancient reasonable user" with respect to water was sufficient in India to establish a right in the absence of any law of the land on the use of water.[10]

Another class of examples of procedure cropped up in "new" land frontiers. In the Bengal delta, newly formed sandbanks ("alluvial secretions" in the language of the courts) in the great rivers were usually the most fertile land for cultivation. These lands were technically without established ownership and led to violent conflicts over possession as well as protracted adjudication. The potential for violence arose from the fact that though the first-mover right was in principle respected by the courts, the property itself being new, the claim of the first mover was not protected by a statute of limitations. In other words, if the first mover A was dispossessed forcefully by B soon after A had started cultivating the land, neither party had the means to establish continuous possession over a prescribed number of years because the property had not existed that long.[11]

An especially important set of procedural cases concerned the *lakheraj*, or privileged tenures, of Bengal. The plaintiff was usually a zamindar who filed a suit demanding the right to assess and collect rent on a tenant claiming rent-free tenure. The response of the courts and legislature in these and other matters of tenancy tended to be cautious. By the 1859 act, the twelve-year limitation applied to the validity of the claim, twelve years being counted from the day the landowner came in possession of the property, subject to the condition that no such claims would be entertained if the holder of the rent-free land could demonstrate that the lakheraj had existed from before the Permanent Settlement.[12] As with bodies of water, the court sought a demonstration of an "ancient" right as opposed to "a mere modern appropriation."[13]

There were a few other procedural areas where express departures from English law were made in Indian judgments. In almost all situations, the departure can be explained in terms of an implicit feeling of uncertainty about the Indian social context. For example, departing from English practice, judges disallowed partial payment of a debt as proof of an original debt contract for the purpose of counting the time elapsed from a contract and preferred to "shut out inferences and deductions of all sorts, and to admit nothing short of a direct admission in writing."[14] There were concerns that various acts by a debtor that could be construed as acknowledgment of a debt might in fact be enforced by the relationship between the parties or otherwise not warranted by the contract itself.

The last of the major procedural laws was the Evidence Act. The provisions of the Evidence Act were transplanted from England to India in 1726. The charter of that year established English common and statute law as the law of the three East India Company estates in India. With the expansion of British Indian judicature in the nineteenth century, the rules regarding evidence tended to be followed in diverse ways, in one segment with reference to the English law, in a second segment prevailing in the "mofussil" courts with reference to the Muslim codes, the Hedaya, and in yet a third segment with reference to provincial administrative rules concerning reliability of witness and admissible evidence.[15] In the presence of these practices, "some Judges admitted all kinds of evidence, others tried to regulate their proceedings by . . . English law." The Evidence Act of 1872 was legislation in response to this confusion.

If the Contract Act cases engaged with the terms of contract, the Indian Evidence Act pursued the form of the contract. Deeds and promissory notes, handwritten agreements, forms of oral evidence, and witnesses testifying to family custom were included in the scope. It was an active law because so many claims on property made a reference to a particular tradition or family custom—for example, the practice of primogeniture in an Awadh landlord's household, contested by the younger son (*Garuradhwaja Prasad v. Superundhwaja Prasad*). Trade disputes led to discussions on the admissibility of merchant account books, which came in different versions that did not display consistent information to an outsider. In wagering contracts or marriage contracts (see discussion on contracts above), all agreements were mainly oral, with only a few points such as a loan advanced for a wager being written out. When such agreements turned sour, the court needed to discuss if there was any point in recalling contemporaneous verbal exchanges. In short, contracts were bound to be incomplete not necessarily because of oversight of the parties, but also because of the persistence of tradition, and the personal nature of the relationship between the parties.

Conclusion

The growth in judicial capacity, legislation, and litigation in the late nineteenth century illustrate the fact that the state saw itself as much more than a custodian of Indian notions of law and justice in this phase. It was trying to create a comprehensive framework of substantive and procedural law, while drawing upon Western concepts and Indian case law freely for that purpose. And yet, the legislative drive led to an upsurge in litigation. Apparently, the courts and laws created new problems while solving old ones.

A closer look at case judgments suggest why this was the case. Disputes concentrated in specific areas. One large area of disputation was contracts, and procedures related to contracts. The very existence of procedural law enabled certain types of conflicts to develop. Conflicts developed partly because of the extreme commonness of incomplete and implicit agreements between parties who shared social ties. And partly, the conflicts around procedures developed because of overlaps between the fields covered by contracts and procedures. This is a theme that recurs throughout this book. Even as a new law was instituted because an old one was deemed to have served only a segment of the population, no law was ever taken out of the statute book. Procedural law overlapped with everything else, and therefore was a potent source of litigation. By 1910, the drive to create new laws was slowing, and yet the intensity of litigation showed no tendency to fall.

After introducing this book, in chapter 2 we described the beginnings of the British Indian legal system. We then discussed law as it pertained to specific types of transactions, from land transfer to the formation of corporations. This chapter has, in the spirit of chapter 2, focused on the legal system more broadly, this time discussing the late colonial period. We can now summarize our main arguments and findings, and briefly comment on the persistence (or not) of colonial-era trends.

TEN

Conclusion

The outstanding fact, however, of Indian litigation outside the Presidency towns and certain commercial centres . . . is that most of the litigation relates to land.

—Sir Tej Bahadur Sapru, 1922[1]

Most land parcels in India—90 percent by one estimate—are subject to legal disputes over their ownership.

—McKinsey Global Institute, 2001[2]

We began this book by noting that India's recent rapid growth has occurred in spite of a slow and dysfunctional legal system. We asked, can we trace some of the roots of this problem back to India's colonial history? In approaching this question we took our cues from two sets of influential arguments. One which we called the extractive states hypothesis implies that, because the British did not settle in India, they would have put in place institutions that allowed them to extract wealth rather than promote economic growth. The other, the legal origins hypothesis, suggested a potentially more benign influence of British rule. India could have benefited from the importation of British legal tradition. We argued that both hypotheses are useful, though neither fits the Indian case neatly.

The extractive states hypothesis helpfully pointed us toward the British objective of political and economic management and control, a clue we also got from the historiography on colonial empires. But we also recognized that the colonial state's ability to access and appropriate resources was limited by the huge imbalance in numbers between British officials and soldiers and the Indian population. Survival, rather than extraction, was often the Raj's biggest worry. And, while British legal tradition *was* imported, for instance, to regulate the corporation or factory, British Indian law also drew on and preserved what it viewed to be indigenous law. Still, the legal origins hypothesis helpfully nudged us to view colonial law from the perspective of economic efficiency, the approach also favored by the New Institutional Economics.

With these points of departure, we discussed the structure of the British-Indian judiciary, and law pertaining to property and contract in land, labor, and credit. We also studied new institutional forms such as the corporation and the factory. Throughout, our focus was on "law in practice," so we relied heavily on case law. Did we see today's debates and issues emerge in the colonial period? For instance, can present-day difficulties of "doing business" be traced back to British India?

Surely, the answer to these questions cannot be a simple yes. Indian economy and society have changed profoundly since independence. The postcolonial state, in all its phases, has been far more welfarist and interventionist than the Raj ever was. India is now a robust democracy. Various subaltern groups have increasingly found voice. Population has grown rapidly. The international environment has changed. Looking for historical roots is a tricky matter, with potential for oversimplification and mechanical extrapolation. Still, acknowledging these risks, we will end this book with some conjectures.

Perhaps the clearest continuity between colonial and postcolonial India is in the persistence of conflict over rights in land. In the colonial period the state began documenting and recognizing within its "rule of law" the complex network of rights that might be associated with a single parcel of land. There were multiple points of ambiguity and tension—between individual and family, family and "community," "community" and "immigrant," landlord and tenant, and between all these entities and the state. There were at least three major difficulties. First, there was a problem of knowledge. How could a distant state of foreign origin know the minutiae of local relationships? Second, legislation had to impose uniformity, but how was this to be achieved without doing violence to local diversity and existing rights? And most of all, the indigenous actors, whether peasants, landlords, laborers, or "tribals," were by no means passive—they fought for their rights in various arenas, including the courts, which they often overwhelmed. The one thing the colonial state did clearly (usually) was define who was liable for the land tax. Much else, in particular, the right to use and the right to transfer, was up for grabs. And the Raj was reactive rather than proactive, legislating defensively on tenancy and land transfer. Over time, conflict on the ground began to be reflected in the complexity of legislation. By the end of the colonial period land rights were a huge area of contest and confusion, legal and otherwise. At the dawn of Indian independence, there was a widely shared sense of "unfinished business."[3]

Various states (provinces) in independent India attended to this unfinished business with uneven success. They enacted an enormous number of laws to abolish zamindari, impose ceilings on landholding, restrict land transfer, and protect tenants. Much of this legislation was well intentioned, aiming to protect the underprivileged. In some cases it did. For instance, Operation Barga, aimed at providing security to sharecroppers in West Bengal, appears to have enhanced growth and equity.[4] But landowners often evaded these laws. Tenancy went underground, or tenants were periodically switched from plot to plot, to prevent them from acquiring rights of occupancy. Land was given to fictitious people so that ceilings on ownership would not apply. Complex laws, defective systems of registration of ownership, sale, and mortgage, and weak enforcement of law have made land transactions hazardous.[5] The World Bank estimates that in Mumbai it takes more than three years to resolve a "standard land dispute" between two domestic businesses.[6] The report by McKinsey Global Institute cited at the beginning of this chapter concluded that land market distortions (including undertaxation and low user charges) have reduced the growth rate of the Indian economy by 1.3 percentage points per year.[7] While the precise number is of course debatable, the magnitude of the problem is widely acknowledged.[8]

In chapter 5 we described how the colonial state applied different "personal" laws to Hindus and Muslims. We also recognized that these laws undermined women's ownership of property and their rights vis-à-vis the family more broadly. Though gender equity was the goal of some late colonial-era legislation, there was, again, much left to do when India became independent.[9] The state initiated change via, for instance, the Hindu Succession Act of 1956, and more recently the Hindu Succession (Amendment) Act of 2005.[10] Still, further reform is required to protect the rights of women. Unfortunately, now as much as ever, this discussion is politically fraught. There is consensus on the need for gender equity, but specific policy initiatives or court decisions can create enormous controversy regarding religious freedom and identity.[11] Even as we write, debate rages on whether or not the country should have a "uniform civil code," a discussion that has been reopened by the new federal government elected in 2014.[12] The colonial-era decision to link "family law" to religion has had long-term consequences.

Another controversial topic in India today is the extent of employment protection provided to workers in India's formal manufacturing sector. To some, this inflexibility is an important reason why the manufacturing sector has created relatively few jobs even in the last two decades of rapid growth. Others argue that labor law is not a binding constraint and that it can be easily evaded by employers.[13] But most participants in the debate agree that the law is needlessly complex. In this instance the link to the colonial era, while present, can be overstated. It is true that during the colonial period factory acts provided protections for workers, the right to form unions was clarified, and the state began to play an active role in regulating capital-labor relations. But, as we have argued in chapter 6, much of labor law in colonial India was to "manage" workers rather than to empower them. In contrast, the controversial amendments of the 1947 Industrial Disputes Act in 1976 and 1982, which limited employers' ability to fire workers, came in a period when almost every political party called itself socialist and the Indian constitution itself was amended to declare India a socialist republic. We do not see this as continuation of a colonial-era trend.

In relation to corporation and company law, colonial-era legislation, precisely because it was borrowed and did not have indigenous roots, was easily altered for better and for worse. In chapter 8 we discussed conflicts of interest at the heart of the managing-agency structure. Shareholders were particularly vulnerable to insiders. This situation has not persisted. The managing agency was abolished in 1970. And, as of June 2014, in the World Bank's indices, India ranks seventh best out of 186 countries in the extent to which minority investors are protected. Another dimension in which there was a break from colonial precedent was in regulation of the formal manufacturing sector, in pursuit of policies of import substitution. The extent of regulation was captured in the popular expression "License-Permit Raj." Again, though the government did take a more interventionist position vis-à-vis industry in the late colonial period, the sheer extent of intrusive regulation in independent India was a postcolonial innovation.[14]

Finally, there is a striking similarity between the late colonial period and today in what the Law Commission *Report 253* (January 2015) has called "litigation culture."[15] Plaintiffs file frivolous suits which impose costs on others, lawyers engage in delaying tactics, and judges are too indulgent in granting adjournments. Pratap Bhanu Mehta, a respected legal scholar, has commented: "For me one of the big puzzles is how passive judges generally are during the trial process. . . . Extensions, adjournments, and delays are routinely granted almost as if they are a matter of right."[16] Similarly, Tej Bahadur Sapru told the Civil Justice Committee (1924–25) that litigants sought adjournments on dubious grounds, and that while "strong judges" resisted this, there weren't many such. Also, he noted, "considerable time is wasted in perfectly idle appeals from interlocutory orders."[17] A recent report on civil justice in the UK has argued along the same lines that lawyers and litigants have excessive control over the process. Quoting this document, the Law Commission (January 2015) comments that there is "an uncanny similarity to the problems facing the civil justice system in India today."[18] India is poorly served by this inheritance.

TIMELINE

1600	Formation of the East India Company
1677	Charter to company accords limited sovereignty
1658–1707	Reign of Aurangzeb or Alamgir and creator of the code Fatawa-e-Alamgiri
1687	Charter to company admits town administration
1726	Charter to company admits mayor's courts
1757	Battle of Plassey (Palashi)
1764	Battle of Buxar (Baksar)
1765	Acquisition of "dewanny" of Eastern India by the company
1770	Famine in Bengal
1772	Parliamentary regulation of company's government in India
1772	Supreme Court of Calcutta
1773–84	Warren Hastings head of company state in India
1775	Execution of Nandakumar
1786–93	Lord Cornwallis governor general of India
1793	Bengal Regulations
1793	Permanent Settlement
1802	Madras Regulations
1818	Defeat of Maratha ruler (Peshwa)
1832	Bengal Regulations
1834–8	T. B. Macaulay Law Member of Council
1837	Property in Land Act
1843	Slavery Abolition Act
1849	Annexation of Punjab
1850	Caste Disabilities Removal Act
1850	Regulation of Joint Stock Companies Act
1856	Annexation of Awadh
1857	Indian Mutiny
1857	Incorporation and Regulation of Joint Stock Companies Act
1859	Code of Civil Procedure
1859	Bengal Rent Act
1859	Workmen's Breach of Contract Act
1859	Indigo or Blue Mutiny
1860	Penal Code

1860	Joint Stock Banking Companies Act
1861	High Courts Act
1865	Indian Succession Act
1866	High courts established in major cities
1866	Indian Companies Act
1870	Hindu Wills Act
1872	Punjab Laws Act
1872	Indian Evidence Act
1872	Indian Contract Act
1875	Bombay Stock Exchange established
1877	Specific Relief Act
1879	Deccan Agriculturists' Relief Act
1881	Probate and Administration Act
1881	Negotiable Instruments Act
1881	Indian Factories Act
1882	Transfer of Property Act
1882	Indian Companies Act
1885	Bengal Tenancy Act
1885	Annexation of Upper Burma
1886	Indian Registration Act
1888	Design and Invention Act
1889	Merchandise Marks Act
1896–7	Famine in the Deccan Plateau
1898–9	Famine in the Deccan Plateau
1900	Punjab Land Alienation Act
1908	Madras Estates Land Act
1908	Code of Civil Procedure
1911	Indian Factories Act
1913	Indian Companies Act
1913	Wakf Act
1918	Usurious Loans Act
1923	Workmen's Compensation Act
1926	The Indian Trade Unions Act
1926	Workmen's Breach of Contract Act withdrawn
1932	Indian Partnership Act
1934	Indian Factories Act
1936	Indian Companies Act
1937	Shariat Act
1947	Indian Independence
1947	Partition of India

NOTES

CHAPTER ONE

1. Three comparative indices directly or indirectly focus on institutional quality, and all rank India low in international comparisons. These are the Global Competitiveness Index, the Global Innovation Index, and the World Bank's Ease of Doing Business Index. The last mentioned ranks India very low on the ease of contract enforcement. http://www.weforum.org/reports/global-competitiveness-report-2014–2015; https://www.globalinnovationindex.org/content.aspx?page=GII-Home; http://www.doingbusiness.org/reports (all three accessed 20 July 2015).

2. Douglass North, *Institutions, Institutional Change and Economic Performance* (Cambridge: Cambridge University Press, 1991).

3. There is debate on how the "quality" of institutions should be measured, and whether they are driven by other more fundamental factors such as expansion of education. See E. Glaeser et al., "Do Institutions Cause Growth?," *Journal of Economic Growth* 9, no. 3 (2004): 271–303. S. Ogilvie and A. W. Carus emphasize the need for context-specific and nuanced discussion of *when* specific institutions (say, parliaments) influence property rights and contract enforcement in ways that promote economic growth. See "Institutions and Economic Growth in Historical Perspective," *Handbook of Economic Growth*, vol. 2A, ed. P. Aghion and S. Durlauf (Amsterdam: Elsevier, 2014): 405–514.

4. D. Acemoglu, S. Johnson, and J. A. Robinson, "The Colonial Origins of Comparative Development: An Empirical Investigation," *American Economic Review* 91, no. 5 (2001): 1369–1401; Acemoglu, Johnson, and Robinson, "Reversal of Fortune: Geography and Institutions in the Making of the Modern World Income Distribution," *Quarterly Journal of Economics* 117, no. 4 (2002): 1231–94; and Acemoglu and Robinson, *Why Nations Fail: The Origins of Power, Prosperity, and Poverty* (New York: Crown Publishers, 2012).

5. R. La Porta et al., "Law and Finance," *Journal of Political Economy* 106, no. 6 (1998): 1113–55; E. Glaeser et al., "Courts," *Quarterly Journal of Economics* 118, no. 2 (2003): 453–517; S. Djankov et al., "Debt Enforcement around the World," *Journal of Political Economy* 116, no. 6 (2008): 1105–49.

6. Aron Balas et al., "The Divergence of Legal Procedures," *American Economic Journal: Economic Policy* 1, no. 2 (2009): 138–62; N. Lamoreaux and J. Rosenthal, "Legal Regime and Contractual Flexibility: A Comparison of Business's Organizational Choices

in France and the United States during the Era of Industrialization," *American Law and Economic Review* 7, no. 1 (2005): 28–61; A. Musacchio, "Can Civil Law Countries Get Good Institutions? Lessons from the History of Creditor Rights and Bond Markets in Brazil," *Journal of Economic History* 68, no. 1 (2008): 80–108; A. Musacchio and J. D. Turner, "Does the Law and Finance Hypothesis Pass the Test of History?," *Business History* 55, no. 4 (2013): 524–42. D. Berkowitz, K. Pistor, and J. Richard highlight the importance of the circumstances in which a legal transplant occurred in their widely cited paper "The Transplant Effect," *American Journal of Comparative Law* 51, no. 1 (2003): 163–203.

7. The literature is large. For a recent example and a survey, see R. Birla, *Stages of Capital: Law, Culture, and Market Governance in Late Colonial India* (Durham, NC: Duke University Press, 2006). A rich scholarship which describes the emergence of legal pluralism in colonial societies, is another example. See L. Benton, *Law and Colonial Cultures: Legal Regimes in World History, 1400–1900* (Cambridge: Cambridge University Press, 2002).

8. H. Berman, *Law and Revolution* (Cambridge, MA: Harvard University Press, 1983), 556.

9. For instance, one recent article documents and compares across countries the length of time it takes to evict a tenant or collect on a bounced check, and finds that the legal system was relatively efficient in countries which inherited their legal traditions from English common law. Glaeser et al., "Courts."

10. R. M. A. Branson, *Digest of Cases reported in the Indian Law Reports*, vols 1–3 (Bombay: Education Society's Press, 1884).

11. D. K. Khanna, *The Complete and Consolidated Digest: Indian Civil Cases 1901, to 1908*, vols. 1–6 (Delhi: Delhi Central Press, 1910); B. D. Bose, *Digest of Indian Law Cases Containing High Court Reports, 1862–1909; and Privy Council Reports of Appeals from India, 1836–1909, with an Index of Cases, Compiled under the Orders of the Government of India*, vols. 1–6 (Calcutta: Government Press, 1912).

CHAPTER TWO

1. Cited in C. Ilbert, *The Government of India: A Brief Historical Survey of Parliamentary Legislation Relating to India* (Oxford: Clarendon Press, 1922), 17.

2. Ilbert, *The Government of India*, 33.

3. S. Smith, "Fortune and Failure: The Survival of Family Firms in Eighteenth Century India," in *Family Capitalism*, ed. Geoffrey Jones and Mary B. Rose (London: Routledge, 1993), 44–65; L. Subrahmanian, "Merchants in Transit: Risk-Sharing Strategies in the Indian Ocean," in *Cross Currents and Community Networks: The History of the Indian Ocean World*, ed. H. P. Ray and E. A. Alpers (Delhi: Oxford University Press, 2005), 263–85; K. Mukund, *The View from Below: Indigenous Society, Temples and the Early Colonial State in Tamilnadu, 1700–1835* (Hyderabad: Orient Longman, 2005); M. C. Setalvad, *The Common Law in India* (London: Steven and Sons, 1960).

4. C. Dobbin, "The Parsi Panchayat in Bombay City in the Nineteenth Century," *Modern Asian Studies* 4, no. 2 (1970): 149–64; D. L. White, "Parsis in the Commercial World of Western India, 1700–1750," *Indian Economic and Social History Review* 24, no. 2 (April 1987): 183–203.

5. A. A. A. Fyzee, *Outlines of Muhammadan Law*, 5th ed. (New Delhi: Oxford University Press, 2009), 1. Hanafi is the largest among the four schools of jurisprudence in Sunni Islam.

6. S. A. Kugle, "Framed, Blamed and Renamed: The Recasting of Islamic Jurisprudence in Colonial South Asia," *Modern Asian Studies* 35, no. 2 (2001): 257–313; M. R. Anderson, "Islamic Law and the Colonial Encounter in British India," in *Institutions and*

Ideologies: A SOAS South Asia Reader, ed. D. Arnold and P. Robb (Richmond: Curzon Press, 1993), 165–85.

7. The peshwa was the Maratha ruler based in western India.

8. V. T. Gune, *The Judicial System of the Marathas* (Poona: Sangam, 1953), 19.

9. H. Franks, *Panchayats of the Peshwas* (publisher not known, undated), 5.

10. W. H. Sykes, "Statistics of Civil and Criminal Justice in British India, Chiefly from the Year 1836 to 1840," *Journal of the Statistical Society of London* 6, no. 2 (1843): 94–119.

11. A. Steele, *The Law and Custom of Hindoo Castes within the Dekhun Provinces subject to the Presidency of Bombay chiefly affecting Civil Suits* (London: W. H. Allen, 1868).

12. F. Buchanan, *A Journey from Madras, through the countries of Mysore, Canara, and Malabar, etc.*, vol. 2 of 3 (London: E. Caddell for the East India Company, 1807), passim.

13. On the provincial setup in Mughal India, see N. Manucci, *Storia do Mogor*, vol. 3 of 3 (London: John Murray, 1907), 420–21; and J. Sarkar, *Mughal Administration* (Calcutta: M. C. Sarkar, 1920), 48–49.

14. Montgomery Martin, *The History, Antiquities, Topography, and Statistics of Eastern India . . . collated from the Original Documents of the E.I. House*, vol. 1 of 3 (London: W. H. Allen, 1838), 316.

15. W. Dampier, "Report on the State of the Police in the Lower Provinces for the first six months of 1842," *Calcutta Review* 1 (1844): 189–217.

16. British Parliamentary Papers, *Papers relating to Police, Civil and Criminal Justice under Governments of Bengal, Fort-St.-George and Bombay, 1810–19* (London: HMSO, 1819), 17.

17. J. E. Colebrooke, *A Digest of the Regulations and Laws, enacted by the Governor General in Council for the civil government of the territories under the Presidency of Bengal, etc.* (Supplement containing a collection of the Regulations enacted anterior to the year MDCCXCIII, and completing each article of the Digest to the close of the year MDCCCVI) (Calcutta, 1807).

18. H. Cowell, *History and Constitution of the Courts and Legislative Authorities in India* (Calcutta: Thacker Spink, 1905), 159.

19. Steele, *Law and Custom of Hindoo Castes*.

20. Lord Moira's judicial minute, 1815, in British Parliamentary Papers, *Papers*, 158.

21. C. Ilbert, "Application of European Law to Natives of India," *Journal of the Society of Comparative Legislation* 1 (1896–97): 212–26. Cited text appears on 215–16.

22. British Parliamentary Papers, *Papers*, 292.

23. Ibid., 291.

24. Ibid., 291, discusses these costs.

25. Ibid., 292.

26. Ibid., 93.

27. Ibid., 294.

28. E. Perry, *Cases Illustrative of Oriental Life, the Application of English Law to India, Decided in H. M. Supreme Court at Bombay* (London: S. Sweet, 1853), 122–23.

CHAPTER THREE

1. Daniel Thorner, *The Agrarian Prospect in India: Five Lectures on Land Reform Delivered in 1955 at the Delhi School of Economics* (Delhi: Allied Publishers, 1976), 13. The word *kaccha* (Hindi) in this context means weak or impermanent.

2. David Washbrook, "Law, State and Agrarian Society in Colonial India," *Modern Asian Studies* 15, no. 3 (1981): 649–721. Quoted text is on page 676.

3. There is an enormous literature on land rights in colonial India. The classic works in the field are B. H. Baden-Powell, *A Manual of the Land Revenue Systems and Land Tenures of British India* (Calcutta: Government Press, 1882); and Baden-Powell, *The*

Land Systems of British India (Oxford: Clarendon Press, 1892). Another useful resource is D. Kumar, ed., *The Cambridge Economic History of India*, vol. 2: *1757–1970* (Cambridge: Cambridge University Press, 1983). We have found D. Rothermund's succinct and insightful overview especially useful. See *Government, Landlord, and Peasant in India* (Wiesbaden: Franz Steiner Verlag, 1978). B. B. Chaudhuri, *Peasant History of Late Pre-colonial and Colonial India* (Noida: Pearson Longman, 2008), surveys land rights, though his focus is not on law and institutions. We cite more recent work at appropriate points in this and the next chapter.

4. See P. J. Marshall, *Problems of Empire* (London: George Allen and Unwin, 1968), 60.

5. T. Besley, "Property Rights and Investment Incentives: Theory and Evidence from Ghana," *Journal of Political Economy* 103, no. 5 (1995): 903–37.

6. The Bengal and Madras Presidencies were enormous regions, covering substantial swaths of eastern and southern India, respectively.

7. The figure for civil servants is from P. J. Marshall, *East Indian Fortunes: The British in Bengal in the Eighteenth Century* (Oxford: Clarendon Press, 1976), 15. O. Prakash estimates the population of Bengal province alone at twenty million in 1700, in "Bullion for Goods: International Trade and the Economy of Early Eighteenth Century Bengal," *Indian Economic and Social History Review* 13, no. 2 (1976): 159–86. Reference to p. 174.

8. When the true value of the item being auctioned is unclear, the highest bidder will be likely to overestimate it—the "winner's curse."

9. F. G. Wrigley, *The Eastern Bengal and Assam Code, Containing the Regulations and Local Acts in Force in the Province of Eastern Bengal and Assam*, vol. 1 (Calcutta: Government Press, 1907), 5.

10. R. Guha, *A Rule for Property in Bengal: An Essay on the Idea of the Permanent Settlement* (Paris: Mouton and Co., 1963), 106.

11. P. Robb, *Ancient Rights and Future Comfort: Bihar, the Bengal Tenancy Act of 1885 and British Rule in India* (Richmond, UK: Curzon Press, 1997), 66.

12. See H. Cowell, *History and Constitution of the Courts and Legislative Authorities in India*, 2nd ed. (Calcutta: Thacker Spink, 1884), chap. 7, for a description of the back-and-forth between civil and revenue courts in Bengal.

13. W. H. Macnaghten, *Reports of Cases Determined in the Court of Sudder Dewanny Adawlat, with Tables of the Names of the Cases and Principal Matters*, vol. 1 (Calcutta: Bishop's College Press, 1827), 174. In 1802 the collector (official in charge of revenue administration) of Moorsheedabad (Murshidabad) brought a case against the claim that Bishennath and Sheonath Rai held land to the extent of 4,536 bighas (a bigha is a third of an acre) free of land tax obligations because it was devoted to a religious establishment. The grant had been made by Ranee Bhuwani, formerly zamindar of Rajshahy. But the maintenance of the religious establishment was to be done by her family. The zamindari had then been sold. What was the status of these 4,536 bighas, now in the possession of her grandsons? The collector's argument was twofold: first, the ranee could not make a grant to herself, and second, to the extent the grant had been made after the diwani (when the company took the reins of power) without the permission of the government, it was invalid. The defendants argued that the grant had been made before the diwani. The district courts ruled for the collector, arguing the ranee had perpetrated fraud by making a grant to herself. The provincial court disagreed and ruled in favor of the defendants, barring 888 bighas, which had been awarded after the diwani. On appeal by the collector to the Sudder Dewanny Adalat,

the highest relevant court, it added another 558 bighas to the 888. The remainder, roughly 72% of the disputed land, was ruled to be tax free.

14. Zamindars did complain about taxes imposed to pay for education and roads, in 1871. See N. Mukherjee, *A Bengal Zamindar: Jaykrishna Mukherjee of Uttarpara and His Times, 1808–1888* (Calcutta: Firma K. L. Mukopadhyay, 1975), 262–67.

15. A. N. Chowdhury-Zilly, *The Vagrant Peasant: Agrarian Distress and Desertion in Bengal, 1770 to 1830* (Wiesbaden: Franz Steiner Verlag, 1982).

16. A. Bhaduri, "The Evolution of Land Relations in Eastern India under British Rule," *Indian Economic and Social History Review* 13, no. 1 (1976): 45–53. In 1819 legislation was passed recognizing the rights of the *patnidar*, who had, in effect, received a permanent settlement of his own from the zamindar. A market for these rights developed.

17. B. Stein, *Thomas Munro: The Origins of the Colonial State and His Vision of Empire* (New York: Oxford University Press, 1989), provides a description of Munro's career and influence.

18. United Kingdom, House of Commons, *Report of the Select Committee of the House of Commons on the Affairs of the East India Company* (London: Cox and Son, 1833), 81, after declaring the Permanent Settlement in Bengal a failure, identified the reasons for this: a "mere hereditary steward" of the land or "Officer of the Government" had been declared the owner, and it had been assumed that "the rights of all parties claiming an interest in the Land were sufficiently established by usage to enable the Courts to protect individual rights." No "efficient measures" had been taken to prevent the zamindar from making exorbitant demands on his tenants.

19. N. Hatekar, "Information and Incentives: Pringle's Ricardian Experiment in the Nineteenth Century Deccan Countryside," *Indian Economic and Social History Review* 33, no. 4 (1996): 437–57.

20. See D. Kumar, *Land and Caste in South India: Agricultural Labour in the Madras Presidency during the Nineteenth Century* (New York: Cambridge University Press, 1965), for a detailed account of Raiyatwari in the Madras Presidency; and R. Kumar, *Western India in the Nineteenth Century* (London: Routledge and Kegan Paul, 1968), on the Bombay Presidency.

21. India, Department of Agriculture and Revenue, *Returns of Agricultural Statistics of British India* (Calcutta: Superintendent of Government Printing, 1886–90), 5–8.

22. Madras, *A Brief Report on the Entire Operations of the Inam Commission from its Commencement* (Madras: Government Press, 1869), 14.

23. Ibid., 4.

24. Ibid., 8.

25. Bombay, *Reports of Cases decided in the High Courts of Bombay 1873* (Bombay: Government Central Press, 1874), 471.

26. S. Islam, *The Permanent Settlement in Bengal: A Study of Its Operation, 1790–1819* (Dacca: Bangla Academy, 1979), 25.

27. P. J. Marshall, *Bengal: The British Bridgehead* (Cambridge: Cambridge University Press, 1987), 144.

28. See D. Kumar, *Land and Caste*, 93.

29. Acemoglu and Robinson, "Why Nations Fail."

30. D. Kumar, "The Fiscal System," in *The Cambridge Economic History of India*, vol. 2, *1757–1970*, ed. D. Kumar (New Delhi: Orient Longman, 1984), 905–44. Cited figures appear on 918.

31. As a proportion of GDP, governmental revenues for the period 1920–30 averaged 5% in India, 19% in the UK, and 29% in Japan; Tirthankar Roy, *The Economic History of India, 1857–1947* (New Delhi: Oxford University Press, 2011), 255.

32. Great Britain, House of Commons, *Revenue: Appendix to the Report from the Select Committee of the House of Commons on the Affairs of the East India Company, Minutes of Evidence* (London: J. L. Cox and Son, 1833), 131.

33. A. C. Banerjee and B. K. Ghosh, "Introduction," in *Bengal Ryots: Their Rights and Liabilities; Being an Elementary Treatise on the Law of Landlord and Tenant*, by Sunjeeb Chunder Chatterjee (Columbia, MO: South Asia Books, 1977), xiii.

34. Great Britain, House of Commons, *Revenue: Appendix to the Report*, 128.

35. A *pargana* is a set of villages, an administrative unit smaller than a district. S. Chatterjee, *Bengal Ryots*, 33.

36. Ibid., 35.

37. S. Islam, *The Permanent Settlement in Bengal*, 64.

38. S. Chatterjee, *Bengal Ryots*, 89.

39. Ibid., 90.

40. Mukherjee, *Bengal Zamindar*, 343.

41. R. Ray, *Change in Bengal Agrarian Society, c. 1760–1870* (New Delhi: Manohar, 1979).

42. Sharecroppers were cultivators who paid a fraction of the output, often half, as rent.

43. Ray, *Change in Bengal Agrarian Society*, 271.

44. F. Buchanan, *A Geographical, Statistical, and Historical Description of the District or Zila of Dinajpur, in the Province or Soubah of Bengal* (Calcutta: Baptist Mission Press, 1833).

45. Ibid., 236.

46. Ibid., 235.

47. Ibid., 238.

48. An alternative view is that the jotedar was more an agent of the zamindar than a rival. R. Datta, "Agricultural Production, Social Participation and Domination in Late Eighteenth-Century Bengal: Towards an Alternative Explanation," *Journal of Peasant Studies* 17, no. 1 (1989): 68–113. Still, the need to share surplus would dilute the zamindar's incentive to invest.

49. Macnaghten, *Reports of Cases*, 302.

50. These were tendencies rather than hard-and-fast rules. Tribals had been subject to Hindu cultural influences and sometimes did practice peasant agriculture. We revisit their situation in more detail in the next chapter.

51. J. C. Jha, *The Tribal Revolt of Chotanagpur* (Patna: Kashi Prasad Jayaswal Research Institute, 1987), 1; K. K. Datta, *Unrest against British Rule in Bihar, 1831–59* (Bihar: Superintendent Secretariat Press, 1957), 14.

52. Banerjee and Ghosh, "Introduction," xxxiii.

53. The darpatnidar was a creation of the process of subinfeudation, which had been given legal recognition. He or she was an intermediary between the zamindar and the cultivator, who held land in perpetuity subject to paying the fixed assigned rent to the next higher rung in the ladder of intermediaries. See *Ishwar Ghose v. James Hills*, September 24, 1862, in Bengal, High Court, *Decisions under the Rent Laws of the Court of the Sadr Dewani Adalat and the High Court of Judicature at Fort William in Bengal*, vol. 1 (Calcutta: George Wyman and Co., 1865), 77–84. Quoted text is on 77.

54. *Thakooranee Dossee v. Bisheshur Mookerjee and Others*, in L. A. Goodeve and J. V. Woodman, *Full Bench Rulings of the High Court at Fort William, from Its Institution In 1862 to the Commencement of the Bengal Law Reports* (Calcutta: Thacker Spink, 1874), 202–345. See A. Sen, "Agrarian Structure and Tenancy Laws in Bengal, 1850–1900," in

Perspectives in Social Sciences 2: Three Studies on the Agrarian Structure in Bengal, 1850–1947, ed. A. Sen, P. Chatterjee, and S. Mukherji (Delhi: Oxford University Press, 1982); and Rothermund, *Government, Landlord, and Peasant*, 99.

55. Goodeve and Woodman, *Full Bench Rulings*, 224, 225.

56. For discussion of the notion of custom in the context of the Great Rent Case as well as more broadly see A. Sartori, "A Liberal Discourse of Custom in Colonial Bengal," *Past and Present* 212 (2011): 163–97.

57. Goodeve and Woodman, *Full Bench Rulings*, 225.

58. Rothermund, *Government, Landlord, and Peasant*, 99.

59. K. K. Sen Gupta, "The Agrarian League of Pabna, 1873," *Indian Economic and Social History Review* 7, no. 3 (1970): 253–68; K. K. Sen Gupta, "Agrarian Disturbances in 19th Century Bengal," *Indian Economic and Social History Review* 8, no. 2 (1971): 192–212; K. K. Sen Gupta, "Bengali Intelligentsia and the Politics of Rent, 1873–1885," *Social Scientist* 3, no. 2 (1974): 27–34.

60. J. Dacosta, *Remarks and Extracts from Official Reports on the Bengal Tenancy Bill* (London: W. H. Allen, 1884). The quotations from the raja are on 43 and 44. On Darbhanga, see S. Henningham, "Bureaucracy and Control in India's Great Landed Estates: The Raj Darbhanga of Bihar, 1879 to 1950," *Modern Asian Studies* 17, no. 1 (1983): 35–55.

61. Dacosta, *Remarks and Extracts*, 38.

62. Ibid., 36.

63. Bengal, *Report of the Government of Bengal on the Proposed Amendment on the Law of Landlord and Tenant in that Province, With a Revised Bill and Appendices*, vol. 1 (Calcutta: Government Press, 1883), 9.

64. S. B. Cook argues that a group of officials of Irish descent, whose sympathies were with the tenant, had an important influence on the discussion. See *Imperial Affinities: Nineteenth Century Analogies and Exchanges between India and Ireland* (New Delhi: Sage Publications, 1993).

65. M. Finucane and R. F. Rampini, *The Bengal Tenancy Act: Being Act VIII of 1885, with Notes and Annotations, Judicial Rulings, and the Rules Made by the Local Government and the High Court, Under the Act, for the Guidance of Revenue Officers and the Civil Courts* (Calcutta: Thacker, Spink, and Co., 1886), chap. 5, sec. 20, pp. 61, 63.

66. Bengal, *Final Report on the Survey and Settlement Operations in the District of Jessore* (Calcutta: Bengal Secretariat Book Depot, 1925), 155.

67. Ibid., 124. In a famous gazetteer for the district of Bakarganj, J. C. Jack reported that abwabs were roughly a quarter of the rent. See Bengal, *Bengal District Gazetteers: Bakarganj* (Calcutta: Bengal Secretariat, 1918), 73.

68. Bengal, *Report on the Land Revenue Administration of the Presidency of Bengal for the Year 1934–35* (Calcutta: Bengal Secretariat Book Depot, 1935), 18.

69. Bengal, *Bengal District Gazetteers: Bakarganj*, 104.

70. Bengal, *Bengal District Gazetteers: Muzaffarpur* (Calcutta: Bengal Secretariat Book Depot, 1907), 125.

71. See the testimony of C. J. Mackay to the Civil Justice Committee in India, Civil Justice Committee, *Appendix No. 2: Oral evidence*, vol. 1, *Bengal, Assam, United Provinces* (Calcutta: Government of India Central Publication Branch, 1925), 7.

72. India, Civil Justice Committee, *Report* (Calcutta: Government of India Central Publication Branch, 1925), 541.

73. In 1938 the government of Bengal appointed the Land Revenue Commission, under Francis Floud, to study the land revenue system in Bengal. It is usually referred to as

the Floud Commission. Its influential report was published in 1940 as Bengal, *Report of the Land Revenue Commission Bengal* (Calcutta: Government Press, 1940). Cited text appears on 166.

74. Bengal, *Bengal District Gazetteers: Bakarganj*, 73.

75. Ibid., 95. Tapan Raychaudhuri, who used Jack's gazetteer extensively, highlighted the extraordinary levels of subinfeudation in Bakarganj, pointing out that there were 162 names for various types of tenures and subtenures. He argues that, in addition to land reclamation, the desire to enhance social status also drove the phenomenon of sub-infeudation. See T. Raychaudhuri, "Permanent Settlement in Operation, Bakarganj District, East Bengal," in *Land Control and Social Structure in Indian History*, ed. R. E. Frykenberg (Delhi: Manohar, 1979), 163–74.

76. Mukherjee, *Bengal Zamindar*, 91. To be sure, there are also many accounts of zamind-ars, in Bengal and elsewhere, who neglected their estates. See P. Price, "Warrior Caste 'Raja' and Gentleman 'Zamindar': One Person's Experience in the Late Nineteenth Century," *Modern Asian Studies* 17, no. 4 (1983): 563–90, for an account of a Madras zamindar for whom managing an estate would have been infra dig.

77. Mukherjee, *A Bengal Zamindar*, 102, goes so far as to say that in popularizing potato and sugarcane cultivation in Hooghly District the zamindar engineered what would today be called a green revolution.

78. Mukherjee, *A Bengal Zamindar*, 100.

79. M. Olson, *The Logic of Collective Action: Public Goods and the Theory of Groups* (Cambridge, MA: Harvard University Press, 1965).

80. G. A. Grierson, *Notes on the District of Gaya* (Calcutta: Bengal Secretariat, 1893), 80, emphasized the importance of incentives. According to him, landlords and tenants in Gaya did not lack "original sin"—it was "self-interest" that kept them cooperating.

81. B. B. Chaudhuri, "The Movement of Rents in Eastern India, 1793–1930," *Indian Historical Review* 3, no. 2 (1978): 308–90. Especially 333–36.

82. As the Permanent Settlement fell out of favor, after some zamindari estates defaulted in the Madras Presidency, the government converted them into raiyatwari.

83. Richard Clarke, *The Regulations of the Government of Fort St. George in Force at the End of 1847; to Which are Added the Acts of the Government of India in Force in that Presidency* (London: J. and H. Cox, 1848), 133.

84. Ibid., 422.

85. P. O'Sullivan and J. M. C. Mills, *Reports of the Cases Decided in the High Court of Madras in 1870 and 1871* (Madras: Higginbotham and Co., 1872), 164–74.

86. Ibid., 164.

87. Madras, *The Indian Law Reports Madras Series: Containing Cases Determined by the High Court at Madras and by the Judicial Committee of the Privy Council on Appeal from that Court*, vol. 13 (Madras: Government Press, 1890), 60–65.

88. Ibid., 64–65.

89. Madras, *The Indian Law Reports Madras Series: Containing Cases Determined by the High Court at Madras and by the Judicial Committee of the Privy Council on Appeal from that Court*, vol. 20 (Madras: Government Press, 1897), 299. Madras, *Madras Estates Land Act Committee (Main Report)* (Madras: Government Press, 1938), chap. 10, has a detailed discussion of these and other cases.

90. A raiyat was entitled to a permanent occupancy right on any land currently in his possession with an exception for "old waste," one component of which was land that had not been cultivated for ten years. See M. Krishnamacharaiar, *The Madras Estates*

Land Act: being Act I of 1908 as amended by Act IV of 1909, with commentaries, and an introduction, historical, analytical and critical (Madras: Government Press, 1917), x.

91. *Suryanarayana and Others v. Patanna and Others*, in Madras, *The Indian Law Reports Madras Series: Containing Cases Determined by the High Court at Madras and by the Judicial Committee of the Privy Council on Appeal from that Court*, vol. 41 (Madras: Government Press, 1918), 1012–21. Cited text is on page 1012. Madras, *Madras Estates Land Act Committee (Main Report)*, chap. 11 has a very detailed discussion of inams.

92. For a discussion of zamindar-tenant tensions in Tamil Nadu and the events leading up to the formation of the Prakasam Committee, see C. Baker, "Tamilnad Estates in the Twentieth Century," *Indian Economic and Social History Review* 13, no. 1 (1976): 1–44.

93. Madras, *Madras Estates Land Act Committee (Memoranda Submitted to the Committee Part II), (Raiyats)* (Madras: Government Press, 1938), 11.

94. Presumably, they had not supported their zamindar or his candidate. Ibid., 12.

95. Ibid., 180–81, 231, 239.

96. See, for instance, Madras, *Madras Estates Land Act Committee (Irrigation Reports from Zamindars)* (Madras: Government Press, 1938), 1, 5, 11.

97. The use of the certificate procedure was permitted to a much smaller extent in Bengal, and it was virtually eliminated in 1938.

98. Bengal, *Report of the Land Revenue Commission*, 163, 166.

99. Rothermund, *Government, Landlord, and Peasant*, 157.

100. H. R. Crosthwaite, *Report on the Land Revenue Settlement of the Jubbulpore District in the Central Provinces effected during the years 1907 to 1912* (Nagpur: Government Press, 1912), 26.

101. Rothermund, *Government, Landlord, and Peasant*, 129–38.

102. Bengal, *Report of the Government of Bengal on the Proposed Amendment on the Law of Landlord and Tenant in that Province*, 3.

103. D. Kumar, *Land and Caste*, 85.

104. *Seturatnam Aiyer v. Venkatachela Goundan and Others*, in Madras, *The Indian Law Reports Madras Series: Containing Cases Determined by the High Court at Madras and by the Judicial Committee of the Privy Council on Appeal from that Court*, vol. 43 (Madras: Government Press, 1920), 567–78. Quoted text is on 567.

105. In a classic paper Joseph Stiglitz argued that, on the one hand, a wage-labor arrangement, where payment is independent of effort, leaves the employer with the problem of monitoring his workers. On the other hand a fixed-rent arrangement gives the worker the right incentives, but exposes him to risk. Sharecropping is a good compromise. The argument assumes the absence of economies of scale. These did not emerge in India until later in the twentieth century, with tractors, combined harvesters, and the like. See Joseph Stiglitz, "Risk and Incentives in Sharecropping," *Review of Economic Studies* 41, no. 2 (1974): 219–55. For a discussion of tenancy in Punjab see N. Bhattacharya, "The Logic of Tenancy Cultivation: Central and South-East Punjab, 1870–1935," *Indian Economic and Social History Review* 20 (1983): 121–70.

106. H. S. M. Ishaque, *Agricultural Statistics by Plot to Plot Enumeration in Bengal, 1944–45*, pt. 1 (Calcutta: Government Press, 1946), 47. We computed the figure of 22% using totals provided in columns 12 of table 1 (for the numerator) and column 7 (for the denominator).

107. Bombay, *Statistical Atlas of Bombay State (Provincial Part)*, rev. ed. (Bombay: Bureau of Economics and Statistics, 1950), 58.

108. Ibid., 198. The authors computed the percentages from detailed figures provided here.
109. B. S. Baliga, *Studies in Madras Administration*, vol. 2 (Madras: India Press, 1960), 121.
110. P. Chatterjee, *Bengal, 1920–47: The Land Question* (Calcutta: K. P. Bagchi and Co., 1984), 82.
111. Washbrook, "Law, State and Agrarian Society," 656.
112. S. Kapur and S. Kim, "British Colonial Institutions and Economic Development in India" (NBER Working Paper 12613, 2006), provide evidence that raiyatwari areas were more productive in the colonial period. Their findings are subject to concerns about the quality of data on yields. See, for instance, A. Heston, "Official Yields per Acre in India: 1886–1947; Some Questions of Interpretation," *Indian Economic and Social History Review* 10, no. 4 (1973): 303–32; A. Heston, "A Further Critique of Historical Yields per Acre in India," *Indian Economic and Social History Review* 15, no. 2 (1978): 187–210.

CHAPTER FOUR

1. Letter to local governments and administrations from Denzil Ibbetson, officiating secretary to the government of India, October 26, 1895, in India, *Selection of Papers on Agricultural Indebtedness and the Restriction of the Power to Alienate Interests in Land*, vol. 1 (Simla: Government Press, 1898), 450. Ibbetson was quoting another official whom he identifies only as "a former Chief Commissioner of the Central Provinces."
2. See L. Dumont, "The 'Village Community' from Munro to Maine," *Contributions to Indian Sociology* 9 (1966): 67–89.
3. In some of the most quoted lines in Indian history, Charles Metcalfe wrote: "The village communities are little republics, having nearly everything they can want within themselves, and almost independent of any foreign relations. They seem to last where nothing else lasts." These lines are quoted in M. Elphinstone, *History of India*, vol. 1, 2nd ed. (London: John Murray, 1842), 123.
4. H. Maine, *Village-Communities in the East and West* (New York: Henry Holt and Company, 1889), 106.
5. Land had been transferable earlier as well, but less easily. The buyer was getting a share of collectively owned property, not necessarily a discrete piece of land. See S. Guha, *The Agrarian Economy of the Bombay Deccan, 1818–1941* (Delhi: Oxford University Press, 1985), 9.
6. See T. W. Coats, "An Account of the Present State of the Township of Lony: An Illustration of the Institutions, Resources and c. of the Marrata Cultivators," *Transactions of the Literary Society of Bombay* 3 (1823):183–220; R. Kumar, *Western India in the Nineteenth Century* (London: Routledge and Kegan Paul, 1968); A. Steele, *The Law and Custom of Hindoo Castes within the Dekhun Provinces subject to the Presidency of Bombay chiefly affecting Civil Suits* (London: W. H. Allen, 1868).
7. As we will see below, richer regions relied more heavily on indigenous lenders.
8. Steele, *Law and Custom of Hindoo Castes*, in his compilation of "Customary Law," reports on page 265 that village councils would require repayment "according to the debtor's circumstances."
9. For an analysis of damdupat, see M. Oak and A. V. Swamy, "Only Twice as Much: A Rule for Regulating Lenders," *Economic Development and Cultural Change* 58, no. 4 (2010): 775–803.
10. See P. V. Kane, *History of Dharmasastra* (*Ancient and Medieval Religious and Civil Law*) (Poona: Bhandarkar Oriental Research Institute, 1962).
11. D. Hardiman, *Feeding the Baniya: Peasants and Usurers in Western India* (Delhi: Oxford

University Press, 1996), 108. Family lore has it that the grandfather of one of the authors of the present work, who hailed from this region, upheld his Pious Obligation after his father's death in the influenza epidemic of 1919, even though this was no longer required by law.

12. W. H. Sykes, "Administration of Civil Justice in British India for a period of Four Years, chiefly from 1845 to 1848, both years inclusive," *Journal of the Statistical Society of London* 16 (1853): 103–36; see 123. Sykes noted that in the period 1845–48, only 0.07% of 336, 968 cases decided were adjudicated by panchayats and describes them as "scarcely operative."

13. Bombay, *Report of the Committee on the Riots in Poona and Ahmednagar 1875* (Bombay: Government Press, 1876), 31. The "facility" that seems to have most troubled Wingate was the lender's right to seize land in lieu of repayment. The threat of imprisonment of the debtor was not a source of controversy.

14. See David Washbrook, "Law, State and Agrarian Society in Colonial India," *Modern Asian Studies* 15, no. 3 (1981): 686.

15. T. Metcalf, *Ideologies of the Raj* (Cambridge: Cambridge University Press, 1995), 66. The Raj was happy to borrow from British precedent when it came to the factory or the corporation, as we discuss in later chapters.

16. W. B. Oldham, referring to his tenure as deputy commissioner of the Santhal Parganas, lamented that the tribals had been given "this new and fatal boon of transferability." India, *Selection of Papers on Agricultural Indebtedness*, 3:303.

17. I. J. Catanach, *Rural Credit in Western India, 1875–1930: Rural Credit and the Cooperative Movement in the Bombay Presidency* (Berkeley: University of California Press, 1970). N. Charlesworth, "The Myth of the Deccan Riots of 1875," *Modern Asian Studies* 6, no. 4 (1972): 401–21; see 416. Charlesworth moderated his position in a later work, *Peasants and Imperial Rule: Agriculture and Agrarian Society in the Bombay Presidency, 1850–1935* (Cambridge: Cambridge University Press, 1985).

18. Bombay, *Report of the Deccan Agriculturists' Relief Commission* (Bombay: Government Press, 1912), 6, argued that "a large number of saokars [professional moneylenders], including of course the best, have wound up, or are winding up their business with agriculturists."

19. L. Chaudhary and A. Swamy, "Protecting the Borrower: An Experiment in Colonial India" (mimeo, Williams College, MA, 2014). This section of the paper draws on this joint work, and we thank Latika Chaudhary for her help. We have also drawn on R. Kranton and A. V. Swamy, "The Hazards of Piecemeal Reform: British Civil Courts and the Credit Market in Colonial India," *Journal of Development Economics* 58, no. 1 (1999): 1–24.

20. S. Cole, "Fixing Market Failures or Fixing Elections? Agricultural Credit in India," *American Economic Journal: Applied Economics* 1, no. 1 (2009): 219–50.

21. Quoted in India, *Note on Land Transfer and Agricultural Indebtedness in India* (Simla: Government Press, 1895), 65.

22. S. S. Raghavaiyangar, *Memorandum on the Progress of the Madras Presidency during the last forty years of British Administration* (Madras: Government Press, 1883), 309. Raghavaiyangar has been viewed very negatively by critics of British rule, who view him as biased in its favor. This does not worry us in this context; if anything, this makes his criticism of the high costs associated with the British-introduced judicial system more persuasive.

23. Ibid., app. VI, E, pp. cccxvi–cccxvii.

24. Ibid., 309.

25. See, for instance, the high costs of screening of borrowers and administration for informal lenders, as described by I. Aleem, "Imperfect Information, Screening, and the Costs of Informal Lending: A Study of a Rural Credit Market in Pakistan," *World Bank Economic Review* 4, no. 3 (1990): 329–49. Microfinance lenders today typically charge in excess of 20% per annum, see A. Banerjee et al., "The Miracle of Microfinance? Evidence from a Randomized Evaluation," *American Economic Journal: Applied Economics* 7, no. 1 (2015): 22–53.

26. This is subject to the caveats regarding the power of the tenant and tenants paying fixed rents, as discussed in the previous chapter.

27. In the early years land may not have had much value because of high land taxes. See A. Bhaduri, "The Evolution of Land Relations in Eastern India under British Rule," *Indian Economic and Social History Review* 13, no. 1 (1976): 45–53. But over the nineteenth century, the burden of land taxes fell dramatically. Such restrictions as there were on the transfer of zamindari lands came when the state stepped in to preserve a zamindari when it was disintegrating due to mismanagement or until a minor came of age.

28. This and the previous quote are from Letter 3565 L.R. dated July 16,1894, from C. E. Buckland, secretary to the government of Bengal to secretary of the government of India, Revenue and Agricultural Department, in India, *Selection of Papers on Agricultural Indebtedness*, 1:284.

29. India, *Selection of Papers on Agricultural Indebtedness*, 1:290. Ironically, the agriculturist-moneylender of Bengal was later, in independent India, identified as central to a "semifeudal" structure that was inhibiting growth. A. Bhaduri, "A Study in Agricultural Backwardness under Semi-feudalism," *Economic Journal* 83 (1973): 120–37, argued that the rich peasant lender was also a landlord, who earned rents as well as interest from his sharecroppers. Increases in his sharecropper's output could be harmful to the rich peasant, because they might reduce his interest receipts.

30. India, *Selection of Papers on Agricultural Indebtedness*, 1:285.

31. Bengal, *Indian Law Reports*, Calcutta Series, vol. 23 (Calcutta, 1896), 179–86.

32. Ibid., 180.

33. Ibid. Both quotes are from page 186.

34. This paragraph is based on H. McPherson, *Final Report on the Survey and Settlement Operations in the District of the Sonthal Parganas, 1898–1907* (Calcutta: Secretariat Book Depot, 1909), and all the quotations are from page 40.

35. Also, an interest rate ceiling of 24% was imposed, damdupat was put in place, and compound interest was banned. Ibid., 40.

36. Ibid., 135.

37. Ibid., 138.

38. Ibid., 139.

39. Also see M. C. McAlpin, *Report on the Condition of the Sonthals in the Districts of Birbhum, Bankura, Midnapore and North Balasore* (Calcutta: Firma K. L. Mukhopadhyay, 1981, first published 1909); H. M. L. Allanson, *Final Report on the Survey and Settlement Operations in the District of Sonthal Parganas (Third Programme), 1898–1910* (Calcutta: Bengal Secretariat Press, 1912).

40. We adapt this classification from R. Fox, *Lions of the Punjab: Culture in the Making* (Berkeley: University of California Press, 1985), 28. Any such categorization is somewhat arbitrary. This one does not include hill districts like Kangra.

41. The first of these projects was begun in 1886, and all but one was completed by 1921: I. Ali, *The Punjab under Imperialism, 1885–1947* (Princeton, NJ: Princeton University

Press, 1988), 9; and I. Ali, "Malign Growth? Agricultural Colonization and the Roots of Backwardness in the Punjab," *Past and Present* 114 (1987): 114.

42. Grants of land in the Canal Colonies were a rich resource of patronage for the Raj and they were used to consolidate its power in Punjab, which was disproportionately represented in the British-Indian army. See Ali, *Punjab under Imperialism* for a good discussion.

43. G. Campbell, "Tenure of Land in India," in *Systems of Land Tenure in Various Countries*, by Cobden Club (London: Macmillan and Co., 1870), 195. As in the raiyatwari areas, theory could deviate from practice, and, in concessions to facts on the ground, ownership rights were conferred on some holders of large areas of land, especially in southwestern Punjab.

44. B. H. Baden-Powell, *A Manual of the Land Revenue Systems and Land Tenures of British India* (Calcutta: Government Press, 1882), 413.

45. Ibid., 404.

46. Fox, *Lions of the Punjab*, 120.

47. See D. Gilmartin, *Empire and Islam: Punjab and the Making of Pakistan* (Berkeley: University of California Press, 1988), chap. 1, for a discussion of the notion of "tribes" in Punjab.

48. Customary law in the context of shared property rights was especially relevant for common land and "waste" in the Punjab. See M. Chakravarty-Kaul, *Common Lands and Customary Law: Institutional Change in North India over the Past Two Centuries.* (Delhi: Oxford University Press, 1996).

49. Compiled by J. M. Douie, *Punjab Land Administration Manual*, rev. ed. (Lahore: Government Press, 1931), 6. Also see H. C. Calvert, *Wealth and Welfare of the Punjab: Being Some Studies in Punjab Rural Economics* (Lahore: Civil and Military Gazette Press, 1922), 123–24.

50. Calvert, *Wealth and Welfare*, 123.

51. Douie, *Punjab Land Administration*, 7.

52. In *Nadir Ali Shah v. Wali* the high court in Lahore considered the following dispute. Nadir Ali Shah had received a small amount of land, eight kanals (an acre) as "gift" from Khanun in 1918. He then bought a much larger amount, two hundred kanals, from Amir in 1919. Wali later claimed the right to preempt and buy both properties and filed two suits. Regarding the eight kanals, judgments were passed in Wali's favor. But what about the second purchase? Nadir Ali Shah's argument was that at the time he made the second purchase he was in possession of land in the village, and as such, could not be preempted. Wali's argument was that since the Nadir Ali Shah's first purchase only gave him a "defeasible right" that was subsequently declared invalid, he really had no right at all. The high court argued that there was nothing in the Punjab Pre-Emption Act to "qualify the term 'owner' so as to mean a person who was not in danger of losing his right at the suit of a pre-emptor." So Nadir Ali Shah's ploy worked, and his purchase of the two hundred kanals was declared valid. The Punjab Pre-Emption Act of 1913 was amended in 1928 with the explicit intention of preventing such ruses. See Ibid, 10; and Punjab, *Indian Law Reports Lahore Series: Containing Cases Determined by the High Court at Lahore and by the Judicial Committee of the Privy Council on Appeal from that Court*, vol. 5 (Lahore: Government Book Depot, 1924), 486–91.

53. Punjab, High Court, *Note on the Administration of Civil Justice in the Punjab* (Lahore: Superintendent of Government Printing, 1939), 1.

54. See Calvert, *Wealth and Welfare*, chap. 8. An official named S. S. Thorburn explicitly

compared Punjab in 1872 with the Bombay Deccan in 1852 in *Musalmans and Money-Lenders in the Punjab* (Edinburgh: William Blackwood and Sons, 1886), 62.

55. India, *Note on Land Transfer*, 48.

56. India, *Selection of Papers on Agricultural Indebtedness*, 2:2.

57. Ibid., 2. Italics and quotation marks are in the original.

58. For instance, permission might be given if the buyer was planning to open a factory. A deathbed gift to Brahmin might be permitted, subject to a ceiling on the amount (Douie, *Punjab Land Administration*, 13, 14).

59. Douie, *Punjab Land Administration*, 8.

60. See the 1900 version of the act and commentary in S. G. Singh, *The Punjab Land Alienation Act (XIII of 1900)* (Lahore: Albion Press, 1901), 20.

61. This paragraph is based on Douie, *Punjab Land Administration*, 15–16.

62. G. Cassan, "Identity Based Policies and Identity Manipulation: Evidence from Colonial Punjab," *American Economic Journal: Economic Policy* 7, no. 4 (2015): 103–31; M. M. Islam, "The Punjab Land Alienation Act and the Professional Moneylenders," *Modern Asian Studies* 29, no. 2 (1995): 271–91.

63. See Punjab, *Report on the Administration of Civil Justice in the Punjab and Its Dependencies during the Year 1905* (Lahore: Civil and Military Gazette Press, 1906), 5. The figure rose slightly for the next two years to 61,072 and 70, 289. The report for 1908 attributes this change in trend partly to a change in classification, and partly to a rumor that the extension on limitation passed in the Punjab Act of 1904 had been eliminated by the Indian Limitation Act of 1908. See Punjab, *Report on the Administration of Civil Justice in the Punjab and Its Dependencies during the Year 1908* (Lahore: Civil and Military Gazette Press, 1909), 2.

64. Ibid., 2. The report also notes, on the same page, that in Gujranwala as well, "the old moneylender is gradually being replaced by the agriculturist."

65. B. Singh and H. C. Calvert, *An Inquiry into Mortgages of Agricultural Land in the Kot Kapura Utar Assessment Circle of the Ferozepur District in the Punjab* (Lahore: Civil and Military Gazette Press, 1925).

66. Punjab, *Report of the Punjab Provincial Banking Enquiry Committee* (Lahore: Government Press, 1930), 117.

67. Calvert, *Wealth and Welfare*, 128. Some of the increase in numbers must reflect inflation. The real value of a thousand rupees was falling.

68. M. Darling, *Punjab Peasant in Prosperity and Debt* (Columbia, MO: South Asia Books, 1978; first published 1947). The ratios reported in the text are computed from the table on page 18.

69. The figures for other regions were Madras, 0.91; Bengal, 0.41; Bombay, 0.53; Bihar and Orissa, 1.29; North-West Frontier, 1.69; Delhi and Ajmer-Merwara, 2.25; and Central Provinces and Berar, 0.46.

70. The ratio of mortgage debt to total agricultural debt was 43% in Punjab, which was in no way exceptional compared to other regions (Berar, 61.5%; United Provinces, 56%; Madras, 50%; Bengal, 45%; Bihar and Orissa, 40%; Bombay Presidency, 28% to 36%; Sind, 27.5%; and Central Provinces including Berar, 27.5%). Also, the Punjab figure pertains only to usufructuary mortgages. Malcolm Darling, *Punjab Peasant*, 8, urges caution in using these figures and merely provides them to suggest that Punjab was not "abnormal."

71. India, Civil Justice Committee, *Report* (Calcutta: Government of India Central Publication Branch, 1925), 16.

72. These figures pertain to cases where small-cause procedures, which could expedite the process, were not used. See Civil Justice (Rankin) Committee, *Report*, 16–17.

73. Madras, *Report of the Madras Provincial Banking Enquiry Committee* (Madras: Government Press, 1930), 181.

74. In the Madras Presidency, in mofussil courts outside of village courts, decrees were fully executed in only 16.56% of cases. In another 7% they were partly executed, and in the remaining cases they were totally infructuous. The percentage of totally infructuous decrees was also high in subordinate courts in Lahore (48%), Allahabad (41%), and Central Provinces and Berar (47%). See India, Civil Justice Committee, *Report*, 376.

75. This was common practice for professional trader-lenders, who were usually reluctant to get involved in agricultural production. For an exception see D. Cheesman, *Landlord Power and Rural Indebtedness in Colonial Sind, 1865–1901* (Richmond, Surrey: Curzon Press, 1997), 64.

76. Bengal, *Report of the Bengal Provincial Banking Enquiry* (Calcutta: Government Press, 1930), 174.

77. Bombay, *Report of the Bombay Provincial Banking Enquiry Committee* (Bombay: Government Press, 1930), 188.

78. Elizabeth Whitcombe has a fascinating discussion of how zamindars in the United Provinces used legal or other means to obstruct the new owner of their property. *Agrarian Conditions in Northern India*, vol. 1, *The United Provinces under British Rule, 1860–1900* (Berkeley: University of California Press, 1972), 227–31.

79. Madras, *Report of the Madras Provincial Banking Enquiry*, 177.

80. Central Provinces, *Report of the Central Provinces Provincial Banking Enquiry Committee, 1929–30* (Nagpur: Government Press, 1930), 88.

81. Calcutta High Court, *Calcutta Law Journal* 4 (1906): 22–37. Quoted text is on page 24.

82. Madras, *Report of the Madras Provincial Banking Enquiry*, 179.

83. Bengal, *Report of the Bengal Provincial Banking Enquiry*, 165.

84. Madras, *Report of the Madras Provincial Banking Enquiry*, 173.

85. Ibid., 174.

86. Bengal, *Report of the Bengal Provincial Banking Enquiry*, 165.

87. Ibid., 166.

88. Ibid., 176.

89. These included the Punjab Regulation of Accounts Act of 1930, the Madras Debtors' Protection Act of 1934, the Bihar Moneylenders' Act of 1938, the U.P. Usurious Loans Act of 1934, the Punjab Relief of Indebtedness Act of 1934, the C.P. [Central Provinces] and Berar Relief of Indebtedness Act of 1939, the Madras Agriculturists' Relief Act of 1938, the Assam Debt Conciliation Act of 1936, and the U.P. Agriculturists' Relief Act of 1934 (Reserve Bank of India, *All-India Rural Credit Survey: Report of the Committee of Direction*, vol. 2, *The General Report* [Bombay: Reserve Bank of India, 1954], 122; K. G. Sivaswamy, *Legislative Protection and Relief of Agriculturist Debtors in India* [Poona: Gokhale Institute of Politics and Economics, 1939], 202, 217, 260).

90. Bengal, Legislative Department, *The Bengal Agricultural Debtors Act, 1935* (Calcutta: Government Press, 1936), 10.

91. Ibid., 7.

92. Ibid., 11.

93. See, for instance, Bengal, High Court, *Report on the Administration of Civil Justice in the Province of Bengal in 1938* (Calcutta: Government Press, 1939), 6.

94. Reserve Bank of India, *All-India Rural Credit Survey*, 123.
95. Ibid., 124.
96. Ibid.
97. This instance is described in Chaudhary and Swamy, "Protecting the Borrower."

CHAPTER FIVE

1. W. A. Montriou, *Cases of Hindu Law before H. M. Supreme Court, during the first Thirty Years of the Court's Establishment* (Calcutta: D'Rozario and Co., 1853), 338.
2. "Testamentary": related to a will.
3. T. Besley and M. Ghatak, "Property Rights and Economic Development." In *Handbook of Development Economics*, vol. 5, ed. Dani Rodrik and Mark Rosenzweig (Amsterdam: North-Holland, 2010), 4525–94.
4. It is difficult to give the word "coparcener" more precise legal content because of differences within Hindu law on the nature of the right, among other reasons.
5. R. Birla, *Stages of Capital: Law, Culture, and Market Governance in Late Colonial India* (Durham, NC: Duke University Press, 2006), 5.
6. See, for example, E. Newbigin, *The Hindu Family and the Emergence of Modern India: Law, Citizenship and Community* (Cambridge: Cambridge University Press, 2013); and for an extension of the idea to the area of women's property, R. Sturman, *The Government of Social Life in Colonial India: Liberalism, Religious Law and Women's Rights* (Cambridge: Cambridge University Press, 2012).
7. For more discussion, T. Roy, *Company of Kinsmen: Enterprise and Community in South Asian History* (New Delhi: Oxford University Press, 2010).
8. A. C. Mitra, *The Hindu Law of Inheritance, Partition, Stridhan, and Wills with leading cases from 1825 to 1888* (Calcutta: Calcutta Central Press, 1888), 3.
9. Agnatic relations are descendants (male or female, by blood or adopted) from a common male ancestor; cognates are descendants through females.
10. Prossonno Coomar Tagore, *Table of Succession according to Hindu Law of Bengal* (Calcutta: Albion Press, 1864).
11. J. Cochrane, *Hindu Law: Defence of the Daya Bhaga* (London: W. H. Allen, 1872).
12. Ibid., 430.
13. Nemai Churn Mullick, Sudder Dewanny judgment, cited by Cochrane, *Hindu Law*, 12.
14. For a large compilation see A. C. Mitra, *Hindu Law*.
15. R. West and H. R. Abdul Majid, *A Digest of the Hindu Law of Inheritance, Partition, and Adoption Embodying the Replies of the Sastris with Introductions and Notes* (London: Sweet and Maxwell, 1919), 4.
16. *Myna Boyee v. Ootaram*, cited in West and Majid, *Digest*.
17. T. Strange, *Responsa Prudentum or Opinions of Pundits*, vol. 2 of 2 (London: Payne and Foss, 1825), 369.
18. Montriou, *Cases of Hindu Law*.
19. *John Cochrane v. Hurrehkishno Daas, Bhowani Daas and Duarcah Dass*, in Montriou, *Cases of Hindu Law*, 360–63.
20. Strange, *Responsa Prudentum*, 2:17.
21. Ibid., 2:342–43.
22. Ibid. 2:220.
23. J. B. Norton, *A Selection on the Hindu Law of Inheritance* (Madras: C. D'Cruz, 1870).
24. Ibid., 267–69.
25. Anon., "The memorial of Ramchunder Surmona, late Professor of Law in the Sanscrit

College, Calcutta, to the Court of Directors of the East-India Company," pamphlet (Calcutta: William Rushton, 1838)

26. E. Perry, *Cases Illustrative of Oriental Life, the Application of English Law to India, Decided in H. M. Supreme Court at Bombay* (London: S. Sweet, 1853), 138.

27. See L. A. Goodeve and J. A. Woodman, *Full Bench Rulings of the High Court at Fort William, from Its Institution In 1862 to the Commencement of the Bengal Law Reports* (Calcutta: Thacker Spink, 1874), 48–53.

28. The 1849 judgment is discussed in Perry, *Cases*, 133–38.

29. Ibid., 144.

30. A. A. A. Fyzee, *Outlines of Muhammadan Law*, 5th ed. (New Delhi: Oxford University Press, 2009), 45.

31. Ibid., 46–47.

32. Perry, *Cases*, 113–14.

33. *Gossain*, colloquial variant of *goswami*, is a term for Vaishnavite sects.

34. On cases involving such issues, see A. C. Mitra, *Hindu Law*, 16–20.

35. B. K. Acharya, *Codification in British India* (Calcutta: S. K. Banerji and Sons, 1914), 269.

36. Ibid., 318.

37. Ibid., 230.

38. C. Ilbert, *The Government of India: Being a Digest of the Statute Law Relating Thereto* (Oxford: Clarendon Press, 1907), 335.

39. J. Pouchepadass, *Land, Power and Market: A Bihar District under Colonial Rule* (New Delhi: Sage, 2000).

40. J. A. Schoenblum, "The Role of Legal Doctrine in the Decline of the Islamic Waqf: A Comparison with the Trust," *Vanderbilt Journal of Transnational Law* 32 (1999): 1191–1227.

41. T. Kuran and A. Singh, "Economic Modernization in Late British India: Hindu-Muslim Differences," *Economic Development and Cultural Change* 61, no. 3 (2013): 503–38.

42. Asaf A. A. Fyzee, "Recent Developments in Muhammadan Law in India," *International and Comparative Law Quarterly* 13, supplement (1964): 46–50. Cited text appears on 47, 50.

43. Schoenblum, "Role of Legal Doctrine." Cited text appears on 1208.

44. G. C. Kozlowsky, cited by Schoenblum, "Role of Legal Doctrine," 1223.

45. Fyzee, "Recent Developments."

46. India, *Seventh Report on the Transfer of Property Act 1882* (Delhi: Law Commission, 1977), 11.

CHAPTER SIX

1. India, *Abridged Report of the Royal Commission on Agriculture in India* (Bombay: Government Press, 1928); India, *Report of the Royal Commission on Labour in India* (London: HMSO, 1931).

2. India, *Report of the Royal Commission on Labour*, 323.

3. In Coorg (Kodagu), in southern India, penal contracts were permitted until 1931. The Employers and Workmen (Disputes) Act of 1860 was formally repealed only in 1932 but was not in use. M. Anderson, "India, 1850–1930: The Illusion of Free Labor," in *Masters, Servants, and Magistrates in Britain and the Empire, 1562–1955*, ed. D. Haynes and P. Craven (Chapel Hill: University of North Carolina Press, 2004), 422–54. See footnote 152 on page 448.

4. India, *Abridged Report of the Royal Commission on Agriculture*, 434.
5. E. Domar, "The Causes of Slavery and Serfdom: A Hypothesis," *Journal of Economic History* 30, no. 1 (1970): 18–32.
6. D. Galenson, "The Rise of Free Labor: Economic Change and the Enforcement of Service Contracts in England, 1351–1875," in *Capitalism in Context: Essays on Economic Development and Cultural Change in Honor of R. M. Hartwell*, ed. J. A. James and M. Thomas (Chicago: University of Chicago Press. 1994), 115.
7. See, for instance, D. Kumar, *Land and Caste in South India: Agricultural Labour in the Madras Presidency during the Nineteenth Century* (Cambridge: Cambridge University Press, 1965); B. Hjejle, "Slavery and Agricultural Bondage in South India in the Nineteenth Century," *Scandinavian Economic History Review* 15, nos. 1–2 (1967): 71–126; and I. Chatterjee and R. Eaton, eds., *Slavery and South Asian History* (Bloomington: Indiana University Press, 2006).
8. See P. Bardhan, "Labor-Tying in a Poor Agrarian Economy: A Theoretical and Empirical Analysis," *Quarterly Journal of Economics* 98, no. 3 (1983): 501–14, for a model of labor tying along these lines.
9. R. K. Das, *History of Indian Labour Legislation* (Calcutta: University of Calcutta, 1941), 159–60, lists the names used for bonded laborers in different locations, including *hali* in Gujarat, *kamiauti* in Bihar, and *vetti* in parts of the Madras Presidency. J. Breman, "The Hali System in South Gujarat," in *The World of the Rural Laborer in Colonial India*, ed. Gyan Prakash (Bombay: Oxford University Press, 1992); and G. Prakash, *Bonded Histories: Genealogies of Labor Servitude in Colonial India* (Cambridge: Cambridge University Press, 1990), are widely cited works on Gujarat and South Bihar, respectively. U. Patnaik and M. Dingwaney, eds., *Chains of Servitude: Bondage and Slavery in India* (Madras: Sangam Books, 1985), provide a bibliography with many useful references from both colonial and postcolonial periods.
10. On Madras, R. Ahuja, "The Origins of Colonial Labor Policy in Late Eighteenth-Century Madras," *International Review of Social History* 44, no. 2 (1999): 159–95; and R. Ahuja, "Labor Relations in Early Colonial Madras, c. 1750–1800," *Modern Asian Studies* 36, no. 4 (2002): 793–826.
11. According to Ahuja, "Origins," 183–84, "Police Regulations" were passed in 1811, modeled on English law, including vagrancy acts. The company resorted to forced labor in Bengal as well, especially when troops were on the march. Legal sanction for this was provided by a Bengal regulation passed in 1806; Das, *History*, 161. Though these regulations were later modified, a Bengal zamindar complained in 1847 that rules prohibiting use of forced labor were "mere moonshine." This episode is described in detail in N. Mukherjee, *A Bengal Zamindar: Jaykrishna Mukherjee of Uttarpara and His Times, 1808–1888* (Calcutta: Firma K. L. Mukopadhyay, 1975), 116. See Anderson, "India," 429n42, for a discussion of coercive regulation in early nineteenth-century Bombay.
12. N. G. Cassels, "Social Legislation under the Company Raj: The Abolition of Slavery, Act V of 1843," *South Asia* 11, no. 1 (1988): 59–87.
13. D. Kumar, *Land and Caste*, 68.
14. Hjejle, "Slavery and Agricultural Bondage."
15. Ibid.
16. Prakash, *Bonded Histories*, argues that the identification of slavery as a feature of Indian social relations was one dimension of its identification as "Other" by company and Raj. They viewed debt bondage, in contrast, as a more tolerable contract into which the laborer enters voluntarily. Prakash questions the link between the

debt and unfreedom of the *kamia* (bonded laborer) of South Bihar, arguing that this connection itself was a creation of colonial-era discourse and legislation.

17. Madras, *Report of the Administration of the Madras Presidency, during the years 1879–80* (Madras: Government Press, 1880), app. B, pp. xxxviii and xl.

18. Prakash, *Bonded Histories*, 169.

19. Das, *History*, 161.

20. India, *Abridged Report of the Royal Commission on Agriculture*, 435. For a very recent description of bonded labor among granite workers in India, see Liberty Voice, "Slavery in India," October 18, 2013, http://guardianlv.com/2013/10/slavery-in-india -bonded-labor, accessed May 5, 2014.

21. Galenson, "Rise of Free Labor"; and R. J. Steinfeld, *Coercion, Contract and Free Labor in the Nineteenth Century* (Cambridge: Cambridge University Press, 2001).

22. Master-and-servant law was not just on paper. It was used extensively. See S. Naidu and N. Yuchtman, "Coercive Contract Enforcement: Law and the Labor Market in Nineteenth Century Industrial Britain," *American Economic Review* 103, no. 1, (2013): 107–44.

23. Das, *History*, 257.

24. Anderson, "India," 432n55.

25. For a list of locations where the WBOC was used, see Anderson, "India," 431n52. Section 492 of the Indian Penal Code also permitted a month of imprisonment for breach of contract by a worker whose transportation over a long distance had been paid by an employer. This was repealed in 1925. It was used to a lesser extent than the WBOC.

26. See D. Galenson, "The Rise and Fall of Indentured Servitude in the Americas," *Journal of Economic History* 44, no. 1 (1984): 1–26; and F. Grubb, "The Statutory Regulation of Involuntary Servitude: An Incomplete Contract Approach," *Explorations in Economic History* 37 (2000): 42–75.

27. See R. P. Behal, *One Hundred Years of Servitude: Political Economy of Tea Plantations in Colonial Assam* (New Delhi: Tulika Books, 2014), for a comprehensive history of tea plantations in the Brahmaputra Valley.

28. See B. Gupta and A. V. Swamy, "Unfree Labor: Did Indenture Reduce Labor Supply to Tea Plantations in Assam?" (mimeo, University of Warwick, 2014). This section of this chapter draws heavily on this ongoing joint work. We thank Bishnupriya Gupta for her help.

29. In principle, of course, the worker could also go home. This was less likely, given the distances and costs involved.

30. The exception was Sylhet, in the Surma Valley, where it was extended a few years later. P. Griffiths, *The History of the Indian Tea Industry* (London: Weidenfield and Nicholson, 1967), 269.

31. Ibid., 270.

32. Clause 172 of the act as of 1893 specified that the right to private arrest was available only if there was no magistrate within five miles. David Crole, *Tea: A Textbook of Tea Planting and Manufacture* (London: Crosby, Lockwood, and Son, 1897), 220.

33. These articles were compiled and published in 1972 in K. L. Chattopadhyay and S. K. Kundu, eds., *Slavery in British Dominion*, by D. Ganguli (Calcutta: Jijnasa, 1972). The first quotation is on a page without a number, after xii. The next two are on pages 42 and 44, respectively.

34. J. Buckingham and C. Dowding, *Tea-garden Coolies in Assam: A letter by the Hon'ble J. Buckingham, . . . replying to a communication on the subject, which appeared in the*

"Indian churchman"; *The whole reprinted with introduction and an answer by the Rev. Charles Dowding* (London: W. Thacker, 1894).

35. F. A. Hetherington, *The Diary of A Tea Planter* (Sussex, England: Book Guild Limited, 1994), 92. Cited in Gupta and Swamy, "Unfree Labor."

36. See A. R. Ramsden, *Assam Planter: Tea Planting and Hunting in the Assam Jungle* (London: J. Gifford Limited, 1945); J. Kinney, *Old Times in Assam* (Calcutta: Star Press, 1896), 91; and W. Fraser, *Recollections of a Tea Planter* (London: Tea and Rubber Mail, 1935).

37. See R. P. Behal and P. Mohapatra, "Tea and Money versus Human Life: The Rise and Fall of the Indenture System in the Assam Tea Plantations, 1840–1908," in *Plantations, Peasants and Proletarians in Colonial Asia*, ed. E. Valentine Daniel, H. Bernstein, and T. Brass (London: Frank Cass, 1992), for a detailed discussion of the labor shortage issue.

38. Griffiths, *History*, 278.

39. Quoted in India, *Report of the Assam Labour Enquiry Committee, 1906* (Calcutta: Government Press, 1906), 3.

40. Gupta and Swamy, "Unfree Labor," note that among adult workers imported in 1899, 12.5% and 90% were under the Special Act in Surma and Brahmaputra Valleys, respectively.

41. Ibid.

42. India, *Report of the Assam Labour Enquiry Committee, 1906*, 4.

43. Anderson, "India," 448.

44. R. P. Behal, "Power Structure, Discipline, and Labour in Assam Tea Plantations under Colonial Rule," *International Review of Social History* 51, no. 2 (2006): 143–72. See pages 168–69.

45. Griffiths, *History*, 282.

46. See Eastern Bengal and Assam, *Report of the Duars Committee 1910* (Shillong: Government Press, 1910), 17.

47. Ibid., 60.

48. W. Grey, manager of Nakhati Tea Estate in the Dooars, had also spent fifteen months managing an estate in Lakhimpur in Assam's Brahmaputra Valley, where, as we have noted, the harsh Special Act was widely used. He told the Duars Committee: "I have experience of Assam and consider that the Duars system is far preferable. The managers prefer it and the coolies prefer it." Ibid., 63. Also see managers' comments on pages 68, 69, 71, 72.

49. Ibid., 44.

50. Official reports and nationalist critics differed in their sense of how effectively these regulations were enforced. A report on the working of the Special Act claimed there were a very small number of complaints for 1888–89. For instance, there were only six cases of alleged "forcible or fraudulent recruitment" in Sibsagar in Upper Assam, which had a labor population of eighty thousand. See India, *Special Report on the Working of Act 1 of 1882 in the Province of Assam during the Years 1886–89* (Calcutta: Government Press, 1890), 31. In contrast, an article in the *Bengalee* in 1886 by Dwarkanath Ganguli reported that the procedures for ensuring that workers understood their contracts were perfunctory (Chattopadhyay and Kundu, *Slavery*, 4) and argued, no doubt with some exaggeration, that "it is doubtful if one in a thousand knows what Assam really is."

51. India, *Special Report on the Working of Act 1 of 1882*, 105.

52. R. Raman, *Global Capital and Peripheral Labour: The History and Political Economy of*

Plantation Workers in India (New York: Routledge, 2010), 93–94, discusses plantations in South India where the legislative history parallels that of Assam to some extent. After initially using the WBOC, planters pushed for a stronger measure. The Madras Planters' Labour Act (1903) was modeled on the Assam Act of 1901 but did not include the private arrest provision.

53. D. V. Rege, *Report on an Enquiry into the Conditions of Plantation Workers in India* (Simla: Government Press, 1948), 28–29.

54. W. A. Lewis, "Economic Development with Unlimited Supplies of Labor," *Manchester School* 22, no. 2 (1954) 139–91.

55. S. Wolcott, "Industrial Labour in Late Colonial India," in *A New Economic History of Colonial India*, ed. L. Chaudhary, B. Gupta, T. Roy, and A. Swamy (London: Routledge, 2015), fig. 3.

56. Ibid. The jute comparison is less reliable because Wolcott's benchmark wage is for tea plantation workers, who were already migrants.

57. Tirthankar Roy, *The Economic History of India, 1857–1947* (New Delhi: Oxford University Press, 2011), 198.

58. Workers had previously been assembled under one roof for production of luxury textiles for the nobility. See D. B. Mitra, *The Cotton Weavers of Bengal, 1857–1933* (Calcutta: Firma KLM, 1978).

59. There was, at least rhetorically, some caution regarding importation of British law. United Kingdom, *Report of the Indian Factory Labour Commission* (London: HMSO, 1908), 5, emphasized that it might "most injurious" to mechanically copy English law, because Indian conditions were different.

60. D. Chakrabarty, "Sasipada Banerjee: A Study in the Nature of the First Contact of the Bengali Bhadralok with the Working Classes of Bengal," *Indian Historical Review* 2 (1976): 339–64.

61. See J. C. Kydd, *A History of Factory Legislation in India* (Calcutta: Calcutta University Press, 1920), 4n1.

62. Quoted by Kydd, *History*, 6. For complaints from the jute manufacturers in Dundee regarding working conditions in jute mills in Calcutta see T. S. Gordon, *Jute and Empire: The Calcutta Jute Wallahs and the Landscapes of Empire* (Manchester: Manchester University Press, 1998).

63. N. S. Bengallee, *The Life of Sorabjee Shapoorjee Bengallee, C.I.E.: With Illustrations, Letters, and a Sketch in English* (Bombay: Times of India Press, 1900), 52.

64. L. Chakravarty, "Emergence of an Industrial Labour Force in a Dual Economy: British India, 1880–1920," *Indian Economic and Social History Review* 15 (1978): 249–327. Cited text is on 250.

65. India, *Report of the Royal Commission on Labour*, 4.

66. This could be because higher wages improve workers' nutritional status, reduce turnover, or improve discipline. See A. Weiss, *Efficiency Wage Models of the Labor Market: Models of Unemployment, Layoffs, and Wage-Dispersion* (Princeton, NJ: Princeton University Press, 1991), for a survey of efficiency wage models. Even Mahatma Gandhi's notion of the capitalist as merely a trustee of society's wealth and his view of capitalists and workers as "co-partners" were inconsistent with the notion of a market-determined wage. See R. Chandavarkar, *Imperial Power and Popular Politics: Class, Resistance, and the State in India, c. 1850–1950* (Cambridge: Cambridge University Press, 1998), 286.

67. Anecdotal evidence supports this view. M. Read, *From Field to Factory: An Introductory Study of the Indian Peasant Turned Factory Hand* (London: Student Christian Move-

ment, 1927), 41, describes an occasion when she visited a factory (she does not say exactly where, just "North India") with an inspector, and found many children below age nine, in violation of law. When confronted with this evidence, the European manager, summoned from his home, merely scratched his head and said, "Caught this time." J. H. Kelman, *Labour in India: A Study of the Conditions of Indian Women in Modern Industry* (London: George Allen and Unwin, 1923), 225, describes how jobbers and women workers, in collaboration, could easily evade restrictions on hours of work.

68. India, *Report of the Labour Investigation Committee* (Delhi: Government Press, 1946), 45.

69. D. Chakrabarty, *Rethinking Working Class History: Bengal, 1890–1940* (Princeton, NJ: Princeton University Press, 1989), 78–79.

70. Wolcott, "Industrial Labour."

71. India, *Report of the Royal Commission on Labour*, 333; M. D. Morris, *The Emergence of an Industrial Labor Force in India: A Study of the Bombay Cotton Mills, 1854–1947* (Berkeley: University of California Press, 1965), 178.

72. R. Chandavarkar, "Workers' Politics and the Mill Districts in Bombay between the Wars," *Modern Asian Studies* 15, no. 3 (1981): 603–47, especially 603.

73. H. M. Trivedi, *Labour and Factory Legislation in India* (Bombay: Law Publishers, 1945), is a very useful compendium providing the text of various labor laws enacted up to that date. The text quoted appears on 491.

74. According to India, *Report of the Royal Commission on Labour*, 321, membership in a union was "everywhere loosely defined and many unions retain on their books members who have long ceased to pay subscriptions."

75. See V. De Sousa, "Modernizing the Colonial Labor Subject in India," *CLCWeb: Comparative Literature and Culture* 12, no. 2, article 3 (2010), http://docs.lib.purdue.edu /clcweb/vol12/iss2/3, accessed on May 14, 2014, for an elaboration of this point.

76. India, *Report of Royal Commission on Labour*, 322.

77. Tirthankar Roy, "Sardars, Jobbers, Kanganies: The Labour Contractor and Indian Economic History," *Modern Asian Studies* 42, no. 5 (2007): 971–98, and Tirthankar Roy, "Labor Institutions, Japanese Competition, and the Crisis of Cotton Mills in Interwar Mumbai," *Economic and Political Weekly* 43, no. 1 (2008): 37–45.

78. Quoted by R. K. Das, "Women and Labour in India I," *International Labor Review* 24 (1931): 376–409; see 396.

79. C. Joshi, *Lost Worlds: Indian Labour and its Forgotten Histories* (London: Anthem Press, 2005), 147–54, details the range ways of ways in which jobbers in Kanpur's textile mills could take advantage of workers.

80. R. Chandavarkar, *History, Culture, and the Indian City* (Cambridge: Cambridge University Press, 2009), 129. By conceding a lot of power to the jobbers the managers had reduced their ability to negotiate with the workers.

81. Ibid., 94.

82. "It was the pressure of this rivalry within the labour movement in Ahmedabad, rather than, for instance, the power of capitalist interests within the Congress, which drove the highly repressive policies towards labour—including the formulation and passage of the Bombay Trade Disputes Act of 1938, and directed primarily against the communist unions—adopted by the provincial Congress ministry in Bombay between 1937 and 1939." Ibid., 304.

83. C. A. Myers, *Labor Problems in the Industrialization of India* (Cambridge, MA: Harvard University Press, 1958), 140.

84. On how the workers came to organize (or not) see S. Basu, "The Paradox of the

Peasant Worker: Reconceptualizing Workers' Politics in Bengal, 1890–1939," *Modern Asian Studies* 41, no. 1 (2008): 47–74; Chakrabarty, *Rethinking*; and R. Chandavarkar, *The Origins of Industrial Capitalism in India: Business Strategies and the Working Classes in Bombay, 1900–1940* (Cambridge: Cambridge University Press, 1994).

85. S. Sen, *Women and Labour in Late Colonial India: The Bengal Jute Industry* (Cambridge: Cambridge University Press, 1999); and S. Sen, "Gender and Class: Women in Indian Industry, 1890–1990," *Modern Asian Studies* 42, no. 1 (2008): 75–116.

86. Das, "Women and Labour," 382.

87. Morris, *Emergence*, 66.

88. The prohibition was introduced in the Factories Act of 1911. Ibid., 67n96.

89. S. Sen, *Women and Labour*, 5.

90. Ibid., 5.

91. S. Sen, "Gender and Class," 82.

92. R. Mukerjee, *The Indian Working Class* (Bombay: Hind Kitabs, 1951), 94–95. The ban on underground work by women was passed in India in 1929 but as early as 1842 in England, according to Read, *From Field to Factory*, 48.

93. S. Sen, "Gender and Class," 94.

94. Ibid., 95.

95. Joshi, *Lost Worlds*, 86.

96. Ibid., 84.

CHAPTER SEVEN

1. See S. Tofaris, "Hindu Law and the English Law of Contract: A Century of Interaction, 1772–1872," RINDAS Series Working Paper, Ryukoku University, 2013, for a discussion and an example of the second position.

2. Tarkapanchanan was famous not only for his scholarship, but also for a fiercely independent character that had placed him in potentially dangerous situation with a powerful local potentate. In the eighteenth century, the company's Indologists often found it difficult to persuade Brahmin scholars to share knowledge with Europeans. Some Brahmins among those who did collaborate were excommunicated and remained on the pay of Europeans lifelong. The others were sufficiently big names to ignore the threat. Tarkapanchanan was one of the latter. Possibly on William Jones's recommendation, the company paid him the princely sum of Rs. 500 per month during the time he compiled the book, and Rs. 300 per month for the rest of his life. Few European officers earned such a salary in the 1770s. Among the visitors to his home were three Calcutta judges, William Jones, J. H. Harrington, and Colebrooke. For a biography, R. K. Gupta, *Naba Charit* [New biographies, in Bengali] (Calcutta: Gurudas Chattopadhyay, 1886), 1–39.

3. H. T. Colebrooke, *Treatise on Obligations and Contracts* (London: Black, Kingsbury, Purbury and Allen, 1818).

4. J. Tarkapanchanan, *Digest on Hindu Law of Contracts and Successions with a Commentary*, trans. H. T. Colebrooke, vols. 1–2 (Madras: Higginbothams, 1874), 11.

5. Ibid., 20.

6. Ibid., 352.

7. Ibid., 14.

8. T. Strange, *Hindu Law with reference to Such Portions of it as Concern the Administration of Justice in the King's Courts in India*, 5th ed. (Madras: Higginbothams, 1875), 262.

9. Cited by R. and L. Rocher, *The Making of Western Indology: Henry Thomas Colebrooke and the East India Company* (London: Routledge, 2012), 38.

10. F. W. Macnaghten, *Considerations on Hindoo Law as it is current in Bengal* (Serampore: Mission Press, 1824), 404.

11. S. Davar, *Elements of Indian Mercantile Law* (Bombay: publisher unknown, 1917).

12. A wagering contract was an agreement between two parties placing a bet on an uncertain event. Sometimes, bets were placed on behalf of a third party with the principal's capital. A wagering contract would encompass both types of deal.

13. Strange, *Hindu Law*, 306.

14. K. Mukund, *The View from Below: Indigenous Society, Temples and the Early Colonial State in Tamilnadu, 1700–1835* (Hyderabad: Orient Longman, 2005).

15. *Gopikrishna Goswami v. Ramnidhi Lahiri*, in K. Haldar et al., *Sadar Dewanny Adawlater Nishponno Mokoddomar Reporter Chumbak* [Abstracts of cases settled in the Sadar Dewanny Court, in Bengali] (Calcutta: Boikunthanath Das, 1857), 62–70.

16. *Babu Bulaki Lal and others v. Ganesh Lal and others*, 1853, in Haldar et al., *Sadar Dewanny*, 373–74.

17. *Jawahar Misra v. Bhagu Misra*, 1855, in Haldar et al., *Sadar Dewanny*, 362–73.

18. *Syed Mahomed Bakur v. Blanchard, Spence, and others*, 1848; *Motee Loll Seal v. Mudden Thakoor*, 1856; *Frith and Sandes v. Chunder Monee Debea*, 1856; and *E. D. De Sarun v. Woma Churn Sett*, 1858; see L. A. Goodeve and J. V. Woodman, *Full Bench Rulings of the High Court at Fort William, from Its Institution In 1862 to the Commencement of the Bengal Law Reports* (Calcutta: Thacker Spink, 1874).

19. Goodeve and Woodman, *Full Bench Rulings*: 675–87.

20. J. D. M. Derrett, "The Administration of Hindu Law by the British," *Comparative Studies in Society and History* 4, no. 1 (November 1961): 10–52.

21. Reverend Samuel John Hill, London Missionary Society, in British Parliamentary Papers, *East India Indigo Commission, Minutes of Evidence* (London: HMSO, 1861), 105.

22. Munshi Latafat Hossain, landlord, before the Indigo Commission, cited in Tirthankar Roy, "Indigo and Law in Colonial India," *Economic History Review* 64, no. S1 (2011): 60–75.

23. Secretary of state to the government of India, 1861, cited in Tirthankar Roy, "Indigo and Law."

24. Lieutenant governor of Bengal, 1854; for full citation see Tirthankar Roy, "Indigo and Law."

25. B. Chowdhury, *Growth of Commercial Agriculture in Bengal, 1757–1900* (Calcutta: Quality Printers, 1964).

26. James Cockburn, magistrate and planter, Indigo Commission; for full citation, see Tirthankar Roy, "Indigo and Law."

27. On planter violence, see E. Kolsky, *Colonial Justice in British India: White Violence and the Rule of Law* (Cambridge: Cambridge University Press, 2010), 58–63.

28. As we see in a number of other contexts, letting the intermediaries pay themselves by "corruption" was in fact quite common and possibly suggests a scenario where it was difficult for the principal to monitor the intermediary. For example, between the company and the intermediary (*gumastha*) who dealt with the peasant who cultivated poppy, or the weaver. See R. Kranton and A. V. Swamy, "Contracts, Hold-Up, and Exports: Textiles and Opium in Colonial India," *American Economic Review* 98, no. 3 (2008): 967–89.

29. S. Bhattacharya, "The Indigo Revolt of Bengal," *Social Scientist* 5, no. 12 (1978): 13–23; R. Sah, "Features of British Indigo in India," *Social Scientist* 9, nos. 2/3 (1980): 67–79; B. Kling, *The Blue Mutiny: The Indigo Disturbances in Bengal, 1859–1862* (Philadelphia: University of Pennsylvania Press, 1966), 148; S. Bose, *Peasant Labour*

and Colonial Capital: Rural Bengal since 1770 (Cambridge: Cambridge University Press, 1993), 48; B. Hartmann and J. K. Boyce, A Quiet Violence: View from a Bangladesh Village (London: Zed Books, 1987), 13; R. Ray, "The Changing Fortunes of the Bengali Gentry under Colonial Rule: Pal Chaudhuris of Mahesganj, 1800–1950," Modern Asian Studies 21, no. 3 (1987): 511–19.

30. Kling, Blue Mutiny, 148.

31. I. Ray, "The Indigo Dye Industry in Colonial Bengal: A Re-examination," Indian Economic and Social History Review 41, no. 2 (2004): 199–224.

32. Sah, "Features of British Indigo."

33. Bhattacharya, "Indigo Revolt."

34. British Parliamentary Papers, Copy of the Legislative Despatch on the Breach of Contracts (East India) Bill, together with a Copy of the Bill (London: HMSO, 1862), 1.

35. W. H. Rattigan, "The Influence of English Law and Legislation upon the Native Laws of India," Journal of the Society of Comparative Legislation, n.s., 3, no. 1 (1901): 46–65.

36. G. Rankin, Background to Indian Law (Cambridge: Cambridge University Press, 1946), 91.

37. Specific performance refers to obligatory fulfillment of the contract, as opposed to payment of damages when the contract is not performed.

38. British Parliamentary Papers, East India Contract Law: Copies of Papers showing the present position of the Question of a Contract Law for India, And, of all Reports of the Indian Law Commissioners on the Subject of Contracts (London: HSMO, 1868), 96.

39. Ibid., 69.

40. R. N. Gooderson, "English Contract Problems in Indian Code and Case Law," Cambridge Law Journal 16, no. 1 (1958): 67–84.

41. On this subject, John Phillips, "Protecting Those in a Disadvantageous Negotiating Position: Unconscionable Bargains as a Unifying Doctrine," Wake Forest Law Review 45, no. 3 (2010): 837–61.

42. See J. E. Hogg, "Partnership Law in the Empire," Journal of Comparative Legislation and International Law 18, no. 2 (1918): 232–41.

43. R. N. Gooderson, "Turpitude and Title in England and India," Cambridge Law Journal 16, no. 2 (1958): 199–217.

CHAPTER EIGHT

1. Reference to managing agency in Malaya can be found in K. S. Sandhu and A. Mani, Indian Communities in Southeast Asia (Singapore: Institute of Southeast Asian Studies, 2006), 291.

2. N. Lindley, The Law of Partnership, vol. 1 of 2, 5th ed. (Jersey City: F. D. Linn, 1888), 248–49.

3. India, Law Commission, Seventh Report on the Partnership Act (New Delhi: Government Press, 1957).

4. M. A. Pickering, "The Company as a Separate Legal Entity," Modern Law Review 31, no. 5 (1968): 481–511. Cited text appears on 509.

5. R. Harris, "The English East India Company and the History of Company Law," in VOC 1602–2002—400 Years of Company Law, ed. Ella Gepken-Jager, Gerard van Solinge, and Levinus Timmerman (Dordrecht: Kluwer Legal Publishers, 2005), 219–47. Cited text appears on 246.

6. M. D. Morris, "Modern Business Organisation and Labour Administration: Specific Adaptations to Indian Conditions of Risk and Uncertainty, 1850–1947," Economic and Political Weekly 14, no. 40 (1979): 1680–87.

7. R. Birla, *Stages of Capital: Law, Culture, and Market Governance in Late Colonial India* (Durham, NC: Duke University Press, 2006), 5.

8. A chit fund is the Indian term for a rotating savings and credit association, or ROSCA. The members donate a fixed sum every month (say) over a year (say). Each month a subset of members receives a lump sum.

9. E. Perry, *Cases Illustrative of Oriental Life, the Application of English Law to India, Decided in H. M. Supreme Court at Bombay* (London: S. Sweet, 1853), 546–50.

10. Based on R. S. Rungta, *Rise of Business Corporations in India, 1851–1900* (Cambridge: Cambridge University Press, 1970), 64–68. See also K. M. Ghosh, *The Indian Company Law: A Book for Lawyers and Business Men* (Calcutta: Eastern Law House, 1940).

11. Rungta, *Rise of Business Corporations*, 115.

12. Lindley, *Law of Partnership*, 2:656.

13. T. Parsons, *A Treatise on the Law of Partnership* (Boston: Little, Brown, 1867), 155.

14. R. T. Reid and C. F. Farran, eds., *Reports of Cases Decided in the High Court of Bombay, 1866-67* (Bombay: Education Society Press, 1868), 185–86.

15. P. S. Sangal, "Ultra Vires and Companies: The Indian Experience," *International and Comparative Law Quarterly* 12, no. 3 (1963): 967–88.

16. S. Davar, *Business Organization* (Calcutta: Butterworths, 1939), 35.

17. On these and other contrasts between the two cities in the operation of the agency system, see A. F. Brimmer, "The Setting of Entrepreneurship in India," *Quarterly Journal of Economics* 69, no. 4 (1955): 553–76.

18. For example, the pioneering study of concentration by M. M. Mehta, *Combination Movement in Indian Industry* (Bombay: Friends' Book Depot, 1952); and India, *Report of the Monopolies Enquiry Commission* (New Delhi: Ministry of Commerce and Industry), 1965.

19. R. K. Goel, "Delegation of Directors' Powers and Duties: A Comparative Analysis," *International and Comparative Law Quarterly* 18, no. 1 (1969): 152–77. Cited text appears on 168.

20. Ibid.

21. P. S. Lokanathan, *Industrial Organisation in India* (London: George Unwin, 1936), 331.

22. S. Davar, *Inefficient Managing Agency System* (Bombay: Davar's College, 1939), 9.

23. India, *Selections from the Debates on the Reform of Company Law in the Central Assembly and Parliament in 1936 and 1954–55* (New Delhi: Ministry of Commerce and Industry, 1960), 11.

24. When the share value of the agent firm fell again, the losses were set off against the dividend income earned by these individuals. The income tax commissioner challenged that move, and in the process the story of the transfer of control came to the courts.

25. Maria Misra, *Business, Race, and Politics in British India, 1850–1960* (Oxford: Oxford University Press, 1998).

26. W. F. Agnew, *The Law of Trusts in British India* (Calcutta: Thacker Spink, 1920).

27. See Marina Martin, "An Economic History of the Hundi" (doctoral diss., Department of Economic History, London School of Economics and Political Science, 2012), for a recent history of regulation of the instrument.

28. Marwari Chamber of Commerce, *Rules and Regulations about Hundi Chithi and Seed-Wheat* (Bombay: Marwari Chamber of Commerce, 1916).

29. P. B. Venkatasubramanian, "The Law of Trademarks in India," *World Development* 7, no. 7 (1979): 737–46.

30. India, *Selections from the Debates*, 74.

31. India, *Report of the Monopolies Enquiry Commission* (New Delhi: Ministry of Commerce and Industry, 1965); R. K. Hazari, *The Structure of the Corporate Private Sector* (London: Asia Publishing, 1966).

32. Hazari, *Structure*.

33. An early instance of this was the use of Life Insurance Corporation funds by Haridas Mundhra to inflate the shares of five Indo-British companies that he had recently acquired (1955–56), in independent India's first major financial scandal.

CHAPTER NINE

1. C. Ilbert, "Application of European Law to Natives of India," *Journal of the Society of Comparative Legislation* 1 (1896–97): 223.

2. Ibid.

3. India, *Royal Commission to consider Reform of Judicial Establishments, Judicial Procedure and Laws of India: First Report* (London: HMSO, 1856).

4. An 1825 book on Indian law written by an army captain, writer, and director of the East India Company, Archibald Galloway, proposed a streamlined judiciary for India. *Observations on the Law and Constitution of India* (London: Kingsbury, Parbury and Allen, 1825). Galloway estimated that the number of judges required to clear the backlog of cases, already quite heavy, was 245 (p. 344). The actual number must have been smaller than this. The implied officers/population ratio for Bengal is added to the other numbers in figure 9.4.

5. British Parliamentary Papers, *Papers relating to Police, Civil and Criminal Justice under Governments of Bengal, Fort-St.-George and Bombay, 1810–19*. London: HMSO, 1819.

6. India, *Royal Commission to consider Reform of Judicial Establishments*, 19.

7. For population, P. C. Mahalanobis and D. Bhattacharya, "Growth of Population in India and Pakistan, 1801–1961," *Artha Vijnana* 18, no. 1 (1976): 1–10.

8. Indian Law Commission, "Proposed Act for Amending the Law regarding the Limitation of Suits," in *Copies of Special Reports of the Indian Law Commissioners* (London: House of Commons, 1843), 3–47.

9. B. K. Acharya, *Codification in British India* (Calcutta: S. K. Banerji and Sons, 1914).

10. N. H. Thomson, *Act XIV of 1859 Regulating the Limitation of Civil Suits in British India* (Calcutta: Thacker Spink, 1870).

11. Ibid., 153.

12. Ibid., 198–99; see also discussion of lakheraj tenures by W. Markby, *Lectures on Indian Law* (Calcutta: Thacker Spink, 1873).

13. Thomson, *Act XIV of 1859*, 200.

14. Ibid., 249.

15. Ibid., 83–84.

CHAPTER TEN

1. India, Civil Justice Committee, *Report* (Calcutta: Government of India Central Publication Branch, 1925), xxii.

2. McKinsey Global Institute, *India: the Growth Imperative* (2001), 4, http://www.mckinsey.com/insights/india/growth_imperative_for_india, accessed July 29, 2015.

3. This expression is taken from Louis J. Walinsky, ed. *Agrarian Reforms as Unfinished Business: The Selected Papers of Wolf Ladejinsky* (New York, Oxford University Press 1977).

4. A. V. Banerjee, P. J. Gertler, and M. Ghatak, "Empowerment and Efficiency: Tenancy Reform in West Bengal, *Journal of Political Economy* 110, no. 2 (2002): 239–80.

5. In January 2015 a business magazine reported a dispute in which a man who bought a piece of land found that it had already been sold twice to others. See T. Lasseter, "India's Stagnant Courts Resist Reform," January 8, 2015, http://www.bloomberg.com /news/articles/2015-01-08/indias-courts-resist-reform-backlog-at-314-million-cases, accessed July 27, 2015. For a recent proposal by a senior government official, Arvind Panagariya, to revise tenancy laws to facilitate land leasing, see "Land-Leasing: A Big Win-Win Reform for the States," 2015, http://niti.gov.in/content/view_blogs_arch .php?blog=1, accessed August 24, 2015.

6. World Bank, *Doing Business in India: Registering Property in India—Mumbai*, 2015, http://www.doingbusiness.org/data/exploreeconomies/mumbai/registering -property/, accessed July 13, 2015.

7. McKinsey Global Institute, *India: The Growth Imperative*, 4.

8. A. V. Banerjee and L. Iyer, in a daring and creative analysis, have suggested that regions where the British-introduced land tenure systems favored "landlords" have done worse, since independence, than places where the system favored "peasants." See "History, Institutions, and Economic Performance: The Legacy of Colonial Land Tenure Systems in India," *American Economic Review* 95, no. 4 (2005): 1190–1213. V. Iversen, R. Palmer-Jones, and K. Sen, "On the Colonial Origins of Agricultural Development in India: A Re-examination of Banerjee and Iyer, 'History, Institutions and Economic Performance,'" *Journal of Development Studies* 49, no. 12 (2013): 1631– 46, point out that Banerjee and Iyer's results do not hold if one region, the Central Provinces, in which it is unclear whether land tenure was de facto peasant based or landlord based, is dropped.

9. E. Newbigin, "A Post-colonial Patriarchy? Representing Family in the Indian Nation State," *Modern Asian Studies* 44, no. 1 (2010): 121–44.

10. K. Deininger, A. Goyal, and H. Nagarajan, "Inheritance Law Reform and Women's Access to Capital" (World Bank Policy Research Working Paper 5338, 2010).

11. This is best exemplified by the Shah Bano case of 1985. For a discussion see S. Mullally, "Feminism and Multicultural Dilemmas in India," *Oxford Journal of Legal Studies* 24, no. 4 (2004): 671–92.

12. For a collection of recent newspaper articles, see http://articles.economictimes .indiatimes.com/keyword/uniform-civil-code, accessed July 26, 2105.

13. For contrasting views on this subject see A. Panagariya, *India: The Emerging Giant* (New York: Oxford University Press, 2000), especially 287–93; and P. Bardhan, "The Labour Reform Myth," September 8, 2014, http://www.ideasforindia.in/article.aspx ?article_id=339, accessed July 28, 2015.

14. J. N. Bhagwati and P. Desai, *Planning for Industrialization* (New York: Oxford University Press, 1970).

15. India, Law Commission, *Report 253: Commercial Division and Commercial Appellate Division of High Courts and Commercial Courts Bill*, January 2015, 25, http:// lawcommissionofindia.nic.in/reports/Report_No.253_Commercial_Division _and_Commercial_Appellate_Division_of_High_Courts_and__Commercial_Courts _Bill,_2015.pdf, accessed July 29, 2015.

16. Pratap Bhanu Mehta, "India's Judiciary: The Promise of Uncertainty," in *Public Institutions in India: Performance and Designs*, ed. D. Kapur and P. B. Mehta (New Delhi: Oxford University Press, 2005), 185.

17. Civil Justice Committee, *Report*, xiv, xvi.

18. India, Law Commission, *Report 253*, 2015, 29.

GLOSSARY

abwab A fine or tax.

adawlut, adalat Court of law.

adivasi India's "tribals" or indigenous people.

agnate Descendant from a male ancestor.

bandhu Literally, friend or related (from "bandhan," or relation in Sanskrit), the term in Hindu law referring to a person related to a deceased through female links.

bania Hindu trader—derived from the Sanskrit *vanijya*, for business.

benami A transaction in which the person whose name is on the documentation is not the actual beneficiary.

bigha The standard measurement of land (except South India). In the nineteenth century, one bigha was officially 0.33 acres.

Brahmin Member of the highest Hindu caste, often a priest.

cognate Descendants from a female ancestor.

collector The official responsible for collection of land revenue in a district. He also had a wide range of other administrative responsibilities.

Congress Indian nationalist political party. Jawaharlal Nehru and Mahatma Gandhi were among its important leaders.

cooly, coolie Generic term for unskilled hired laborers.

coparcener Person with a right to some portion of family property.

dadan Money advanced for the supply of merchandise.

damdupat A ceiling on loan repayment at a single point in time. The interest repaid could not exceed the principal.

Dayabhaga School of Hindu law applicable in Bengal.

dewanny, dewani, diwani In the precolonial north Indian state, the king's dewan was in charge of the civil administration, including collection of revenues, sending money to the royal treasury, and submission of the accounts to the king. In 1765, the English East India Company was appointed the dewan of the province of Bengal, Bihar, and Orissa, technically belonging to the Mughal Empire.

Dharmasastra Ancient Hindu texts on law and morality.

doab The tract between two confluent rivers.

gomasta Agent.

gossain Colloquial of Goswami, is a generic term for Vaishnavite sects who trace their origin to a single preacher. Some of them followed distinctive personal law.

Hanafi The largest among the four schools of jurisprudence in Sunni Islam.

hundi Banker's draft, bill of exchange.

ilaqa Neighborhood or locality.

inam Land on which the owner paid low or no tax to the state.

indenture An employment contract specifying a legally binding fixed term of employment. Originating in apprenticeship in early modern England, the contract was used extensively in nineteenth-century employment in India.

jagir, jagirdar In north India, the precolonial term *jagir* referred to an assignment of a part of the revenues of the state to a superior officer. Jagirdar, in this sense, was a tax collector on behalf of the state.

jobber Intermediary between employer and worker in recruitment and workplace interactions.

jotedar In Bengal, a tenant of the zamindar who might have considerable power at the village-level.

kamia Laborer in debt bondage in Bihar and Orissa.

lakheraj Land exempt from payment of revenue.

lex loci The principle that the relevant law is the one that holds in the location in which the disputants transacted.

mahajan Moneylender.

Marwari Trader or lender from Marwar in Rajasthan.

maulvi Law officers and experts of Islamic law.

mirasdar Landowner with a secure right, and member of the village corporate body.

Mitakshara Major school of Hindu law.

Mughal Literally, of the Mongols, the term referred to the Timurid house of Babar, who started an Empire in India.

munsif Indian judicial official in lower court.

nawab The viceroy or chief officer of the Mughal provincial administration, in charge of internal security and criminal justice; also called subadar. In the first quarter century of the company's rule in Bengal (1765–1790), criminal justice was left to the nazim.

nazim *See* nawab.

panchayet, panchayat Literally, a council of five, and an institution for dispensing justice. Usually associated with the self-administration in the villages, the word was also used in the context of caste or community courts, for example, the Parsi panchayet.

pandit, pundit Sanskrit root word for a learned man. Ordinarily the term would refer to a scholar of Sanskrit and ancient texts.

pargana, pergunnah Group of villages.

patnidar, darpatnidar In Bengal, holders of tenure beneath a zamindar. The patnidar was a de facto owner, subject to paying the zamindar a rent fixed in perpetuity. The darpartinadar had a similar arrangement with the patnidar.

patta A grant or lease document stating the amount of land that could be used by the holder and sometimes specifying the rent thereon.

patwari An officer of the revenue system who maintained the land registers and rent accounts of a village.

Permanent Settlement *See* settlement.

peshwa Maratha prime minister, de facto ruler.

Pious Obligation Responsibility of male descendants to repay an ancestor's debts.

presidency The territory administered by the principal factories of the East India Company, and later, the three principal administrative divisions within British India:

Bombay, Madras, and Bengal. The three presidency towns were Bombay, Calcutta, and Madras.

princely states States that retained independence in colonial India, as opposed to British India, which consisted of territories ruled by the Crown. Civil law in the princely states differed in some respects from those in British India; a complete history of the comparison is yet to be written.

Privy Council The highest court of appeal, based in London.

raiyat, ryot Occupant of the soil; either a tenant or an owner-farmer.

raiyatwari, ryotwari A revenue system where the peasants contracted directly with the government for the payment of revenue in exchange for perpetual right on land.

raja King.

regulation The term applied to laws passed by the governor general or the governor between approximately 1793, when the first compilation of ad hoc laws was made, and 1833, when these officers became solely responsible for legislation in India.

sahukar, sowcar, savkar, saokar Moneylenders.

sapinda Individuals who share a common ancestor. A more restricted meaning is possession of the right to offer ritual oblation (pinda) to enable deceased ancestors to attain salvation.

sardar Intermediary between employer and worker, primarily in recruitment, but also in workplace interactions.

settlement A term in general use in the British Indian land revenue administration. It meant an arrangement whereby the tax obligation of the landholder was calculated and kept constant for a fixed term. In some zamindari areas, there was a Permanent Settlement, meaning the tax was fixed in perpetuity. In others, it might be raised at intervals of several decades. In the ryotwari areas, settlements were carried out periodically, accompanied by extensive land surveys.

shastri Hindu scholar.

sudder and mufassil or mofussil The two terms formed a pair, and meant, respectively, the center and the branches. The Sudder Dewanny Adawlut was the chief civil court under the East India Company. *See also* adawlut.

tahsil The administrative unit just below a district. Several tahsils constituted a district.

talukdar Meaning varies by location, but usually substantial landholder.

ultra vires When an authority exceeds its bounds in issuing a law.

vakil, vakeel Originally a negotiator or political agent, in the British Indian courts system, the term referred to the lawyers.

zamindar In Mughal India, the zamindar was a local revenue officer, usually resident of a large village. The rights to land tended to be hereditary, and the condition of service was civil rather than military. East India Company changed the meaning into a person who held land in perpetuity upon the promise to pay the government a rent. The cultivators of soil under that arrangement were the tenants of the zamindar.

zamindari *See* settlement.

REFERENCES

Acemoglu, D., S. Johnson, and J. A. Robinson. "The Colonial Origins of Comparative Development: An Empirical Investigation." *American Economic Review* 91, no. 5 (2001): 1369–1401.

———. "Reversal of Fortune: Geography and Institutions in the Making of the Modern World Income Distribution." *Quarterly Journal of Economics* 117, no. 4 (2002): 1231–94.

Acemoglu, D., and J. Robinson. *Why Nations Fail: The Origins of Power, Prosperity, and Poverty.* New York: Crown Publishers, 2012.

Acharya, B. K. *Codification in British India.* Calcutta: S. K. Banerji and Sons, 1914.

Agnew, W. F. *The Law of Trusts in British India.* Calcutta: Thacker Spink, 1920.

Ahuja, R. "Labour Relations in Early Colonial Madras, c. 1750–1800." *Modern Asian Studies* 36, no. 4 (2002): 793–826.

———. "The Origins of Colonial Labour Policy in Late Eighteenth-Century Madras." *International Review of Social History* 44, no. 2 (1999): 159–95.

Aleem, I. "Imperfect Information, Screening, and the Costs of Informal Lending: A Study of a Rural Credit Market in Pakistan." *World Bank Economic Review* 4, no. 3 (1990): 329–49.

Ali, I. "Malign Growth? Agricultural Colonization and the Roots of Backwardness in the Punjab." *Past and Present* 114 (1987): 110–32.

———. *The Punjab under Imperialism, 1885–1947.* Princeton, NJ: Princeton University Press, 1988.

Allanson, H. M. L. *Final Report on the Survey and Settlement Operations in the District of Sonthal Parganas (Third Programme), 1898–1910.* Calcutta: Bengal Secretariat Press, 1912.

Anderson, M. "India, 1850–1930: The Illusion of Free Labor." In *Masters, Servants, and Magistrates in Britain and the Empire, 1562–1955,* edited by D. Haynes and P. Craven, 422–54. Chapel Hill: University of North Carolina Press, 2004.

———. "Islamic Law and the Colonial Encounter in British India." In *Institutions and Ideologies: A SOAS South Asia Reader,* edited by D. Arnold and P. Robb, 165–85. Richmond: Curzon Press, 1993.

Anon. "The memorial of Ramchunder Surmona, late Professor of Law in the Sanscrit College, Calcutta, to the Court of Directors of the East-India Company." Pamphlet. Calcutta: William Rushton, 1838.

Baden-Powell, B. H. *A Manual of the Land Revenue Systems and Land Tenures of British India.* Calcutta: Government Press, 1882.

————. *The Land Systems of British India.* Oxford: Clarendon Press, 1892.

Baker, C. "Tamilnad Estates in the Twentieth Century." *Indian Economic and Social History Review* 13, no. 1 (1976): 1–44.

Balas, A., R. La Porta, F. Lopez-de-Silanes, and A. Shleifer. "The Divergence of Legal Procedures." *American Economic Journal: Economic Policy* 1, no. 2 (2009): 138–62.

Baliga, B. S. *Studies in Madras Administration.* Vol. 2. Madras: India Press, 1960.

Banerjee, A., E. Duflo, R. Glennerster, and C. Kinnon. "The Miracle of Microfinance? Evidence from a Randomized Evaluation." *American Economic Journal, Applied Economics* 7, no. 1 (2015): 22–53.

Banerjee, A. C., and B. K. Ghosh. "Introduction." In *Bengal Ryots: Their Rights and Liabilities; Being an Elementary Treatise on the Law of Landlord and Tenant,* by S. C. Chatterjee (Columbia, MO: South Asia Books, 1977): i–xxxv.

Banerjee, A. V., P. J. Gertler, and M. Ghatak. "Empowerment and Efficiency: Tenancy Reform in West Bengal." *Journal of Political Economy* 110, no. 2 (2002): 239–80.

Banerjee, A. V., and L. Iyer. "History, Institutions, and Economic Performance: The Legacy of Colonial Land Tenure Systems in India." *American Economic Review* 95, no. 4 (2005): 1190–1213.

Bardhan, P. "Labor-Tying in a Poor Agrarian Economy: A Theoretical and Empirical Analysis." *Quarterly Journal of Economics* 98, no. 3 (1983): 501–14.

————. "The Labour Reform Myth." September 8, 2014. http://www.ideasforindia.in /article.aspx?article_id=339. Accessed July 28, 2015.

Basu, S. "The Paradox of the Peasant Worker: Reconceptualizing Workers' Politics in Bengal, 1890–1939." *Modern Asian Studies* 41, no. 1 (2008): 47–74.

Behal, R. P. "Power Structure, Discipline, and Labour in Assam Tea Plantations under Colonial Rule." *International Review of Social History* 51, no. 2 (2006): 143–72.

————. *One Hundred Years of Servitude: Political Economy of Tea Plantations in Colonial Assam.* New Delhi: Tulika Books, 2014.

Behal, R. P., and P. Mohapatra. "Tea and Money versus Human Life: The Rise and Fall of the Indenture System in the Assam Tea Plantations, 1840–1908." In *Plantations, Peasants and Proletarians in Colonial Asia,* edited by E. Valentine Daniel, H. Bernstein, and T. Brass. London: Frank Cass, 1992.

Bengal. *Bengal District Gazetteers: Bakarganj.* Calcutta: Bengal Secretariat, 1918.

————. *Bengal District Gazetteers: Muzaffarpur.* Calcutta: Bengal Secretariat Book Depot, 1907.

————. *Final Report on the Survey and Settlement Operations in the District of Jessore.* Calcutta: Bengal Secretariat Book Depot, 1925.

————. *Indian Law Reports.* Calcutta Series, vol. 23. Calcutta, 1896.

————. *Report of the Bengal Provincial Banking Enquiry Committee.* Calcutta: Government Press, 1930.

————. *Report of the Government of Bengal on the Proposed Amendment on the Law of Landlord and Tenant in that Province, With a Revised Bill and Appendices.* Vol. 1. Calcutta: Government Press, 1883.

————. *Report of the Land Revenue Commission Bengal.* Calcutta: Government Press, 1940.

————. *Report on the Administration of Civil Justice in the Lower Provinces of Bengal.* Calcutta: Government Press, various years.

————. *Report on the Land Revenue Administration of the Presidency of Bengal for the Year 1934–35.* Calcutta: Bengal Secretariat Book Depot, 1935.

Bengal, High Court. *Decisions under the Rent Laws of the Court of the Sadr Dewani Adalat and* the High Court of Judicature at Fort William in Bengal. Vol. 1. Calcutta: George Wyman and Co., 1865.

———. Report on the Administration of Civil Justice in the Presidency of Bengal. Calcutta: Bengal Secretariat Book Depot, various years.

———. Report on the Administration of Civil Justice in the Province of Bengal. Calcutta: Government Press, various years.

Bengal, Legislative Department. The Bengal Agricultural Debtors Act, 1935. Calcutta: Government Press, 1936.

Bengallee, N. S. The Life of Sorabjee Shapoorjee Bengallee, C.I.E.: With Illustrations, Letters, and a Sketch in English. Bombay: Times of India Press, 1900.

Benton, L. Law and Colonial Cultures: Legal Regimes in World History, 1400–1900. Cambridge: Cambridge University Press, 2002.

Berkowitz, D., K. Pistor, and J. Richard. "The Transplant Effect." American Journal of Comparative Law 51, no. 1 (2003): 163–203.

Berman, H. Law and Revolution. Cambridge, MA: Harvard University Press, 1983.

Besley, T. "Property Rights and Investment Incentives: Theory and Evidence from Ghana." Journal of Political Economy 103, no. 5 (1995): 903–37.

Besley, T., and M. Ghatak. "Property Rights and Economic Development." In Handbook of Development Economics, vol. 5, edited by D. Rodrik and M. Rosenzweig, 4525–94. Amsterdam: North-Holland, 2010.

Bhaduri, A. "The Evolution of Land Relations in Eastern India under British Rule." Indian Economic and Social History Review 13, no. 1 (1976): 45–53.

———. "A Study in Agricultural Backwardness under Semi-feudalism." Economic Journal 83 (1973): 120–37.

Bhagwati J. N., and P. Desai. Planning for Industrialization. New York: Oxford University Press, 1970.

Bhattacharya, N. "The Logic of Tenancy Cultivation: Central and South-East Punjab, 1870–1935." Indian Economic and Social History Review 20 (1983): 121–70.

Bhattacharya, S. "The Indigo Revolt of Bengal." Social Scientist 5, no. 12 (1978): 13–23.

Birla, R. Stages of Capital: Law, Culture, and Market Governance in Late Colonial India. Durham, NC: Duke University Press, 2006.

Bombay. Report of the Bombay Provincial Banking Enquiry Committee. Bombay: Government Press, 1930.

———. Report of the Committee on the Riots in Poona and Ahmednagar 1875. Bombay: Government Press, 1876.

———. Report of the Deccan Agriculturists' Relief Commission. Bombay: Government Press, 1912.

———. Reports of Cases decided in the High Courts of Bombay 1873. Bombay: Government Press, 1874.

———. Statistical Atlas of Bombay State (Provincial Part). Rev. ed. Bombay: Bureau of Economics and Statistics, 1950.

Bose, B. D. Digest of Indian Law Cases Containing High Court Reports, 1862–1909; and Privy Council Reports of Appeals from India, 1836–1909, with an Index of Cases, Compiled under the Orders of the Government of India. Vols. 1–6. Calcutta: Government Press, 1912.

Bose, S. Peasant Labour and Colonial Capital: Rural Bengal since 1770. Cambridge: Cambridge University Press, 1993.

Branson, R. M. A. Digest of Cases reported in the Indian Law Reports. Vols. 1–3. Bombay: Education Society's Press, 1884.

Breman, J. "The Hali System in South Gujarat." In *The World of the Rural Labourer in Colonial India*, edited by G. Prakash. Bombay: Oxford University Press, 1992.

Brimmer, A. F. "The Setting of Entrepreneurship in India." *Quarterly Journal of Economics* 69, no. 4 (1955): 553–76.

British Parliamentary Papers. *Copy of the Legislative Despatch on the Breach of Contracts (East India) Bill, together with a Copy of the Bill*. London: HMSO, 1862.

———. *East India Contract Law: Copies of Papers showing the present position of the Question of a Contract Law for India, And, of all Reports of the Indian Law Commissioners on the Subject of Contracts*. London: HMSO, 1868.

———. *East India Indigo Commission, Minutes of Evidence*. London: HMSO, 1861.

———. *Papers relating to Police, Civil and Criminal Justice under Governments of Bengal, Fort-St.-George and Bombay, 1810–19*. London: HMSO, 1819.

Buchanan, F. *A Geographical, Statistical, and Historical Description of the District or Zila of Dinajpur, in the Province or Soubah of Bengal*. Calcutta: Baptist Mission Press, 1833.

———. *A Journey from Madras, through the countries of Mysore, Canara, and Malabar, etc.* Vol. 2 of 3. London: E. Caddell for the East India Company, 1807.

Buckingham, J., and C. Dowding. *Tea-garden Coolies in Assam: A letter by the Hon'ble J. Buckingham, . . . replying to a communication on the subject, which appeared in the "Indian churchman"; The whole reprinted with introduction and an answer by the Rev. Charles Dowding*. London: W. Thacker, 1894.

Calcutta High Court. *Calcutta Law Journal* 4 (1906): 22–37.

Calvert, H. C. *Wealth and Welfare of the Punjab: Being Some Studies in Punjab Rural Economics*. Lahore: Civil and Military Gazette Press, 1922.

Campbell, G. "Tenure of Land in India." In *Systems of Land Tenure in Various Countries*, by Cobden Club. London: Macmillan and Co., 1870.

Cassels, N. G. "Social Legislation under the Company Raj: The Abolition of Slavery, Act V of 1843." *South Asia* 11, no. 1 (1988): 59–87.

Cassan, G. "Identity Based Policies and Identity Manipulation: Evidence from Colonial Punjab." *American Economic Journal: Economic Policy* 7, no. 4 (2015): 103–31.

Catanach, I. J. *Rural Credit in Western India, 1875–1930: Rural Credit and the Co-operative Movement in the Bombay Presidency*. Berkeley: University of California Press, 1970.

Central Provinces. *Report of the Central Provinces Provincial Banking Enquiry Committee, 1929–30*. Nagpur: Government Press, 1930.

Chakrabarty, D. "Sasipada Banerjee: A Study in the Nature of the First Contact of the Bengali Bhadralok with the Working Classes of Bengal." *Indian Historical Review* 2 (1976): 339–64.

———. *Rethinking Working Class History: Bengal, 1890–1940*. Princeton, NJ: Princeton University Press, 1989.

Chakravarty, L. "Emergence of an Industrial Labour Force in a Dual Economy: British India, 1880–1920." *Indian Economic and Social History Review* 15 (1978): 249–327.

Chakravarty-Kaul, M. *Common Lands and Customary Law: Institutional Change in North India over the Past Two Centuries*. Delhi: Oxford University Press, 1996.

Chandavarkar, R. *History, Culture, and the Indian City*. Cambridge: Cambridge University Press, 2009.

———. *Imperial Power and Popular Politics: Class, Resistance, and the State in India, c. 1850–1950*. Cambridge: Cambridge University Press, 1998.

———. *The Origins of Industrial Capitalism in India: Business Strategies and the Working Classes in Bombay, 1900–1940*. Cambridge: Cambridge University Press, 1994.

————. "Workers' Politics and the Mill Districts in Bombay between the Wars." *Modern Asian Studies* 15, no. 3 (1981): 603–47.

Charlesworth, N. "The Myth of the Deccan Riots of 1875." *Modern Asian Studies* 6, no. 4 (1972): 401–21.

————. *Peasants and Imperial Rule: Agriculture and Agrarian Society in the Bombay Presidency, 1850–1935.* Cambridge: Cambridge University Press, 1985.

Chatterjee, I., and R. Eaton, eds. *Slavery and South Asian History.* Bloomington: Indiana University Press, 2006.

Chatterjee, P. *Bengal, 1920–47: The Land Question.* Calcutta: K. P. Bagchi and Co., 1984.

Chatterjee, S. *Bengal Ryots, Their Rights and Liabilities; Being an Elementary Treatise on the Law of Landlord and Tenant.* Columbia, MO: South Asia Books, 1977. Originally published 1864.

Chattopadhyay, K. L., and S. K. Kundu, eds. *Slavery in British Dominion,* by D. Ganguli. Calcutta: Jijnasa, 1972.

Chaudhary, L., and A. Swamy. "Protecting the Borrower: An Experiment in Colonial India." Mimeo, Williams College, MA, 2014.

Chaudhuri, B. B. "The Movement of Rents in Eastern India, 1793–1930." *Indian Historical Review* 3, no. 2 (1978): 308–90.

————. *Peasant History of Late Pre-colonial and Colonial India.* Noida: Pearson Longman, 2008.

Cheesman, D. *Landlord Power and Rural Indebtedness in Colonial Sind, 1865–1901.* Richmond, Surrey: Curzon Press, 1997.

Chowdhury, B. *Growth of Commercial Agriculture in Bengal, 1757–1900.* Calcutta: Quality Printers, 1964.

Chowdhury-Zilly, A. N. *The Vagrant Peasant: Agrarian Distress and Desertion in Bengal, 1770 to 1830.* Wiesbaden: Franz Steiner Verlag, 1982.

Clarke, R. *The Regulations of the Government of Fort St. George in Force at the End of 1847; to Which are Added the Acts of the Government of India in Force in that Presidency.* London: J. and H. Cox, 1848.

Coats, T. W. "An Account of the Present State of the Township of Lony: An Illustration of the Institutions, Resources and c. of the Marrata Cultivators." *Transactions of the Literary Society of Bombay* 3 (1823):183–220.

Cochrane, J. *Hindu Law: Defence of the Daya Bhaga.* London: W. H. Allen, 1872.

Cohn, B. S. *Colonialism and Its Forms of Knowledge: The British in India.* Princeton, NJ: Princeton University Press, 1996.

Cole, S. "Fixing Market Failures or Fixing Elections? Agricultural Credit in India." *American Economic Journal: Applied Economics* 1, no. 1 (2009): 219–50.

Colebrooke, H. T. *Treatise on Obligations and Contracts.* London: Black, Kingsbury, Purbury and Allen, 1818.

Colebrooke, J. E. *A Digest of the Regulations and Laws, enacted by the Governor General in Council for the civil government of the territories under the Presidency of Bengal, etc. (Supplement containing a collection of the Regulations enacted anterior to the year MDCCXCIII, and completing each article of the Digest to the close of the year MDCCCVI).* Calcutta, 1807.

Cook, S. B. *Imperial Affinities: Nineteenth Century Analogies and Exchanges between India and Ireland.* New Delhi: Sage Publications, 1993.

Cowell, H. *History and Constitution of the Courts and Legislative Authorities in India.* 2nd ed. Calcutta: Thacker Spink, 1884.

————. *History and Constitution of the Courts and Legislative Authorities in India.* Calcutta: Thacker Spink, 1905.

Crole, D. *Tea: A Textbook of Tea Planting and Manufacture*. London: Crosby, Lockwood, and Son, 1897.

Crosthwaite, H. R. *Report on the Land Revenue Settlement of the Jubbulpore District in the Central Provinces effected during the years 1907 to 1912*. Nagpur: Government Press, 1912.

Dacosta, J. *Remarks and Extracts from Official Reports on the Bengal Tenancy Bill*. London: W. H. Allen, 1884.

Dampier, W. "Report on the State of the Police in the Lower Provinces for the first six months of 1842." *Calcutta Review* 1 (1844): 189–217.

Darling, M. *Punjab Peasant in Prosperity and Debt*. Columbia, MO: South Asia Books, 1978. First published 1947.

Das, R. K. *History of Indian Labour Legislation*. Calcutta: University of Calcutta, 1941.

———. "Women and Labour in India I." *International Labor Review* 24 (1931): 376–409.

Datta, K. K. *Unrest against British Rule in Bihar, 1831–59*. Bihar: Superintendent Secretariat Press, 1957.

Datta, R. "Agricultural Production, Social Participation and Domination in Late Eighteenth-Century Bengal: Towards an Alternative Explanation." *Journal of Peasant Studies* 17, no. 1 (1989): 68–113.

Davar, S. *Business Organization*. Calcutta: Butterworths, 1939.

———. *Elements of Indian Mercantile Law*. Bombay: publisher unknown, 1917.

———. *Inefficient Managing Agency System*. Bombay: Davar's College, 1939.

Deininger, K., A. Goyal, and H. Nagarajan. "Inheritance Law Reform and Women's Access to Capital." World Bank Policy Research Working Paper 5338, 2010.

Derrett, J. D. M. "The Administration of Hindu Law by the British." *Comparative Studies in Society and History* 4, no. 1 (November 1961): 10–52.

De Sousa, V. "Modernizing the Colonial Labor Subject in India." *CLCWeb: Comparative Literature and Culture* 12, no. 2, article 3 (2010). http://docs.lib.purdue.edu/clcweb/vol12/iss2/3. Accessed May 14, 2014.

Djankov, S., O. Hart, C. McLiesh, and A. Shleifer. "Debt Enforcement around the World." *Journal of Political Economy* 116, no. 6 (2008): 1105–49.

Dobbin, C. "The Parsi Panchayat in Bombay City in the Nineteenth Century." *Modern Asian Studies* 4, no. 2 (1970): 149–64.

Domar, E. "The Causes of Slavery and Serfdom: A Hypothesis." *Journal of Economic History* 30, no. 1 (1970): 18–32.

Douie, J. M. *Punjab Land Administration Manual*. Rev. ed. Lahore: Government Press, 1931.

Dumont, L. "The 'Village Community' from Munro to Maine." *Contributions to Indian Sociology* 9 (1966): 67–89.

Eastern Bengal and Assam. *Report of the Duars Committee 1910*. Shillong: Government Press, 1910.

Elphinstone, M. *History of India*. Vol. 1. 2nd ed. London: John Murray, 1842.

Finucane, M., and R. F. Rampini, *The Bengal Tenancy Act: Being Act VIII of 1885, with Notes and Annotations, Judicial Rulings, and the Rules Made by the Local Government and the High Court, Under the Act, for the Guidance of Revenue Officers and the Civil Courts*. Calcutta: Thacker, Spink, and Co., 1886.

Fox, R. *Lions of the Punjab: Culture in the Making*. Berkeley: University of California Press, 1985.

Franks, H. *Panchayats of the Peshwas*. Publisher not known, undated.

Fraser, W. *Recollections of a Tea Planter*. London: Tea and Rubber Mail, 1935.

Fyzee, A. A. A. *Outlines of Muhammadan Law*. 5th ed. New Delhi: Oxford University Press, 2009.

———. "Recent Developments in Muhammadan Law in India." *International and Comparative Law Quarterly* 13, supplement (1964): 46–50.

Galenson, D. "The Rise and Fall of Indentured Servitude in the Americas." *Journal of Economic History* 44, no. 1 (1984): 1–26.

———. "The Rise of Free Labor: Economic Change and the Enforcement of Service Contracts in England, 1351–1875." In *Capitalism in Context: Essays on Economic Development and Cultural Change in Honor of R. M. Hartwell*, edited by J. A. James and M. Thomas. Chicago: University of Chicago Press, 1994.

Galloway, A. *Observations on the Law and Constitution of India*. London: Kingsbury, Parbury and Allen, 1825.

Ghosh, K. M. *The Indian Company Law: A Book for Lawyers and Business Men*. Calcutta: Eastern Law House, 1940.

Gilmartin, D. *Empire and Islam: Punjab and the Making of Pakistan*. Berkeley: University of California Press, 1988.

Glaeser, E., R. La Porta, F. Lopez-de-Silanes, and A. Shleifer. "Courts." *Quarterly Journal of Economics* 118, no. 2 (2003): 453–517.

———. "Do Institutions Cause Growth?" *Journal of Economic Growth* 9, no. 3 (2004): 271–303.

Goel, R. K. "Delegation of Directors' Powers and Duties: A Comparative Analysis." *International and Comparative Law Quarterly* 18, no. 1 (1969): 152–77.

Gooderson, R. N. "English Contract Problems in Indian Code and Case Law." *Cambridge Law Journal* 16, no. 1 (1958): 67–84.

———. "Turpitude and Title in England and India." *Cambridge Law Journal* 16, no. 2 (1958): 199–217.

Goodeve, L. A., and J. A. Woodman. *Full Bench Rulings of the High Court at Fort William, from Its Institution In 1862 to the Commencement of the Bengal Law Reports*. Calcutta: Thacker Spink, 1874.

Gordon, T. S. *Jute and Empire: The Calcutta Jute Wallahs and the Landscapes of Empire*. Manchester: Manchester University Press, 1998.

Great Britain, House of Commons. *Revenue: Appendix to the Report from the Select Committee of the House of Commons on the Affairs of the East India Company, Minutes of Evidence*. London: J. L. Cox and Son, 1833.

Grierson, G. A. *Notes on the District of Gaya*. Calcutta: Bengal Secretariat, 1893.

Griffiths, P. *The History of the Indian Tea Industry*. London: Weidenfield and Nicholson, 1967.

Grubb, F. "The Statutory Regulation of Involuntary Servitude: An Incomplete Contract Approach." *Explorations in Economic History* 37 (2000): 42–75.

Guha, R. *A Rule for Property in Bengal: An Essay on the Idea of the Permanent Settlement*. Paris: Mouton and Co., 1963.

Guha, S. *The Agrarian Economy of the Bombay Deccan, 1818–1941*. Delhi: Oxford University Press, 1985.

Gune, V. T. *The Judicial System of the Marathas*. Poona: Sangam, 1953.

Gupta, B., and A. V. Swamy. "Unfree Labor: Did Indenture Reduce Labor Supply to Tea Plantations in Assam?" Mimeo, University of Warwick, 2014.

Gupta, R. K. *Naba Charit* [New biographies, in Bengali]. Calcutta: Gurudas Chattopadhyay, 1886.

Haldar, K., et al. *Sadar Dewanny Adawlater Nishponno Mokoddomar Reporter Chumbak* [Abstracts of cases settled in the Sadar Dewanny Court, in Bengali]. Calcutta: Boikunthanath Das, 1857.

Hardiman, D. *Feeding the Baniya: Peasants and Usurers in Western India*. Delhi: Oxford University Press, 1996.

Harris, R. "The English East India Company and the History of Company Law." In *VOC 1602–2002—400 Years of Company Law*, edited by E. Gepken-Jager, G. van Solinge, and L. Timmerman, 219–47. Dordrecht: Kluwer Legal Publishers, 2005.

Hartmann, B., and J. K. Boyce. *A Quiet Violence: View from a Bangladesh Village*. London: Zed Books, 1987.

Hatekar, N. "Information and Incentives: Pringle's Ricardian Experiment in the Nineteenth Century Deccan Countryside." *Indian Economic and Social History Review* 33, no. 4 (1996): 437–57.

Hazari, R. K. *The Structure of the Corporate Private Sector*. London: Asia Publishing, 1966.

Henningham, S. "Bureaucracy and Control in India's Great Landed Estates: The Raj Darbhanga of Bihar, 1879 to 1950." *Modern Asian Studies* 17, no. 1 (1983): 35–55.

Heston, A. "A Further Critique of Historical Yields per Acre in India." *Indian Economic and Social History Review* 15, no. 2 (1978): 187–210.

———. "Official Yields per Acre in India: 1886–1947; Some Questions of Interpretation." *Indian Economic and Social History Review* 10, no. 4 (1973): 303–32.

Hetherington, F. A. *The Diary of a Tea Planter*. Sussex, England: Book Guild Limited, 1994.

Hjejle, B. "Slavery and Agricultural Bondage in South India in the Nineteenth Century." *Scandinavian Economic History Review* 15, nos. 1–2 (1967): 71–126.

Hogg, J. E. "Partnership Law in the Empire." *Journal of Comparative Legislation and International Law* 18, no. 2 (1918): 232–41.

Ilbert, C. "Application of European Law to Natives of India." *Journal of the Society of Comparative Legislation* 1 (1896–97): 212–26.

———. *The Government of India: Being a Digest of the Statute Law relating thereto*. Oxford: Clarendon Press, 1907.

———. *The Government of India: A Brief Historical Survey of Parliamentary Legislation Relating to India*. Oxford: Clarendon Press, 1922.

India. *Abridged Report of the Royal Commission on Agriculture in India*. Bombay: Government Press, 1928.

———. *Note on Land Transfer and Agricultural Indebtedness in India*. Simla: Government Press, 1895.

———. *Papers and Proceedings Connected with the Passing of the Deccan Agriculturists' Relief Act, XVII. of 1879, From 6th April 1877 to 24th March 1880: Selections from the Records of the Bombay Government No. CLVII—New Series*. Bombay: Government Press, 1882.

———. *Report of the Assam Labour Enquiry Committee, 1906*. Calcutta: Government Press, 1906.

———. *Report of the Labour Investigation Committee*. Delhi: Government Press, 1946.

———. *Report of the Monopolies Enquiry Commission*. New Delhi: Ministry of Commerce and Industry, 1965.

———. *Report of the Royal Commission on Labour in India*. London: HMSO, 1931.

———. *Royal Commission to consider Reform of Judicial Establishments, Judicial Procedure and Laws of India: First Report*. London: HMSO, 1856.

———. *Selection of Papers on Agricultural Indebtedness and the Restriction of the Power to Alienate Interests in Land*. Vol. 1. Simla: Government Press, 1898.

———. *Selections from the Debates on the Reform of Company Law in the Central Assembly and Parliament in 1936 and 1954–55*. New Delhi: Ministry of Commerce and Industry, 1960.

———. *Seventh Report on the Transfer of Property Act 1882*. Delhi: Law Commission, 1977.

———. *Special Report on the Working of Act 1 of 1882 in the Province of Assam during the Years 1886–89*. Calcutta: Government Press, 1890.

India, Civil Justice Committee. *Report*. Calcutta: Government of India Publication Branch, 1925.

———. *Appendix No. 2: Oral evidence*. Vol. 1, *Bengal, Assam, United Provinces*. Calcutta: Government of India Central Publication Branch, 1925.

India, Department of Agriculture and Revenue. *Returns of Agricultural Statistics of British India*. Calcutta: Superintendent of Government Printing, 1886–90.

India, Law Commission. *Report 253: Commercial Division and Commercial Appellate Division of High Courts and Commercial Courts Bill*. 2015. http://lawcommissionofindia .nic.in/reports/Report_No.253_Commercial_Division_and_Commercial_Appellate _Division_of_High_Courts_and__Commercial_Courts_Bill,_2015.pdf. Accessed July 29, 2015.

———. *Seventh Report on the Partnership Act*. New Delhi: Government Press, 1957.

Indian Law Commission. "Proposed Act for Amending the Law regarding the Limitation of Suits." In *Copies of Special Reports of the Indian Law Commissioners*, 3–47. London: House of Commons, 1843.

Ishaque, H. S. M. *Agricultural Statistics by Plot to Plot Enumeration in Bengal, 1944–45*. Pt. 1. Calcutta: Government Press, 1946.

Islam, M. M. "The Punjab Land Alienation Act and the Professional Moneylenders." *Modern Asian Studies* 29, no. 2 (1995): 271–91.

Islam, S. *The Permanent Settlement in Bengal: A Study of Its Operation, 1790–1819*. Dacca: Bangla Academy, 1979.

Iversen, V., R. Palmer-Jones, and K. Sen. "On the Colonial Origins of Agricultural Development in India: A Re-examination of Banerjee and Iyer, 'History, Institutions and Economic Performance.'" *Journal of Development Studies* 49, no. 12 (2013): 1631–46.

Jha, J. C. *The Tribal Revolt of Chotanagpur*. Patna: Kashi Prasad Jayaswal Research Institute, 1987.

Joshi, C. *Lost Worlds: Indian Labour and Its Forgotten Histories*. London: Anthem Press, 2005.

Kane, P. V. *History of Dharmasastra (Ancient and Medieval Religious and Civil Law)*. Poona: Bhandarkar Oriental Research Institute, 1962.

Kapur, S., and S. Kim. "British Colonial Institutions and Economic Development in India." NBER Working Paper 12613, 2006.

Kelman, J. H. *Labour in India: A Study of the Conditions of Indian Women in Modern Industry*. London: George Allen and Unwin, 1923.

Khanna, D. K. *The Complete and Consolidated Digest: Indian Civil Cases, 1901 to 1908*. Vols. 1–6. Delhi: Delhi Central Press, 1910.

Kinney, J. *Old Times in Assam*. Calcutta: Star Press, 1896.

Kling, B. *The Blue Mutiny: The Indigo Disturbances in Bengal, 1859–1862*. Philadelphia: University of Pennsylvania Press, 1966.

Kolsky, E. *Colonial Justice in British India: White Violence and the Rule of Law*. Cambridge: Cambridge University Press, 2010.

Kranton, R., and A. V. Swamy. "The Hazards of Piecemeal Reform: British Civil Courts and the Credit Market in Colonial India." *Journal of Development Economics* 58, no. 1 (1999): 1–24.

———. "Contracts, Hold-Up, and Exports: Textiles and Opium in Colonial India." *American Economic Review* 98, no. 3 (2008): 967–89.

Krishnamacharaiar, M. *The Madras Estates Land Act: being Act I of 1908 as amended by Act IV of 1909, with commentaries, and an introduction, historical, analytical and critical.* Madras: Government Press, 1917.

Kugle, S. A. "Framed, Blamed and Renamed: The Recasting of Islamic Jurisprudence in Colonial South Asia." *Modern Asian Studies* 35, no. 2 (2001): 257–313.

Kumar, D., ed. *The Cambridge Economic History of India.* Vol. 2, *1757–1970.* Cambridge: Cambridge University Press, 1983.

———. *Land and Caste in South India: Agricultural Labour in the Madras Presidency during the Nineteenth Century.* New York: Cambridge University Press, 1965.

———. "The Fiscal System." In *The Cambridge Economic History of India,* vol. 2, *1757–1970,* edited by D. Kumar, 905–44. New Delhi: Orient Longman, 1984.

Kumar, R. *Western India in the Nineteenth Century.* London: Routledge and Kegan Paul, 1968.

Kuran, T., and A. Singh. "Economic Modernization in Late British India: Hindu-Muslim Differences." *Economic Development and Cultural Change* 61, no. 3 (2013): 503–38.

Kydd, J. C. *A History of Factory Legislation in India.* Calcutta: Calcutta University Press, 1920.

Lamoreaux, N., and J. Rosenthal. "Legal Regime and Contractual Flexibility: A Comparison of Business's Organizational Choices in France and the United States during the Era of Industrialization." *American Law and Economics Review* 7, no. 1 (2005): 28–61.

La Porta, R., F. Lopez-de-Silanes, A. Shleifer, and R. Vishny. "Law and Finance." *Journal of Political Economy* 106, no. 6 (1998): 1113–55.

Lasseter, T. "India's Stagnant Courts Resist Reform." January 8, 2015. http://www.bloomberg.com/news/articles/2015-01-08/indias-courts-resist-reform-backlog-at-314-million-cases. Accessed July 27, 2015.

Lewis, W. A. "Economic Development with Unlimited Supplies of Labour." *Manchester School* 22, no. 2 (1954): 139–91.

Liberty Voice. "Slavery in India." October 8, 2013. http://guardianlv.com/2013/10/slavery-in-india-bonded-labor. Accessed May 5, 2014.

Lindley, N. *The Law of Partnership.* Vol. 1 of 2. 5th ed. Jersey City: F. D. Linn, 1888.

Lokanathan, P. S. *Industrial Organisation in India.* London: George Unwin, 1936.

Macnaghten, F. W. *Considerations on Hindoo Law as it is current in Bengal.* Serampore: Mission Press, 1824.

Macnaghten, W. H. *Reports of Cases Determined in the Court of Sudder Dewanny Adawlat, with Tables of the Names of the Cases and Principal Matters.* Vol. 1. Calcutta: Bishop's College Press, 1827.

Madras. *A Brief Report on the Entire Operations of the Inam Commission from its Commencement.* Madras: Government Press, 1869.

———. *The Indian Law Reports Madras Series: Containing Cases Determined by the High Court at Madras and by the Judicial Committee of the Privy Council on Appeal from that Court.* Vol. 13. Madras: Government Press, 1890.

———. *The Indian Law Reports Madras Series: Containing Cases Determined by the High Court at Madras and by the Judicial Committee of the Privy Council on Appeal from that Court.* Vol. 20. Madras: Government Press, 1897.

———. *The Indian Law Reports Madras Series: Containing Cases Determined by the High Court at Madras and by the Judicial Committee of the Privy Council on Appeal from that Court.* Vol. 41. Madras: Government Press, 1918.

———. *The Indian Law Reports Madras Series: Containing Cases Determined by the High Court at Madras and by the Judicial Committee of the Privy Council on Appeal from that Court.* Vol. 43. Madras: Government Press, 1920.

——. *Madras Estates Land Act Committee (Irrigation Reports from Zamindars)*. Madras: Government Press, 1938.

——. *Madras Estates Land Act Committee (Main Report)*. Madras: Government Press, 1938.

——. *Madras Estates Land Act Committee (Memoranda Submitted to the Committee Part II), (Raiyats)*. Madras: Government Press, 1938.

——. *Report of the Administration of the Madras Presidency, during the years 1879–80*. Madras: Government Press, 1880.

——. *Report of the Madras Provincial Banking Enquiry Committee*. Madras: Government Press, 1930.

Madras, Revenue Department. *Report on the Working of the Madras Estates Land Act, 1908, during Fasli 1329*. Madras, 1921.

Mahalanobis, P. C., and D. Bhattacharya. "Growth of Population in India and Pakistan, 1801–1961." *Artha Vijnana* 18, no. 1 (1976): 1–10.

Maine, H. *Village-Communities in the East and West*. New York: Henry Holt and Company, 1889.

Manucci, N. *Storia do Mogor*. Vol. 3 of 3. London: John Murray, 1907.

Markby, W. *Lectures on Indian Law*. Calcutta: Thacker Spink, 1873.

Marshall, P. J. *East Indian Fortunes: The British in Bengal in the Eighteenth Century*. Oxford, Clarendon Press, 1976.

——. *Problems of Empire*. London: George Allen and Unwin, 1968.

——. *Bengal: The British Bridgehead*. Cambridge: Cambridge University Press, 1987.

Martin, Marina. "An Economic History of the Hundi, 1858–1978." PhD diss., Department of Economic History, London School of Economics and Political Science, 2012.

Martin, Montgomery. *The History, Antiquities, Topography, and Statistics of Eastern India . . . collated from the Original Documents of the E.I. House*. Vol. 1 of 3. London: W. H. Allen, 1838.

Marwari Chamber of Commerce. *Rules and Regulations about Hundi Chithi and Seed-Wheat*. Bombay: Marwari Chamber of Commerce, 1916.

McAlpin, M. C. *Report on the Condition of the Sonthals in the Districts of Birbhum, Bankura, Midnapore and North Balasore*. Calcutta: Firma K. L. Mukhopadhyay,1981. First published 1909.

McKinsey Global Institute. *India: the Growth Imperative*. 2001. http://www.mckinsey.com /insights/india/growth_imperative_for_india. Accessed July 29, 2015.

McPherson, H. *Final Report on the Survey and Settlement Operations in the District of the Sonthal Parganas, 1898–1907*. Calcutta: Secretariat Book Depot, 1909.

Mehta, M. M. *Combination Movement in Indian Industry*. Bombay: Friends' Book Depot, 1952.

Mehta, P. B. "India's Judiciary: The Promise of Uncertainty." In *Public Institutions in India: Performance and Designs*, edited by D. Kapur and P. B. Mehta, 158–93. New Delhi: Oxford University Press, 2005.

Menski, W. F. *Comparative Law in a Global Context: The Legal Systems of Asia and Africa*. Cambridge: Cambridge University Press, 2006.

Metcalf, T. *Ideologies of the Raj*. Cambridge: Cambridge University Press, 1995.

Misra, M. *Business, Race, and Politics in British India, 1850–1960*. Oxford: Oxford University Press, 1998.

Mitra, A. C. *The Hindu Law of Inheritance, Partition, Stridhan, and Wills with leading cases from 1825 to 1888*. Calcutta: Calcutta Central Press, 1888.

Mitra, D. B. *The Cotton Weavers of Bengal, 1857–1933*. Calcutta: Firma KLM, 1978.

Montriou, W. A. *Cases of Hindu Law before H. M. Supreme Court, during the first Thirty Years of the Court's Establishment.* Calcutta: D'Rozario and Co., 1853.

Morris, M. D. *The Emergence of an Industrial Labor Force in India: A Study of the Bombay Cotton Mills, 1854–1947.* Berkeley: University of California Press, 1965.

———. "Modern Business Organisation and Labour Administration: Specific Adaptations to Indian Conditions of Risk and Uncertainty, 1850–1947." *Economic and Political Weekly* 14, no. 40 (1979): 1680–87.

Mukerjee, R. *The Indian Working Class.* Bombay: Hind Kitabs, 1951.

Mukherjee, N. *A Bengal Zamindar: Jaykrishna Mukherjee of Uttarpara and His Times, 1808–1888.* Calcutta: Firma K. L. Mukopadhyay, 1975.

Mukund, K. *The View from Below: Indigenous Society, Temples and the Early Colonial State in Tamilnadu, 1700–1835.* Hyderabad: Orient Longman, 2005.

Mullally, S. "Feminism and Multicultural Dilemmas in India." *Oxford Journal of Legal Studies* 24, no. 4 (2004): 671–92.

Murphy, P. W. *Final Report of the Survey and Settlement Operations (under Chapter X of the Bengal Tenancy Act) in the District of Monghyr (South), 1905–12.* Ranchi: Bihar and Orissa Secretariat Printing Office, 1914.

Musacchio, A. "Can Civil Law Countries Get Good Institutions? Lessons from the History of Creditor Rights and Bond Markets in Brazil." *Journal of Economic History* 68, no. 1 (2008): 80–108.

Musacchio, A., and J. D. Turner. "Does the Law and Finance Hypothesis Pass the Test of History?" *Business History* 55, no. 4 (2013): 524–42.

Myers, C. A. *Labor Problems in the Industrialization of India.* Cambridge, MA: Harvard University Press, 1958.

Naidu, S., and N. Yuchtman. "Coercive Contract Enforcement: Law and the Labor Market in Nineteenth Century Industrial Britain." *American Economic Review* 103, no.1 (2013): 107–44.

Newbigin, E. "A Post-colonial Patriarchy? Representing Family in the Indian Nation State." *Modern Asian Studies* 44, no. 1 (2010): 121–44.

———. *The Hindu Family and the Emergence of Modern India: Law, Citizenship and Community.* Cambridge: Cambridge University Press, 2013.

North, D. *Institutions, Institutional Change and Economic Performance.* Cambridge: Cambridge University Press, 1991.

Norton, J. B. *A Selection on the Hindu Law of Inheritance.* Madras: C. D'Cruz, 1870.

Oak, M., and A. V. Swamy. "Only Twice as Much: A Rule for Regulating Lenders." *Economic Development and Cultural Change* 58, no. 4 (2010): 775–803.

Ogilvie, S., and A. W. Carus. "Institutions and Economic Growth in Historical Perspective." In *Handbook of Economic Growth*, vol. 2A, edited by P. Aghion and S. Durlauf, 405–514. Amsterdam: Elsevier, 2014.

Olson, M. *The Logic of Collective Action: Public Goods and the Theory of Groups.* Cambridge, MA: Harvard University Press, 1965.

O'Malley, L. S. S. *Eastern Bengal Gazetteers: Chittagong.* Calcutta: Bengal Secretariat Book Depot, 1908.

O'Sullivan, P., and J. M. C. Mills. *Reports of the Cases Decided in the High Court of Madras in 1870 and 1871.* Madras: Higginbotham and Co., 1872.

Panagariya, A. *India: The Emerging Giant.* New York: Oxford University Press, 2008.

———. "Land-Leasing: A Big Win-Win Reform for the States." 2015. http://niti.gov.in /content/view_blogs_arch.php?blog=1. Accessed August 24, 2015.

Parsons, T. *A Treatise on the Law of Partnership.* Boston: Little, Brown, 1867.

Patnaik, U., and M. Dingwaney, eds. *Chains of Servitude: Bondage and Slavery in India*, Madras: Sangam Books, 1985.

Perry, E. *Cases Illustrative of Oriental Life, the Application of English Law to India, Decided in H. M. Supreme Court at Bombay*. London: S. Sweet, 1853.

Phillips, J. "Protecting Those in a Disadvantageous Negotiating Position: Unconscionable Bargains as a Unifying Doctrine." *Wake Forest Law Review* 45, no. 3 (2010): 837–61.

Pickering, M. A. "The Company as a Separate Legal Entity." *Modern Law Review* 31, no. 5 (1968): 481–511.

Pouchepadass, J. *Land, Power and Market: A Bihar District under Colonial Rule*. New Delhi: Sage, 2000.

Prakash, G. *Bonded Histories: Genealogies of Labor Servitude in Colonial India*. Cambridge: Cambridge University Press, 1990.

Prakash, O. "Bullion for Goods: International Trade and the Economy of Early Eighteenth Century Bengal." *Indian Economic and Social History Review* 13, no. 2 (1976): 159–86.

Price, P. "Warrior Caste 'Raja' and Gentleman 'Zamindar': One Person's Experience in the Late Nineteenth Century." *Modern Asian Studies* 17, no. 4 (1983): 563–90.

Punjab. *Indian Law Reports Lahore Series: Containing Cases Determined by the High Court at Lahore and by the Judicial Committee of the Privy Council on Appeal from that Court*. Vol. 5. Lahore: Government Book Depot, 1924.

———. *Report of the Punjab Provincial Banking Enquiry Committee*. Lahore: Government Press, 1930.

———. *Report on the Administration of Civil Justice in the Punjab and Its Dependencies*. Lahore: Civil and Military Gazette Press, various years.

Punjab, High Court. *Note on the Administration of Civil Justice in the Punjab*. Lahore: Superintendent of Government Printing, various years.

Raghavaiyangar, S. S. *Memorandum on the Progress of the Madras Presidency during the last forty years of British Administration*. Madras: Government Press, 1883.

Raman, R. *Global Capital and Peripheral Labour: The History and Political Economy of Plantation Workers in India*. New York: Routledge, 2010.

Ramsden, A. R. *Assam Planter: Tea Planting and Hunting in the Assam Jungle*. London: J. Gifford Limited, 1945.

Rankin, G. *Background to Indian Law*. Cambridge: Cambridge University Press, 1946.

Rattigan, W. H. "The Influence of English Law and Legislation upon the Native Laws of India." *Journal of the Society of Comparative Legislation*, n.s., 3, no. 1 (1901): 46–65.

Ray, I. "The Indigo Dye Industry in Colonial Bengal: A Re-examination." *Indian Economic and Social History Review* 41, no. 2 (2004): 199–224.

Ray, R. "The Changing Fortunes of the Bengali Gentry under Colonial Rule: Pal Chaudhuris of Mahesganj, 1800–1950." *Modern Asian Studies* 21, no. 3 (1987): 511–19.

———. *Change in Bengal Agrarian Society, c. 1760–1870*. New Delhi: Manohar, 1979.

Raychaudhuri, T. "Permanent Settlement in Operation, Bakarganj District, East Bengal." In *Land Control and Social Structure in Indian History*, edited by R. E. Frykenberg. Delhi: Manohar, 1979.

Read, M. *From Field to Factory: An Introductory Study of the Indian Peasant Turned Factory Hand*. London: Student Christian Movement, 1927.

Rege, D. V. *Report on an Enquiry into the Conditions of Plantation Workers in India*. Simla: Government Press, 1948.

Reid, R. T., and C. F. Farran, eds., *Reports of Cases Decided in the High Court of Bombay, 1866–67*. Bombay: Education Society Press, 1868.

Reserve Bank of India. *All-India Rural Credit Survey: Report of the Committee of Direction.* Vol 2, *The General Report.* Bombay: Reserve Bank of India, 1954.

Robb, P. *Ancient Rights and Future Comfort: Bihar, the Bengal Tenancy Act of 1885 and British Rule in India.* Richmond, UK: Curzon Press, 1997.

Rocher, R., and L. Rocher. *The Making of Western Indology: Henry Thomas Colebrooke and the East India Company.* London: Routledge, 2012.

Rothermund, D. *Government, Landlord, and Peasant in India.* Wiesbaden: Franz Steiner Verlag, 1978.

Roy, T. *Company of Kinsmen: Enterprise and Community in South Asian History.* New Delhi: Oxford University Press, 2010.

———. *The Economic History of India, 1857–1947.* New Delhi: Oxford University Press, 2011.

———. "Indigo and Law in Colonial India." *Economic History Review* 64, no. S1 (2011): 60–75.

———. "Labour Institutions, Japanese Competition, and the Crisis of Cotton Mills in Interwar Mumbai." *Economic and Political Weekly* 43 (2008): 37–45.

———. "Sardars, Jobbers, Kanganies: The Labour Contractor and Indian Economic History." *Modern Asian Studies* 42, no. 5 (2007): 971–98.

Rungta, R. S. *Rise of Business Corporations in India, 1851–1900.* Cambridge: Cambridge University Press, 1970.

Sah, R. "Features of British Indigo in India." *Social Scientist* 9, nos. 2/3 (1980): 67–79.

Sandhu, K. S., and A. Mani. *Indian Communities in Southeast Asia.* Singapore: Institute of Southeast Asian Studies, 2006.

Sangal, P. S. "Ultra Vires and Companies: The Indian Experience." *International and Comparative Law Quarterly* 12, no. 3 (1963): 967–88.

Sarkar, J. *Mughal Administration.* Calcutta: M. C. Sarkar, 1920.

Sartori, A. "A Liberal Discourse of Custom in Colonial Bengal." *Past and Present* 212 (2011): 163–97.

Schoenblum, J. A. "The Role of Legal Doctrine in the Decline of the Islamic Waqf: A Comparison with the Trust." *Vanderbilt Journal of Transnational Law* 32 (1999): 1191–1227.

Sen, A. "Agrarian Structure and Tenancy Laws in Bengal, 1850–1900." In *Perspectives in Social Sciences 2: Three Studies on the Agrarian Structure in Bengal, 1850–1947,* edited by A. Sen, P. Chatterjee, and S. Mukherji. Delhi: Oxford University Press, 1982.

Sen, S. "Gender and Class: Women in Indian Industry, 1890–1990." *Modern Asian Studies* 42, no. 1 (2008): 75–116.

———. *Women and Labour in Late Colonial India: The Bengal Jute Industry.* Cambridge: Cambridge University Press, 1999.

Sen Gupta, K. K. "Agrarian Disturbances in 19th Century Bengal." *Indian Economic and Social History Review* 8, no. 2 (1971): 192–212.

———. "The Agrarian League of Pabna, 1873." *Indian Economic and Social History Review* 7, no. 3 (1970): 253–68.

———. "Bengali Intelligentsia and the Politics of Rent, 1873–1885." *Social Scientist* 3, no. 2 (1974): 27–34.

Setalvad, M. C. *The Common Law in India.* London: Steven and Sons, 1960.

Singh, B., and H. C. Calvert. *An Inquiry into Mortgages of Agricultural Land in the Kot Kapura Utar Assessment Circle of the Ferozepur District in the Punjab.* Lahore: Civil and Military Gazette Press, 1925.

Singh, S. G. *The Punjab Land Alienation Act (XIII of 1900).* Lahore: Albion Press, 1901.

Sivaswamy, K. G. *Legislative Protection and Relief of Agriculturist Debtors in India*. Poona: Gokhale Institute of Politics and Economics, 1939.

Smith, S. "Fortune and Failure: The Survival of Family Firms in Eighteenth Century India." In *Family Capitalism*, edited Geoffrey Jones and Mary B. Rose, 44–65. London: Routledge, 1993.

Steele, A. *The Law and Custom of Hindoo Castes within the Dekhun Provinces subject to the Presidency of Bombay chiefly affecting Civil Suits*. London: W. H. Allen, 1868.

Stein, B. *Thomas Munro: The Origins of the Colonial State and His Vision of Empire*. New York: Oxford University Press, 1989.

Steinfeld, R. J. *Coercion, Contract and Free Labor in the Nineteenth Century*. Cambridge: Cambridge University Press, 2001.

Stiglitz, J. "Risk and Incentives in Sharecropping." *Review of Economic Studies* 41, no. 2 (1974): 219–55.

Stokes, E. *The English Utilitarians and India*. London: Oxford University Press, 1959.

Strange, T. *Hindu Law with reference to Such Portions of it as Concern the Administration of Justice in the King's Courts in India*. 5th ed. Madras: Higginbothams, 1875.

———. *Responsa Prudentum or Opinions of Pundits*. Vol. 2 of 2. London: Payne and Foss, 1825.

Sturman, R. *The Government of Social Life in Colonial India: Liberalism, Religious Law and Women's Rights*. Cambridge: Cambridge University Press, 2012.

Subrahmanian, L. "Merchants in Transit: Risk-Sharing Strategies in the Indian Ocean." In *Cross Currents and Community Networks: The History of the Indian Ocean World*, edited by H. P. Ray and E. A. Alpers, 263–85. Delhi: Oxford University Press, 2005.

Sykes, W. H. "Administration of Civil Justice in British India for a period of Four Years, chiefly from 1845 to 1848, both years inclusive." *Journal of the Statistical Society of London* 16 (1853): 103–36.

———. "Statistics of Civil and Criminal Justice in British India, Chiefly from the Year 1836 to 1840." *Journal of the Statistical Society of London* 6, no. 2 (1843): 94–119.

Tagore, P. C. *Table of Succession according to Hindu Law of Bengal*. Calcutta: Albion Press, 1864.

Tarkapanchanan, J. *Digest on Hindu Law of Contracts and Successions with a Commentary*. Translated by H. T. Colebrooke. Vols 1–2. Madras: Higginbothams, 1874.

Thomson, N. H. *Act XIV of 1859 Regulating the Limitation of Civil Suits in British India*. Calcutta: Thacker Spink, 1870.

Thorburn, S. S. *Musalmans and Money-Lenders in the Punjab*. Edinburgh: William Blackwood and Sons, 1886.

Thorner, D. *The Agrarian Prospect in India: Five Lectures on Land Reform Delivered in 1955 at the Delhi School of Economics*. Delhi: Allied Publishers, 1976.

Tofaris, S. "Hindu Law and the English Law of Contract: A Century of Interaction, 1772–1872." RINDAS Series Working Paper, Ryukoku University, 2013.

Trivedi, H. M. *Labour and Factory Legislation in India*. Bombay: Law Publishers, 1945.

United Kingdom. *Report of the Indian Factory Labour Commission*. London: HMSO, 1908.

United Kingdom, House of Commons. *Report of the Select Committee of the House of Commons on the Affairs of the East India Company*. London: Cox and Son, 1833.

Venkatasubramanian, P. B. "The Law of Trademarks in India." *World Development* 7, no. 7 (1979): 737–46.

Washbrook, D. "Law, State and Agrarian Society in Colonial India." *Modern Asian Studies* 15, no. 3 (1981): 649–721.

Weiss, A. *Efficiency Wage Models of the Labor Market: Models of Unemployment, Layoffs, and Wage-Dispersion*. Princeton, NJ: Princeton University Press, 1991.

West, R., and H. R. Abdul Majid. *A Digest of the Hindu Law of Inheritance, Partition, and Adoption Embodying the Replies of the Sastris with Introductions and Notes*. London: Sweet and Maxwell, 1919.

Whitcombe, E. *Agrarian Conditions in Northern India*. Vol. 1, *The United Provinces under British Rule, 1860–1900*. Berkeley: University of California Press, 1972.

White, D. L. "Parsis in the Commercial World of Western India, 1700–1750." *Indian Economic and Social History Review* 24, no. 2 (1987): 183–203.

Wolcott, S. "Industrial Labour in Late Colonial India." In *A New Economic History of India*, edited by L. Chaudhary, B. Gupta, T. Roy, and A. Swamy. London: Routledge, 2015.

World Bank. *Doing Business in India: Registering Property in India—Mumbai*. 2015. http://www.doingbusiness.org/data/exploreeconomies/mumbai/registering-property. Accessed August 24, 2015.

Wrigley, F. G. *The Eastern Bengal and Assam Code, Containing the Regulations and Local Acts in Force in the Province of Eastern Bengal and Assam*. Vol. 1. Calcutta: Government Press, 1907.

INDEX

Page numbers in italic refer to illustrations.

report on health of women mill workers in 1931–32, 117–18
Royal Commission on Labour in India, 116–17
Rupji, Manohardas, case of, 94–95

S. B. Fraser & Co. v. The Bombay Ice Manufacturing Co. Ltd., 154
Sadar Diwani Adalat, 38
Sajun Mir Ali, 95
sandbanks ("alluvial secretions"), 170
Santal Parganas district, 64–65, 78
Santhal Rebellion, 1855, 4, 38, 64
sapinda rights, 85
Sapru, Tej Bahadur, 173, 176
Sarup Chand Das, 92
"Scheduled Tribes." See adivasis
Scotland, Justice C. J., 46
Sen, Samita, 121
settled raiyat, 40–41, 42
Shaftesbury, Earl of, 116
sharecroppers, 50, 51, 186n42, 189n105, 192n29
Shariat Act of 1937, 102
Sharma, Ramcharan, 88–89, 89–90, 92
Shustri, Mahomed, 93, 94
Sikhs: in British-Indian army, 69; classification as Hindus for purpose of property succession, 98
Sircar, Shama Churn, 86
Skinner, James, 99
Skinner, Thomas, 99
Smyth, D. C., 169
Special Act, 111–14, 200n48, 200n50
Specific Relief Act of 1877, 157
spiritual benefit: and coparcenary rights, 85, 103; and women, 86
Stiglitz, Joseph, 189n105
Stoddart, G. W., 113
Strange, Thomas, 91, 126–27
Subba Reddi v. Doraisami (Bhaba Tarini v. Peary), 101
subinfeudation, 32, 44, 186n53, 188n75
Succession Act of 1865, 97–99
Sudder Dewanny Adawluts (chief civil courts), 18, 23, 86, 91; suits pending in, 1802, 1814, and 1838, 25
Supreme courts: establishment of, 16, 18, 169; merged into high courts in 1862, 148; royal proclamation of 1833 curtailing authority of, 21

Surma Valley tea planters, 112, 113, 114
Syed Ameer Ali, 95
Sylhet, Surma Valley, 112
synthetic partnership, 144, 145

Tagore, Prasanna Kumar, 86
Tarkapanchanan, Jagannath, 124, 126, 203n2
taxes: collection of in Bengal Presidency, 29–34; decline of on land, 34, 192n27; extractive level, 34; sale of land for taxes owed, 32, 34
tax farming, 30
tea garden workers, protests and riots in 1920–22, 113
tea-growing regions and industry: Brahmaputra Valley, Upper Assam, 109; Dooar, North Bengal, 109; and Partition of India, 155; planter agreement on "labor rules" preventing enticement of employees, 114; Surma Valley, Lower Assam, 109
tenant movements, 43–44
tenants, types of: hawala, 44; "Istimrari," 38; jotedars, 37; occupancy tenants, 38–41, 49, 51; protected tenants, 48–49; "settled raiyat, 40–41, 42; tenant-at-will, 46, 50–51, 79; unprotected tenants, 49–51
tenants' rights legislation, 38–44
testimentary power of individuals, 6
Thomas William Skinner v. Durga Prasad, 99
Thomas William Skinner v. Richard Ross Skinner, 99
Thomson, Rivers, 38
Thorner, Daniel, 27
Tilluckchand Doss v. Ramhurry Doss, 90–91
Trade Disputes Act of 1929, 118
trademark law, 157
trader-lender, 58, 68, 71, 195n75
Trade Unions Act of 1926, 104, 118
Transfer of Property Act of 1882, 81, 100–101, 144
Trevor, Justice, 39
Trusts Act of 1882, 155

ulemas (Muslim religious scholars), 18
"undue influence" cases, 138–39
usufructuary mortgages, Punjab, 67
Usurious Loans Act of 1918, 55, 56, 75–76, 139
usury laws, 78